Table of Contents

FREE GIFT!

I am also have one valuable bonus for you - 1000 Worldwide Recipes - cookbook

Please follow this link to get instant access to your Free Cookbook:
http://booknation.top/

Introduction

Instant pots are so popular these days. They managed to impress so many people all over the world, and they've become some of the most appreciated tools in the kitchen.
If you don't have such a pot and you've made the decision to purchase one, there are some things you need to know about it.

First of all, you should know that it may take you a while to get familiarized with this machine. It has a lot of settings and buttons, and you should make sure you understand them before you start cooking in it. This wonderful cookbook you are about to discover contains some simple and easy instant pot recipes specially created for those of you who are using this machine for the first time.

For example, you will learn how to prepare simple beans recipes, vegetable ones, breakfasts, etc.
Make sure you sauté some of the ingredients, as mentioned in the recipes.
Cut ingredients in equal pieces, use enough liquid to cook your dishes and use many spices.

Another thing you must know is that the instant pot is probably one of the easiest to clean machines.
Also, it replaces so many other kitchen machines like rice cookers, slow cookers or even pressure cookers. The best thing is that most of the times you won't even need more pans and pots. Many of the dishes you make in your instant pot just require this machine.

One of the most important aspects you need to know about your new instant pot is that it allows you to make great and tasty foods in a much more effective way.
Your dishes will maintain all their flavors and textures, and they will be cooked in the healthiest way possible.
You won't have to consume all your energy in the kitchen, and you don't need special cooking skills to make magical dishes.

From now on, you won't have to worry about your success in the kitchen because your instant pot will do the hard part!
We are sure we've convinced you that purchasing an instant pot is the best thing you could do.

Then, make sure you prepare all the special recipes we've brought to you through this cooking journal.
As you are about to discover, there are enough recipes to suit all tastes, even the most pretentious ones.

So, what are you waiting for?
Have you got your instant pot?

Instant Pot Breakfast Recipes

Special French Toast

It's probably one of the best breakfast ideas ever! Try it soon and see!

Preparation time: 10 minutes
Cooking time: 30 minutes
Servings: 6
Ingredients:

For the orange sauce:
- ¼ cup orange juice
- ½ cup sugar
- 2 cups cranberries
- A pinch of salt
- ¼ teaspoon cinnamon, ground

For the toast:
- 2 cups milk
- 3 eggs, whisked

- 4 tablespoons melted butter
- ½ cup sugar
- Zest from 1 orange, grated
- A pinch of salt
- 1 teaspoon vanilla extract
- 1 loaf bread, cubed
- 1 cup water

Directions:
1. Heat up a small pot over medium heat, add cranberries, orange juice, ¼ teaspoon cinnamon, a pinch of salt and ½ cup sugar, stir well and cook for 5 minutes.
2. Pour this into a greased pan and leave aside for now.
3. In a bowl, mix butter with milk, ½ cup sugar, eggs, vanilla extract, a pinch of salt and orange zest and stir.
4. Add bread cubes and stir again.
5. Pour this over cranberry, place pan in the steamer basket of your instant pot, add the water on the bottom, cover and cook at High for 25 minutes.
6. Release the pressure, take the pan out, divide the mix among plates and serve.

Enjoy!

Nutrition:
- Calories 300
- Fat 14
- Fiber 2
- Carbs 80
- Sugar 12
- Protein 14

Delicious Vanilla Steel Cut Oats

It's fun and easy to make breakfast idea! Make it tomorrow for breakfast!

Preparation time: 10 minutes
Cooking time: 10 minutes
Servings: 4
Ingredients:

- 1 cup milk
- 1 cup steel cut oats
- 2 and ½ cups water
- 2 tablespoons sugar
- A pinch of salt
- 1 teaspoon espresso powder
- 2 teaspoons vanilla extract
- Whipped cream for serving
- Grated chocolate for serving

Directions:

1. In your instant pot, mix oats with water, sugar, milk, salt and espresso powder and stir.
2. Cover the pot and cook at High for 10 minutes.
3. Release the pressure for 10 minutes, take the lid off, add vanilla extract, stir and leave everything aside for 5 minutes.
4. Divide into bowls and serve with whipped cream and grated chocolate.

Enjoy!

Nutrition:

- Calories 250
- Fat 3.1
- Fiber 5.4
- Carbs 43
- Sugar 4
- Protein 5

Special Mushroom Oatmeal

You have to try this breakfast recipe! It's pretty amazing and tasty!

Preparation time: 10 minutes
Cooking time: 15 minutes
Servings: 4
Ingredients:

- 1 small yellow onion, chopped
- 1 cup steel cut oats
- 2 garlic cloves, minced
- 2 tablespoons butter
- ½ cup water
- 14 ounces canned chicken stock
- 3 thyme springs, chopped
- 2 tablespoons extra virgin olive oil
- ½ cup gouda, grated
- 8 ounces mushroom, sliced
- Salt and black pepper to the taste

Directions:

1. Select Sauté mode on your instant pot, add butter and melt it.
2. Add onions, stir and cook for 3 minutes.
3. Add garlic, stir and cook for 1 minute more.
4. Add oats, stir and cook for 1 minute.
5. Add water, salt, pepper, stock, and thyme, cover the pot and cook at High for 10 minutes.
6. Release the pressure and leave the pot aside.
7. Meanwhile, heat up a pan with the olive oil over medium heat, add mushrooms and cook them for 3 minutes.
8. Add them to the instant pot, also add more salt and pepper to the taste and the gouda, stir and divide among plates.

Enjoy!

Nutrition:

- Calories 300
- Fat 14
- Fiber 6.7
- Carbs 30.2
- Protein 20.5

Delicious Pear Oatmeal

It's pretty amazing and tasty! Try it soon!

Preparation time: 5 minutes
Cooking time: 6 minutes
Servings: 4
Ingredients:

- 1 cup water
- 2 cups milk
- 1 tablespoon soft butter
- A pinch of salt
- ¼ cups brown sugar
- ½ teaspoon cinnamon powder
- 1 cup rolled oats
- ½ cup walnuts, chopped
- 2 cups pear, peeled and chopped
- ½ cup raisins

Directions:

1. In a heatproof dish, mix milk with sugar, butter, salt, oats, cinnamon, raisins, pears and walnuts and stir.
2. Place the dish in the steamer basket of the pot, add 1 cup water in the pot, cover and cook at High for 6 minutes.
3. Release the pressure quick, divide oatmeal into bowls and serve. Enjoy!

Nutrition:

- Calories 250
- Fat 10
- Fiber 11.3
- Carbs 14
- Protein 7

Cinnamon Steel Cut Oats

Your kids will love this simple breakfast make in your instant pot!

Preparation time: 10 minutes
Cooking time: 13 minutes
Servings: 4
Ingredients:

- 1 cup steel oats
- 3 and ½ cups water
- A pinch of salt
- 1 tablespoon butter
- ¾ cup raisins
- 1 teaspoon cinnamon
- ¼ cup brown sugar
- 2 tablespoons white sugar
- 2 ounces cream cheese, soft
- 1 teaspoon milk

Directions:

1. Select Sauté mode on your instant pot, add butter and melt it.
2. Add oats, stir and toast for 3 minutes.
3. Add a pinch of salt and the water, cover the pot and cook at High for 10 minutes.
4. Release the pressure naturally for 5 minutes and uncover the pot.
5. Add raisins, stir and leave aside for now.
6. Meanwhile, in a bowl, mix cinnamon with brown sugar and stir.
7. In another bowl, mix white sugar with cream cheese and milk and stir well.
8. Transfer oats mix to breakfast bowls and top each with cinnamon mix and cream cheese one.

Enjoy!

Nutrition:

- Calories 140
- Fat 3
- Fiber 3
- Carbs 26
- Sugar 4
- Protein 4

Breakfast Banana Cake

You can enjoy it in about 1 hour. It's a great breakfast idea for you and your loved ones!

Preparation time: 10 minutes
Cooking time: 55 minutes
Servings: 5
Ingredients:

- 1 cup water
- 1 and ½ cups sugar
- 2 cups flour
- 3 bananas, peeled and mashed
- 2 eggs
- 1 stick butter, soft
- 2 teaspoon baking powder
- A pinch of salt
- 1 teaspoon cinnamon
- 1 teaspoon nutmeg

Directions:

1. In a bowl, mix eggs with butter and sugar and stir very well.
2. Add salt, baking powder, cinnamon and nutmeg and stir well again.
3. Add bananas and flour and stir again.
4. Grease a spring form pan with some butter, pour the batter in it and cover the pan with a paper towel and tin foil
5. Add 1 cup water to your instant pot, place the pan in the pot, cover and cook at High for 55 minutes.
6. Release the pressure quickly, remove the pan, leave banana breakfast cake to cool down, cut and serve it.

Enjoy!

Nutrition:

- Calories 326
- Fat 11
- Fiber 1.1
- Carbs 55
- Protein 4.3

Breakfast Cobbler

You should try this tasty breakfast as soon as possible!

Preparation time: 10 minutes
Cooking time: 15 minutes
Servings: 4
Ingredients:

- 1 plum, chopped
- 1 pear, chopped
- 1 apple chopped
- 2 tablespoons honey
- ½ teaspoon cinnamon, ground
- 3 tablespoons coconut oil
- ¼ cup pecans, chopped
- ¼ cup coconut, shredded
- 2 tablespoons sunflower seeds

Directions:

1. Put all fruits in a heatproof dish, add coconut oil, cinnamon and honey and toss to coat.
2. Place the dish in the steamer basket of your instant pot, cover and cook at High for 10 minutes.
3. Release the pressure naturally, take out the dish and transfer all fruits to a bowl.
4. In the same baking dish, mix coconut with sunflower seeds and pecans and stir.
5. Transfer these to your instant pot, set it on Sauté mode and toast them for 5 minutes.
6. Add these to fruits in the bowl, toss to coat and serve.

Enjoy!

Nutrition:

- Calories 150
- Fat 7
- Fiber 3
- Carbs 12
- Sugar 7
- Protein 6

Delicious Pomegranate Porridge

The taste is amazing! We adore this simple breakfast!

Preparation time: 5 minutes
Cooking time: 2 minutes
Servings: 2
Ingredients:

1 cup porridge oats
A pinch of salt
1 cup water

¾ cup pomegranate juice
Seeds from 1 pomegranate

Directions:

1. Put oats in your instant pot.
2. Add water, a pinch of salt and pomegranate juice, stir, cover the pot and cook at High for 2 minutes.
3. Release the pressure quick, add pomegranate seeds, stir well, divide into bowls and serve.

Enjoy!

Nutrition:

- Calories 200
- Fat 2.8
- Fiber 4.4
- Carbs 40
- Protein 7.3

Tomato And Spinach Breakfast

It's a perfect combination! You should try it soon!

Preparation time: 10 minutes
Cooking time: 20 minutes
Servings: 6
Ingredients:

- ½ cup milk
- Salt and black pepper to the taste
- 12 eggs
- 3 cups baby spinach, chopped
- 3 green onions, sliced
- 1 cup tomato, diced
- 4 tomato sliced
- ¼ cup parmesan, grated
- 1 and ½ cups water

Directions:

1. Put the water in your instant pot.
2. In a bowl, mix the eggs with salt, pepper and milk and stir well.
3. Put diced tomato, spinach and green onions in a baking dish and stir them.
4. Pour the eggs mix over veggies, spread tomato slices on top and sprinkle parmesan at the end.
5. Arrange this in the steamer basket of your instant pot, cover and cook everything at High for 20 minutes.
6. Release the pressure, open the pot and introduce the baking dish in preheated broiler until the mixture is brown on top.
7. Divide among plates and serve.

Enjoy!

Nutrition:

- Calories 200
- Fat 10.1
- Fiber 1.8
- Carbs 16
- Sugar 1
- Protein 10

Pumpkin Oats Granola

You will never forget the amazing taste this instant pot breakfast has!

Preparation time: 20 minutes
Cooking time: 15 minutes
Servings: 6
Ingredients:

- 3 cups water
- 1 tablespoon soft butter
- 1 cup pumpkin puree
- 1 cup steel cut oats
- ¼ cup maple syrup
- 2 teaspoons cinnamon
- 1 teaspoon pumpkin pie spice
- A pinch of salt

Directions:

1. Select Sauté mode on your instant pot, add butter and melt it.
2. Add oats, stir and cook for 3 minutes.
3. Add pumpkin puree, water, cinnamon, salt, maple syrup and pumpkin spice, stir, cover the pot and cook at High for 10 minutes.
4. Release the pressure naturally for 10 minutes, stir oats granola, leave it aside for 10 minutes, divide it and serve.

Enjoy!
Nutrition:

- Calories 200
- Fat 7
- Fiber 3
- Carbs 33
- Sugar 14
- Protein 5

Delicious Scotch Eggs

We are sure you've heard about this recipe in the past but did you know they taste even better if you make them in your instant pot?

Preparation time: 10 minutes
Cooking time: 15 minutes
Servings: 4
Ingredients:

- 1 pound sausage, ground
- 1 tablespoon vegetable oil
- 4 eggs
- 2 cups water

Directions:

1. Put the eggs in the instant pot, add 1 cup water, cover the pot and cook at High for 6 minutes.
2. Release the pressure for 6 minutes, uncover the pot, remove the eggs and put them in a bowl filled with ice water.
3. Peel the eggs and place them on a working surface.
4. Divide sausage mix into 4 balls, flatten them, place 1 egg in the center of each sausage piece, wrap meat around each egg and put them all on a plate.
5. Set your instant pot on Sauté mode, add the oil and heat it up.
6. Add scotch eggs, brown them on each side and transfer them to a plate.
7. Add the rest of the water to your instant pot, arrange the eggs in the steamer basket of the pot, cover and cook at High for 6 minutes more.
8. Release the pressure quick, divide the eggs among plates and serve.

Enjoy!
Nutrition:

- Calories 300
- Fat 21
- Fiber 0
- Carbs 16
- Protein 12

Poached Eggs

Eggs are healthy and nutritious! Therefore, here's another tasty eggs recipe you can try for breakfast!

Preparation time: 10 minutes
Cooking time: 10 minutes
Servings: 2
Ingredients:

- 1 bunch rucola leaves
- 2 eggs
- 2 bell peppers, ends cut off
- 2 slices mozzarella cheese
- 2 slices whole wheat bread, toasted
- 1 cup water

For the sauce:

- 1 and ½ teaspoons mustard
- 2/3 cup homemade mayonnaise
- Salt to the taste
- 1 teaspoon turmeric powder
- 1 teaspoon lemon juice
- 3 tablespoons orange juice
- 1 tablespoon white wine vinegar

Directions:

1. In a bowl, mix mayo with salt, turmeric, mustard, lemon juice, orange juice and vinegar, stir well, cover the bowl and keep in the fridge for now.
2. Break an egg in each bell pepper, place them in the steamer basket of your instant pot, cover the basket with tin foil, add the water to the pot and cook on Low for 5 minutes.
3. Release the pressure naturally and uncover the pot.
4. Divide toasted bread into 2 plates, add cheese on each, some rucola leaves and top with pepper cups.
5. Drizzle the sauce all over and serve.

Enjoy!

Nutrition:

- Calories 129
- Fat 8
- Fiber 1
- Carbs 9
- Protein 12

Steamed Eggs

This is a simple Korean style breakfast! It's going to be ready in no time for you to enjoy it!

Preparation time: 10 minutes
Cooking time: 5 minutes
Servings: 2
Ingredients:

- 1 and 1/3 cup water
- 2 eggs
- Salt and black pepper to the taste
- A pinch of garlic powder
- A pinch of sesame seeds
- 2 scallions, finely chopped
- Hot rice for serving

Directions:

1. In a bowl, mix the eggs with 1/3 cup water and whisk well.
2. Strain this into a heat proof dish.
3. Add salt, pepper to the taste, sesame seeds, garlic powder and scallions and whisk very well.
4. Put 1 cup water in your instant pot, place the dish in the steamer basket, cover the pot and cook at High for 5 minutes.
5. Release the pressure, uncover the pot, divide the rice among plates and add eggs mix on the side.

Enjoy!

Nutrition:

- Calories 230
- Fat 13
- Fiber 3
- Sugar 1
- Protein 21

Special Eggs Breakfast

It's a special eggs recipe you can easily make in your instant pot!

Preparation time: 10 minutes
Cooking time: 20 minutes
Servings: 6
Ingredients:

- 1 yellow onion, finely chopped
- 6 eggs
- 1 cup ham, cooked and crumbled
- 1 cup kale leaves, chopped
- ½ cup heavy cream
- Salt and black pepper to the taste
- 1 teaspoon herbs de Provence
- 1 cup cheddar cheese, grated
- 1 cup water

Directions:

1. In a bowl, mix eggs with salt, pepper, heavy cream, onion, kale, cheese and herbs, whisk very well and pour into a heat proof dish.
2. Put 1 cup water in your instant pot, place dish in the steamer basket, cover the pot and cook at High for 20 minutes.
3. Release the pressure, uncover the pot, remove the dish, divide eggs between plates and serve.

Enjoy!

Nutrition:

- Calories 189
- Fat 12.3
- Fiber 1
- Carbs 1
- Protein 20.3

Breakfast Quiche

It's a tasty and textured breakfast idea! Try it soon and amaze everyone!

Preparation time: 10 minutes
Cooking time: 30 minutes
Servings: 4
Ingredients:

- ½ cup milk
- 6 eggs, whisked
- Salt and black pepper to the taste
- 4 bacon slices, cooked and crumbled
- 1 cup sausage, already cooked and ground
- ½ cup ham, diced
- 1 cup cheese, shredded
- 2 green onions, chopped
- 1 and ½ cups water

Directions:

1. Put the water in your instant pot and leave it aside for now.
2. In a bowl, mix eggs with salt, pepper, milk, sausage, ham, bacon, onions and cheese and stir everything well.
3. Pour this into a baking dish, cover with some tin foil, place the dish in the steamer basket of your instant pot, cover and cook at High for 30 minutes.
4. Release the pressure for 10 minutes, uncover the pot, take the quiche out and leave it aside for a few minutes to cool down.
5. Cut the quiche, arrange it on plates and serve.

Enjoy!

Nutrition:

- Calories 220
- Fat 3.4
- Fiber 1.1
- Carbs 22
- Protein 15.3

Breakfast Carrot Oatmeal

It's a hearty breakfast you should make today!

Preparation time: 20 minutes
Cooking time: 13 minutes
Servings: 6
Ingredients:

- 1 cup steel cut oats
- 4 cups water
- 1 tablespoon butter
- 3 tablespoons maple syrup
- A pinch of salt
- 2 teaspoons cinnamon
- 1 teaspoon pie spice
- 1 cup grated carrots
- ¼ cup chia seeds
- ¾ cup raisins

Directions:

1. Select the Sauté mode on your instant pot, add butter and melt it.
2. Add oats, stir and toast for 3 minutes.
3. Add carrots, water, maple syrup, cinnamon, spice and a pinch of salt, stir, cover the pot and cook at High for 10 minutes.
4. Release the pressure naturally for 10 minutes, add raisins and chia seeds, stir, leave oatmeal aside for 10 minutes, divide it between bowls and serve right away.

Enjoy!

Nutrition:

- Calories 145
- Fat 3
- Fiber 1.3
- Carbs 25
- Protein 3.5
- Sugar 11

Egg Muffins

This should be very interesting! Pay attention!

Preparation time: 10 minutes
Cooking time: 10 minutes
Servings: 4
Ingredients:

- 1 and ½ cups water
- 1 green onion, chopped
- 4 bacon slices, cooked and crumbled
- 4 tablespoons cheddar cheese, shredded
- ¼ teaspoon lemon pepper
- 4 eggs
- A pinch of salt

Directions:

1. In a bowl, mix eggs with a pinch of salt and lemon pepper and whisk well.
2. Divide green onion, bacon and cheese into muffin cups.
3. Add eggs and stir a bit.
4. Put the water in your instant pot, add muffin cups in the steamer basket, cover the pot and cook at High for 10 minutes.
5. Release the pressure quick, divide the egg muffins among plates and serve them right away.

Enjoy!

Nutrition:

- Calories 70
- Fat 2.4
- Fiber 1
- Carbs 1.5
- Protein 4.6

Delicious Breakfast Risotto

Don't worry! It's going to be a real breakfast feast!

Preparation time: 10 minutes
Cooking time: 12 minutes
Servings: 4
Ingredients:

- 1 and ½ cups Arborio rice
- 1 and ½ teaspoons cinnamon powder
- 1/3 cup brown sugar
- A pinch of salt
- 2 tablespoons butter
- 2 apples, cored and sliced
- 1 cup apple juice
- 3 cups milk
- ½ cup cherries, dried

Directions:

1. Set your instant pot on Sauté mode, add butter and melt it.
2. Add rice, stir and cook for 5 minutes.
3. Add sugar, apples, apple juice, milk, a pinch of salt and cinnamon, stir, cover and cook at High for 6 minutes.
4. Release the pressure naturally for 6 minutes, uncover the pot, add cherries, stir, cover and leave aside for 5 more minutes.
5. Divide into breakfast bowls and serve right away.

Enjoy!
Nutrition:

- Calories 160
- Fat 16
- Fiber 3
- Carbs 30
- Sugar 1
- Protein 11

Breakfast Rice Bowl

It's a healthy breakfast full of taste and flavor!

Preparation time: 5 minutes
Cooking time: 7 minutes
Servings: 4
Ingredients:

- 1 cup brown rice
- ½ cup coconut chips
- 1 cup coconut milk
- 2 cups water
- ½ cup maple syrup
- ¼ cup raisins
- ¼ cup almonds
- A pinch of cinnamon powder
- A pinch of salt

Directions:

1. Put the rice in a pot, add the water, place on stove over medium high heat, cook according to instructions, drain and transfer it to your instant pot.
2. Add milk, coconut chips, almonds, raisins, salt, cinnamon and maple syrup, stir well, cover the pot and cook at High for 5 minutes.
3. Release pressure quick, transfer rice to breakfast bowls and serve right away.

Enjoy!
Nutrition:

- Calories 240
- Fat 7
- Fiber 9.5
- Carbs 45
- Sugar 13
- Protein 13

Special Rice Pudding

This is very tasty! We've tried it, and we loved it! It's your turn!

Preparation time: 10 minutes
Cooking time: 35 minutes
Servings: 4
Ingredients:

- 6 and ½ cups water
- ¾ cup sugar
- 2 cups black rice, washed and rinsed
- 2 cinnamon sticks
- A pinch of salt
- 5 cardamom pods, crushed
- 3 cloves
- ½ cup coconut, grated
- Chopped mango for serving

Directions:

1. Put the rice in your instant pot, add a pinch of salt and the water and stir.
2. In a cheesecloth bag, mix cardamom with cinnamon and cloves and tie it.
3. Place this in the pot with the rice, cover and cook on Low for 35 minutes.
4. Release the pressure naturally, uncover the pot, stir the rice, add coconut and set your pot to sauté mode.
5. Cook for 10 minutes, discard spices bag, transfer to breakfast bowls and serve with chopped mango on top.

Enjoy!

Nutrition:

- Calories 118
- Fat 1
- Fiber 1
- Carbs 21
- Protein 8

Amazing Breakfast Quinoa

It's insanely delicious!

Preparation time: 10 minutes
Cooking time: 10 minutes
Servings: 6
Ingredients:

- 2 and ¼ cups water
- 1 and ½ cups quinoa, rinsed
- 2 tablespoon maple syrup
- A pinch of salt
- ¼ teaspoon cinnamon powder
- ½ teaspoon vanilla extract
- Fresh berries for serving
- Milk for serving
- Almonds, sliced for serving

Directions:

1. In your instant pot, add water, quinoa, vanilla, cinnamon, salt and maple syrup.
2. Stir, cover the pot and cook at High for 10 minutes.
3. Release the pressure naturally, fluff quinoa with a fork, divide it into breakfast bowls, add milk and stir.
4. Top with almonds and berries and serve.

Enjoy!

Nutrition:

- Calories 100
- Fat 3
- Fiber 1
- Carbs 4
- Sugar 3
- Protein 2

Breakfast Quinoa Salad

This quinoa salad will provide you a lot of health benefits! It's just perfect!

Preparation time: 10 minutes
Cooking time: 15 minutes
Servings: 8
Ingredients:

- 2 garlic cloves, minced
- 2 and ¼ cups water
- 1 and ½ cups quinoa, rinsed
- A pinch of salt
- 2 tomatoes, chopped
- 1 cucumber, chopped
- 1 jalapeno pepper, chopped
- 1 cup corn, already cooked
- ½ cup scallions, finely chopped
- 1 and ½ cups chickpeas, already cooked
- 2/3 cup parsley leaves, finely chopped
- 1/3 cup mint leaves, chopped
- 1 avocado, pitted, peeled and diced
- 3 tablespoons veggie stock
- ¼ cup lime juice
- Black pepper to the taste
- ½ teaspoon chipotle chili pepper

Directions:

1. In your pressure cooker, mix quinoa with 1 garlic clove, a pinch of salt and the water, stir, cover and cook at High for 1 minute.
2. Release the pressure, uncover the instant pot, fluff quinoa with a fork and leave it to cool down.
3. Transfer quinoa to a bowl, add tomatoes, cucumber, jalapeno pepper, corn, scallions, chickpeas, parsley, mint, and avocado.
4. In a bowl, mix veggie stock with black pepper to the taste, 1 garlic clove, lime juice and chipotle chili pepper and stir very well.
5. Pour this over salad, toss to coat and serve.

Enjoy!

Nutrition:

- Calories 239
- Fat 6.4
- Fiber 7.7
- Carbs 39
- Protein 9

Breakfast Bread Pudding

It's one of our favorites! It will soon become yours too!

Preparation time: 10 minutes
Cooking time: 25 minutes
Servings: 6
Ingredients:

- 1 cup water
- Cooking spray
- 4 tablespoons butter
- 1 cup onions, thinly sliced
- 1 cup mushrooms, sliced
- 1 cup ham, diced
- ¼ cup sugar
- 3 eggs, whisked
- 2 cups half and half
- ½ teaspoon mustard, dry
- Salt and black pepper to the taste
- 1 cup Swiss cheese, grated
- ½ teaspoon thyme, dried
- 14 ounces loaf and bread, cubed

For the sauce:

- 1 and ½ teaspoons rice wine vinegar
- ½ cup mustard
- 2 tablespoons maple syrup
- Salt and black pepper to the taste

Directions:

1. Heat up a pan over medium heat, add butter and melt it.
2. Add onions, stir and cook for 2 minutes.
3. Add ham, stir again, cook for 2 minutes more, take off heat and leave aside.
4. Spray a pan with some cooking oil.
5. In a bowl, mix eggs with sugar, half and half, thyme, half of the Swiss cheese, salt, pepper, bread cubes, mushroom, ham and onions mix and stir well.
6. Pour this into greased pan, place it in the steamer basket of your instant pot, also add the water in the instant pot, cover with tin foil, cover the pot and cook on High for 25 minutes.
7. Meanwhile, heat up a small pot over medium heat, add dry mustard, salt, pepper, vinegar and maple syrup, stir well and cook for 2-3 minutes.
8. Release pressure from the pot, uncover, take the pan out, sprinkle the rest of the cheese, introduce in preheated broil and brown for a few minutes.
9. Divide bread pudding on plates, drizzle the sauce on top and serve.

Enjoy!

Nutrition:

- Calories 270
- Fat 12
- Fiber 2
- Carbs 14
- Protein 10

Delicious Millet Pudding

It's a tasty and super healthy breakfast pudding!

Preparation time: 10 minutes
Cooking time: 10 minutes
Servings: 4
Ingredients:

- 14 ounces coconut milk
- 7 ounces water
- 2/3 cup millet
- A pinch of salt
- 4 dates, pitted
- Honey for serving

Directions:

1. Put the millet in your instant pot.
2. Add milk, dates and a pinch of salt and stir.
3. Add the water, stir again, cover the pot and cook at High for 10 minutes.
4. Release the pressure naturally, uncover the pot, divide the pudding into bowls, top with honey and serve.

Enjoy!

Nutrition:

- Calories 240
- Fat 2
- Fiber 2.6
- Carbs 25
- Sugar 33
- Protein 8

Special Breakfast Millet Pilaf

Serve this for breakfast right away! It's a special and tasty idea!

Preparation time: 10 minutes
Cooking time: 10 minutes
Servings: 4
Ingredients:

- 1 tablespoon ghee
- 1 teaspoon cardamom, crushed
- 3 teaspoons cumin seeds
- 1 bay leaf
- 1 inch cinnamon stick
- 2 cups organic millet
- 1 white onion, chopped
- Salt to the taste
- 3 cups water

Directions:

1. Set your instant pot on sauté mode, add ghee and heat it up.
2. Add cumin, cinnamon, cardamom and bay leaf, stir and cook for 1 minute.
3. Add onion, stir and cook for 4 minutes.
4. Add millet, salt and water, stir, cover the pot and cook at High for 1 minute.
5. Release the pressure naturally, fluff the mix with a fork, transfer to bowls and serve.

Enjoy!

Nutrition:

- Calories 100
- Fat 3.1
- Fiber 1.3
- Carbs 16
- Protein 2.5

Breakfast Pudding

You will impress everyone with this breakfast pudding!

Preparation time: 5 minutes
Cooking time: 10 minutes
Servings: 4
Ingredients:

- 1 and ½ cups water
- 1/3 cup tapioca pearls
- 1 and ¼ cup whole milk
- Zest from ½ lemon
- ½ cup sugar

Directions:

1. Put 1 cup water in your instant pot.
2. Put tapioca pearls in a heat proof bowl add milk, ½ cup water, lemon zest and sugar.
3. Stir everything, place the bowl in the steamer basket of the pot, cover and cook at High for 10 minutes.
4. Release the pressure, transfer pudding to cups and serve.

Enjoy!

Nutrition:

- Calories 122
- Fat 2
- Fiber 0
- Carbs 21
- Sugar 6
- Protein 5

Breakfast Chia Pudding

This is so healthy and easy to make!

Preparation time: 2 hours
Cooking time: 3 minutes
Servings: 4
Ingredients:

- ½ cup chia seeds
- 2 cups almond milk
- ¼ cup almonds
- ¼ cup coconut, shredded
- 4 teaspoons sugar

Directions:

1. Put chia seeds in your instant pot.
2. Add milk, almonds and coconut flakes, stir, cover and cook at High for 3 minutes.
3. Release the pressure quick, divide the pudding between bowls, top each with a teaspoon of sugar and serve.

Enjoy!

Nutrition:

- Calories 130
- Fat 12
- Fiber 22
- Carbs 2
- Protein 14

Breakfast Hash

It's a rich dish that will give you so much energy!

Preparation time: 10 minutes
Cooking time: 7 minutes
Servings: 4
Ingredients:

- 8 ounces sausage, ground
- 1 package hash browns, frozen
- 1/3 cup water
- 1 yellow onion, chopped
- 1 green bell pepper, chopped
- 1 cup cheddar cheese, grated
- Salt and black pepper to the taste
- 4 eggs, whisked
- Salsa for serving

Directions:

1. Set your instant pot on Sauté mode, add sausage, stir and cook for 2 minutes.
2. Drain excess fat, add bell pepper and onion, stir and cook for 2 more minutes.
3. Add hash browns, water, eggs, salt and cheese, stir, cover and cook on Low for 4 minutes.
4. Release the pressure quick, divide hash among plates and serve with salsa.

Enjoy!

Nutrition:

- Calories 300
- Fat 16
- Fiber 4
- Carbs 30
- Protein 17

Potato Hash

It's always so comforting to have more options! If you are not in the mood to make the hash recipe above, then maybe you'll try this one!

Preparation time: 10 minutes
Cooking time: 8 minutes
Servings: 4
Ingredients:

- 1 cup cheddar cheese, shredded
- 6 eggs, whisked
- Salt and black pepper to the taste
- 6 potatoes, peeled and roughly chopped
- 1 cup ham, chopped
- A drizzle of olive oil
- ¼ cup water
- Toasted bread for serving

Directions:

1. Set your instant pot on Sauté, add the oil and heat it up.
2. Add potatoes, stir and brown them for 3 minutes.
3. Add ham, eggs, cheese, salt, pepper and the water, stir, cover the pot and cook at High for 5 minutes.
4. Release the pressure, transfer hash to plates and serve with toasted bread.

Enjoy!

Nutrition:

- Calories 250
- Fat 12
- Fiber 2
- Carbs 20
- Protein 17

Breakfast Burritos

Get ready to enjoy the best breakfast burritos!

Preparation time: 15 minutes
Cooking time: 15 minutes
Servings: 6
Ingredients:

- 8 ounces pork meat, ground
- Salt and black pepper to the taste
- 1 teaspoon thyme, dry
- 1 teaspoon sage, dry
- 1 teaspoon fennel seed, crushed
- 1 teaspoon brown sugar
- A pinch of nutmeg
- ½ teaspoon red pepper flakes, crushed
- 1 tablespoon water
- 1 and ½ cups water
- 6 tortilla shells
- 8 eggs
- A drizzle of olive oil
- ¼ cup milk
- Cheddar cheese, shredded for serving
- Salsa for serving

Directions:

1. In a bowl, mix pork with salt, pepper, thyme, sage, fennel, pepper flakes, nutmeg, sugar and 1 tablespoon water, stir very well, cover the bowl and keep it in the fridge for now.
2. Brush tortilla shells with some olive oil, arrange them on a baking sheet, cover them with tin foil and seal edges.
3. In a heat proof dish, mix eggs with salt, pepper, and milk and whisk well.
4. Add meat mix, stir and cover the dish with some tin foil.
5. Place dish in the steamer basket of your instant pot, add wrapped tortilla shells on top, add 1 and ½ cups water in the pot, cover and cook at High for 15 minutes.
6. Release the pressure and take tortilla shells and eggs and meat mix out of the pot.
7. Unwrap tortilla shells, fill them with eggs and meat mix and top with salsa and cheddar cheese.
8. Arrange on plates and serve.

Enjoy!

Nutrition:

- Calories 380
- Fat 25
- Fiber 11
- Carbs 19
- Protein 21

Breakfast Sandwiches

You can serve this for breakfast, and you can make an extra serving to take it with you at the office!

Preparation time: 10 minutes
Cooking time: 40 minutes
Servings: 8
Ingredients:

- 2 tablespoons brown sugar
- 4-pound beef roast, cut into small chunks
- Salt and black pepper to the taste
- 2 teaspoons paprika
- 2 and ½ teaspoons garlic powder
- 2 teaspoons mustard powder
- 2 teaspoons onion flakes
- 3 cups beef stock
- 1 tablespoon balsamic vinegar
- 2 tablespoon Worcestershire sauce
- 4 tablespoons butter, soft
- 8 hoagie rolls
- 8 slices provolone cheese

Directions:

1. Put the meat in your instant pot.
2. Add salt, pepper, paprika, 2 teaspoons garlic powder, mustard powder, onion flakes, stock, vinegar and Worcestershire sauce, stir well, cover the pot and cook at High for 40 minutes.
3. Release the pressure quick, transfer meat to a cutting board, strain the liquid and keep it in a bowl.
4. Shred meat and divide among rolls after you've buttered them.
5. Add provolone cheese on top, introduce sandwiches in preheated broiler and broil until cheese melts.
6. Dip sandwiches in the sauce from the pot and serve them.

Enjoy!

Nutrition:

- Calories 340
- Fat 21
- Fiber 2
- Carbs 12
- Protein 34

Simple Breakfast Sausages And Peppers

It's such a simple breakfast idea but it's going to taste wonderful!

Preparation time: 10 minutes
Cooking time: 25 minutes
Servings: 5
Ingredients:

- 15 ounces tomato sauce
- 28 ounces canned tomatoes, diced
- 10 Italian sausages
- 4 green bell peppers, cut into thin strips
- 1 cup water
- 4 garlic cloves, minced
- 1 tablespoon basil, dried
- 1 tablespoon Italian seasoning

Directions:

1. Put tomatoes, tomato sauce, basil, water, garlic, sausages, bell peppers and Italian seasoning in your instant pot and stir gently.
2. Cover the pot and cook at High for 25 minutes.
3. Release the pressure quick, divide the mix between plates and serve.

Enjoy!

Nutrition:

- Calories 400
- Fat 31
- Fiber 1
- Carbs 8
- Protein 23

Delicious Breakfast Tacos

These will be the best tacos you'll ever have!

Preparation time: 10 minutes
Cooking time: 5 minutes
Servings: 4
Ingredients:

- 1 pound turkey meat, ground
- 1 tablespoon Worcestershire sauce
- 1 tablespoon extra virgin olive oil
- 1 and ¼ cups beef stock
- 2 teaspoons corn flour
- 1 and ½ teaspoons cumin, ground
- 1 tablespoon chili powder
- ¼ teaspoon onion powder
- ¼ teaspoon garlic powder
- ¼ teaspoon dried onions
- ½ teaspoon paprika
- ¼ teaspoon oregano, dried
- A pinch of cayenne pepper
- Salt and black pepper to the taste
- Tacos shells for serving

Directions:

1. Set your instant pot on Sauté mode, add oil and heat it up.
2. Add meat and ½ cup stock, stir and brown for a few minutes.
3. Discard excess fat, add the rest of the stock, Worcestershire sauce, flour, cumin, chili powder, garlic and onion powder, dried onions, paprika, oregano, salt, pepper and cayenne pepper, stir, cover the pot and cook at High for 5 minutes.
4. Release the pressure naturally, uncover the pot, stir meat mix and divide it in taco shells.
5. Serve right away.

Enjoy!

Nutrition:

- Calories 240
- Fat 11.5
- Fiber 1
- Carbs 3.4
- Protein 31.1

Breakfast Jam

Serve this with toasted bread slices, and you will feel full all day long!

Preparation time: 20 minutes
Cooking time: 1 hour and 15 minutes
Servings: 12
Ingredients:

- 16 ounces cranberries
- 16 ounces strawberries, chopped
- Zest from 1 lemon
- 4 ounces raisins
- A pinch of salt
- 3 ounces water
- 2 and ½ pounds sugar

Directions:

1. In your instant pot, mix strawberries with cranberries, lemon zest, and raisins.
2. Add sugar, stir and leave pot aside to 1 hour.
3. Add water and a pinch of salt, cover the pot and cook at High for 15 minutes.
4. Release the pressure, leave jam aside for 5 minutes, stir, pour into small jars and enjoy!
5. Serve with toasted bread slices!

Nutrition:

- Calories 60
- Fat 0
- Fiber 0
- Carbs 12
- Protein 1
- Sugar 12

Instant Pot Lemon Marmalade

It's such a delicious marmalade. Serve it in the morning with toasted bread and a glass of milk!

Preparation time: 10 minutes
Cooking time: 15 minutes
Servings: 8
Ingredients:

- 2 pounds lemons, washed and sliced with a mandolin
- 4 pounds sugar
- 1 tablespoon vinegar

Directions:

1. Put lemon slices in your instant pot.
2. Cover the pot and cook the marmalade at High for 10 minutes.
3. Release the pressure, add the sugar, cover the pot again and cook at High for 4 more minutes.
4. Release the pressure again, stir your marmalade, pour it into jars and refrigerate until your serve it.

Enjoy!
Nutrition:

- Calories 60
- Fat 1
- Fiber 0
- Carbs 12
- Sugar 13

Blackberry Jam

The taste is so special! You will enjoy it soon!

Preparation time: 10 minutes
Cooking time: 20 minutes
Servings: 4
Ingredients:

- 4 pints blackberries
- Juice of 1 small lemon
- 5 cups sugar
- 3 tablespoons pectin powder

Directions:

1. Put the blackberries in your instant pot.
2. Add the sugar, stir, select sauté mode and cook for 3 minutes.
3. Transfer the jam to clean jars, close them and place them in the steamer basket of your instant pot.
4. Add water to cover the jars halfway, select Canning mode on your pot, cover and leave them for 20 minutes.
5. Remove jars after 20 minutes, leave them to cool down and keep your jam in the fridge until you serve it in the morning with some toasted bread and some butter.

Enjoy!
Nutrition:

- Calories 63
- Fat 6
- Fiber 7.6
- Carbs 12
- Protein 2
- Sugar 7

Amazing Cheesy Grits

They are delicious, and you don't need to be an expert in the kitchen to make them!

Preparation time: 10 minutes
Cooking time: 10 minutes
Servings: 4
Ingredients:

- 2 tablespoons coconut oil
- 1 and ¾ cup half and half
- 1 cup stone ground grits
- 3 cups water
- 2 teaspoons salt
- 3 tablespoons butter
- 4 ounces cheddar cheese, grated
- Butter for serving

Directions:

1. Set your instant pot on sauté mode, add grits, stir and toast them for 3 minutes.
2. Add oil, half, and half, water, salt, butter and cheese, stir, cover and cook on High for 10 minutes.
3. Release the pressure naturally, leave cheesy grits aside for 15 minutes, transfer to breakfast bowls, add butter on top and serve.

Enjoy!

Nutrition:

- Calories 280
- Fat 13
- Fiber 1
- Carbs 26
- Sugar 2
- Protein 13.2

Tasty Breakfast

It's a unique breakfast idea just for you!

Preparation time: 10 minutes
Cooking time: 25 minutes
Servings: 4
Ingredients:

- 3 cups rooibos tea
- 1 tablespoon cinnamon, ground
- 1 cup red lentils, soaked for 4 hours and drained
- 2 apples, diced
- 1 teaspoon cloves, ground
- 1 teaspoon turmeric, ground
- Maple syrup to the taste
- Coconut milk for serving

Directions:

1. Put lentils in your instant pot, add tea, stir, cover and cook at High for 15 minutes.
2. Release pressure, uncover the pot, add cinnamon, apples, turmeric, and cloves, stir, cover and cook at High for 15 more minutes.
3. Release pressure quick, divide lentils between bowls, add maple syrup to the taste and coconut milk

Enjoy!

Nutrition:

- Calories 140
- Fat 1.2
- Fiber 8.4
- Carbs 35
- Sugar 14
- Protein 5

Chickpeas Spread

Forget about your classic hummus recipe. This is something much better, and the best thing is that you can easily serve it for breakfast!

Preparation time: 5 minutes
Cooking time: 20 minutes
Servings: 8
Ingredients:

- 1 cup chickpeas soaked and drained
- 6 cups water
- 1 bay leaf
- 4 garlic cloves crushed
- 2 tablespoons tahini paste
- Juice of 1 lemon
- ¼ teaspoon cumin
- Salt to the taste
- ¼ cup chopped parsley
- A pinch of paprika
- Extra virgin olive oil

Directions:

1. Put chickpeas and water in your instant pot.
2. Add bay leaf, 2 garlic cloves, cover the pot and cook at High for 18 minutes
3. Release the pressure, discard excess liquid and bay leaf and reserve some of the cooking liquid.
4. Add tahini paste, the cooking liquid you've reserved, lemon juice, cumin, the rest of the garlic and salt to the taste.
5. Transfer everything to your food processor and pulse well.
6. Transfer your chickpeas spread in a serving bowl, sprinkle olive oil and paprika on top and enjoy!

Nutrition:

- Calories 270
- Fat 19
- Fiber 5.1
- Carbs 21.5
- Protein 6.8

Chicken Liver Breakfast Spread

You might find this breakfast idea a bit different, but we can assure you that it is delicious!

Preparation time: 5 minutes
Cooking time: 15 minutes
Servings: 8
Ingredients:

- 1 teaspoon extra virgin olive oil
- ¾ pound chicken liver
- 1 yellow onion, roughly chopped
- 1 bay leaf
- ¼ cup red wine
- 2 anchovies
- 1 tablespoons capers, drained and chopped
- 1 tablespoon butter
- Salt and black pepper to the taste

Directions:

1. Put the olive oil in your instant pot, add onion, salt, pepper, chicken liver, bay leaf and wine.
2. Stir, cover the pot and cook at High for 10 minutes.
3. Release the pressure quick, add anchovies, capers, and butter.
4. Stir, transfer to kitchen blender and pulse very well everything
5. Add salt and pepper to the taste, blend again, transfer to a bowl and serve with toasted bread slices!

Enjoy!

Nutrition:

- Calories 150
- Fat 12
- Fiber 0
- Carbs 5
- Sugar 2
- Protein 4

Mushroom Pate

You only need a few ingredients and an instant pot to prepare a fast and fancy breakfast!

Preparation time: 6 minutes
Cooking time: 18 minutes
Servings: 6
Ingredients:

- 1-ounce dry porcini mushrooms
- 1 pound button mushrooms sliced
- 1 cup boiled water
- 1 tablespoon butter
- 1 tablespoon extra virgin olive oil
- 1 shallot finely chopped
- ¼ cup white wine
- Salt and pepper to the taste
- 1 bay leaf
- 1 tablespoon truffle oil
- 3 tablespoons grated parmesan cheese

Directions:

1. Put dry mushrooms in a bowl, add 1 cup boiling water over them and leave them aside for now.
2. Set your instant pot on sauté mode, add butter and the olive oil and heat them up.
3. Add the shallot, stir and cook for 2 minutes
4. Add dry mushrooms and their liquid, fresh mushrooms, wine, salt, pepper, and bay leaf.
5. Stir, cover the pot and cook at High for 16 minutes.
6. Release the pressure, discard bay leaf and some of the liquid, transfer everything to your blender and pulse until you obtain a creamy spread.
7. Add truffle oil and grated parmesan cheese, blend again, transfer to a bowl and serve.

Enjoy!
Nutrition:

- Calories 220
- Fat 15
- Fiber 0
- Carbs 15
- Sugar 3
- Protein 5

Delicious Ricotta Cheese Spread

Just toast some of your favorite bread, spread this and serve it in the morning with a glass of milk!

Preparation time: 10 minutes
Cooking time: 5 minutes
Servings: 4
Ingredients:

- 10 ounces canned tomatoes and green chilies, chopped
- 1 and ¾ cups Italian sausage, ground
- 4 cups processed cheese, cut into chunks
- 4 tablespoons water

Directions:

1. In your instant pot, mix tomatoes and chilies with water, ground sausage, and cheese.
2. Stir, cover and cook at High for 5 minutes.
3. Release the pressure naturally for 5 minutes, uncover the pot, stir spread, transfer to a bowl and serve it.

Enjoy!

Nutrition:

- Calories 294
- Fat 18
- Fiber 1
- Carbs 4
- Protein 7

Instant Pot Pecan Sweet Potatoes

This is a sweet, fresh and super delicious breakfast dish!

Preparation time: 10 minutes
Cooking time: 10 minutes
Servings: 8
Ingredients:

- 1 cup water
- 1 tablespoon lemon peel
- ½ cup brown sugar
- ¼ teaspoon salt
- 3 sweet potatoes peeled and sliced
- ¼ cup butter
- ¼ cup maple syrup
- 1 cup pecans chopped
- 1 tablespoon cornstarch
- Whole pecans for garnish

Directions:

1. Put the water in your instant pot, add lemon peel, brown sugar and salt and stir.
2. Add potatoes, cover the pot and cook at High for 15 minutes.
3. Release the pressure and transfer the potatoes to a serving plate.
4. Select sauté mode on your instant pot, add the butter and melt it.
5. Add pecans, maple syrup, cornstarch and stir very well.
6. Pour this over the potatoes, garnish with whole pecans and serve!

Enjoy!

Nutrition:

- Calories 230
- Fat 13
- Fiber 4
- Carbs 15
- Protein 6

Pumpkin Butter

This can be refrigerated up to 3 weeks! Therefore, you can enjoy it many mornings from now on!

Preparation time: 15 minutes
Cooking time: 10 minutes
Servings: 18
Ingredients:

- 30 ounces pumpkin puree
- 3 apples, peeled, cored and chopped
- 1 tablespoon pumpkin spice
- 1 cup sugar
- A pinch of salt
- 12 ounces apple cider
- ½ cup honey

Directions:

1. In your instant pot, mix pumpkin puree with pumpkin spice, apple pieces, sugar, honey, cider and a pinch of salt,
2. Stir well, cover the pot and cook at High for 10 minutes.
3. Release the pressure naturally for 15 minutes, transfer the butter to small jars and keep it in the fridge until you serve it.

Enjoy!

Nutrition:

- Calories 50
- Fat 1
- Fiber 0
- Carbs 10
- Sugar 9
- Protein 1

Breakfast Salad

Are you looking for something nutritious to eat in the morning? This is what you were looking for!

Preparation time: 10 minutes
Cooking time: 4 minutes
Servings: 4
Ingredients:

- 6 potatoes, peeled and cubed
- 4 eggs
- 1 and ½ cups water
- 1 cup homemade mayonnaise
- ¼ cup onion, finely chopped
- 1 tablespoon dill pickle juice
- 2 tablespoons parsley, finely chopped
- 1 tablespoon mustard
- Salt and black pepper to the taste

Directions:

1. Put potatoes, eggs and the water in the steamer basket of your instant pot, cover and cook on High for 4 minutes.
2. Release the pressure quick, transfer eggs to a bowl filled with ice water and leave them to cool down.
3. In a bowl, mix mayo with pickle juice, onion, parsley and mustard and stir well.
4. Add potatoes and toss to coat.
5. Peel eggs, chop them, add them to salad and toss again.
6. Add salt and pepper to the taste, stir and serve your salad with toasted bread slices.

Enjoy!

Nutrition:

- Calories 150
- Fat 8
- Fiber 1.3
- Carbs 11
- Protein 3

Breakfast Potatoes

It's a simple, quick and tasty breakfast idea! It the best!

Preparation time: 5 minutes
Cooking time: 7 minutes
Servings: 2
Ingredients:

- 4 gold potatoes, washed
- 2 teaspoons Italian seasoning
- 1 tablespoon bacon fat
- 1 cup chives, chopped for serving.
- Water
- Salt and pepper to the taste

Directions:

1. Put potatoes in your instant pot, add water to cover them, cover the pot and cook at High for 10 minutes.
2. Release the pressure naturally, transfer potatoes to a working surface and leave them to cool down.
3. Peel potatoes, transfer them to a bowl and mash them a bit with a fork.
4. Set your instant pot on sauté mode, add bacon fat and heat up.
5. Add potatoes, seasoning, salt and pepper to the taste, stir, cover the pot and cook at High for 1 minute.
6. Release the pressure quickly, stir potatoes again, divide them between plates and serve with chives sprinkled on top.

Enjoy!

Nutrition:

- Calories 90
- Fat 3
- Fiber 1
- Carbs 11
- Protein 1

Tofu Breakfast

Tofu is perfect for breakfast! Try this simple recipe today!

Preparation time: 10 minutes
Cooking time: 7 minutes
Servings: 4
Ingredients:

- 1 bunch kale leaves, chopped
- 1 leek, cut into halves lengthwise and thinly sliced
- 1 teaspoon paprika
- 1 tablespoon olive oil
- ½ cup water
- Sat to the taste
- A pinch of cayenne pepper
- 2 teaspoons sherry vinegar
- 3 ounces tofu, cubed and baked
- ¼ cup almonds, chopped

Directions:

1. Set your instant pot on Sauté mode, add oil and heat it up.
2. Add leeks, stir and sauté them for 5 minutes.
3. Add paprika, stir and cook for 1 minute.
4. Add water, kale, salt and cayenne, cover the pot and cook at High for 2 minutes.
5. Release the pressure quick, add tofu and vinegar and more salt if needed, stir and transfer to plates.
6. Sprinkle almonds on top and serve right away.

Enjoy!

Nutrition:

- Calories 170
- Fat 12
- Fiber 7
- Carbs 18
- Protein 16

Tofu Scramble

It's really tasty and simple to make! Try it!

Preparation time: 10 minutes
Cooking time: 7 minutes
Servings: 4
Ingredients:

- 1 yellow onion, thinly sliced
- 1 teaspoon walnut oil
- 3 garlic cloves, minced
- ¼ cup veggie stock
- 1 cup carrot, chopped
- 1 block firm tofu, drained
- 12 ounces canned tomatoes, diced
- 1 teaspoon cumin
- 2 tablespoons red pepper, chopped
- 1 tablespoon Italian seasoning
- 1 teaspoon nutritional yeast
- Salt and black pepper to the taste

Directions:

1. Set your instant pot on Sauté mode, add oil and heat it up.
2. Add onion, carrot and garlic, stir and cook for 3 minutes.
3. Crumble tofu, add it to pot and stir.
4. Add stock, red pepper, tomatoes, cumin, Italian seasoning, salt and pepper, stir, cover the pot and cook at High for 4 minutes.
5. Release the pressure quick, transfer to bowls and serve with nutritional yeast on top.

Enjoy!

Nutrition:

- Calories 144
- Fat 5.7
- Fiber 3.1
- Carbs 11.8
- Protein 13

BBQ Tofu

Tofu is a great option for breakfast! So, here is another recipe you can try!

Preparation time: 10 minutes
Cooking time: 10 minutes
Servings: 6
Ingredients:

- 28 ounces firm tofu, cubed
- 12 ounces bbq sauce
- 2 tablespoons extra virgin olive oil
- 4 garlic cloves, minced
- 1 yellow onion, chopped
- 1 celery stalk, chopped
- 1 red bell pepper, chopped
- 1 green bell pepper, chopped
- Salt to the taste
- A pinch of curry powder

Directions:

1. Set your instant pot on Sauté mode, add the oil and heat it up.
2. Add bell peppers, garlic, onion and celery and stir.
3. Add salt and curry powder, stir and cook for 2 minutes.
4. Add tofu, stir and cook 4 minutes more.
5. Add bbq sauce, stir, cover the pot and cook at High for 5 minutes.
6. Release the pressure, uncover the pot, transfer to plates and serve.

Enjoy!

Nutrition:

- Calories 200
- Fat 11
- Fiber 3
- Carbs 14.1
- Protein 14.4

Potatoes And Tofu Breakfast

It's a fresh instant pot breakfast idea! Try it on a hot summer day!

Preparation time: 10 minutes
Cooking time: 4 minutes
Servings: 4
Ingredients:

- 3 purple potatoes, cubed
- 1 yellow onion, chopped
- 2 garlic cloves, minced
- 1 carrot, chopped
- 1 ginger root, grated
- ½ pound firm tofu, cubed
- 3 tablespoons water
- 1 tablespoon tamari
- Mexican spice blend to the taste
- 1 and ½ cups Brussels sprouts

Directions:

1. Set your instant pot on sauté mode, add onion and brown it for 1 minute.
2. Add potatoes, ginger, garlic, tofu, carrots, tamari, spices, Brussels sprouts and water, cover and cook at High for 2 minutes.
3. Release the pressure, uncover the pot, uncover the pot, transfer to plates and serve.

Enjoy!

Nutrition:

- Calories 156
- Fat 10
- Fiber 3
- Carbs 11.4
- Protein 13

Delicious Wild Rice And Farro Pilaf

It's a simple side dish that can be served with a tasty steak!

Preparation time: 10 minutes
Cooking time: 35 minutes
Servings: 12
Ingredients:

- 1 shallot, finely chopped
- 1 teaspoon garlic, minced
- A drizzle of extra virgin olive oil
- 1 and ½ cups whole grain faro
- ¾ cup wild rice
- 6 cups chicken stock
- Salt and black pepper to the taste
- 1 tablespoons parsley and sage, finely chopped
- ½ cup hazelnuts, toasted and chopped
- ¾ cup cherries, dried
- Some chopped chives for serving

Directions:

1. Set your instant pot on Sauté mode, add a drizzle of oil and heat it up.
2. Add onion and garlic, stir and cook for 2-3 minutes.
3. Add farro, rice, salt, pepper, stock and 1 tablespoon mixed sage and parsley, stir, cover the pot and cook on High for 25 minutes.
4. Meanwhile, put cherries in a pot, add hot water to cover, leave aside for 10 minutes and drain them.
5. Release the pressure from the pot for 5 minutes, drain excess liquid, add hazelnuts and cherries, stir gently, divide among plates and garnish with chopped chives.

Enjoy!
Nutrition:

- Calories 120
- Fat 1
- Fiber 1.5
- Carbs 21
- Protein 4.5

Tasty Quinoa Pilaf

If you don't want a rice pilaf, then what about a quinoa one?

Preparation time: 10 minutes
Cooking time: 2 minutes
Servings: 4
Ingredients:

- 2 cups quinoa
- 2 garlic cloves, minced
- 2 tablespoons extra virgin olive oil
- Salt to the taste
- 2 teaspoons turmeric
- 3 cups water
- 1 handful parsley, chopped
- 2 teaspoons cumin, ground

Directions:

1. Set your instant pot on Sauté mode, add oil and heat it up.
2. Add garlic, stir and cook for 30 seconds.
3. Add water, quinoa, cumin, turmeric and salt, stir, cover and cook at High for 1 minute.
4. Release the pressure naturally for 10 minutes, fluff quinoa with a fork, transfer to plates, season with more salt if needed, sprinkle parsley on top and serve as a side dish.

Enjoy!

Nutrition:

- Calories 130
- Fat 0.9
- Fiber 3.2
- Carbs 12
- Protein 6.9

Delicious Quinoa And Almonds Side Dish

This proves that delicious side dishes are so easy to make!

Preparation time: 10 minutes
Cooking time: 11 minutes
Servings: 4
Ingredients:

- ½ cup yellow onion, finely chopped
- 1 tablespoon butter
- 1 celery stalk, chopped
- 1 and ½ cups quinoa, rinsed
- 14 ounces chicken stock
- Salt and black pepper to the taste
- ¼ cup water
- ½ cup almonds, toasted and sliced
- 2 tablespoons parsley, chopped

Directions:

1. Set your instant pot on Sauté mode, add butter and melt it.
2. Add onion and celery, stir and cook for 5 minutes.
3. Add quinoa, water, stock, salt and pepper, stir, cover and cook at High for 3 minutes.
4. Release the pressure for 5 minutes, uncover, fluff with a fork, add almonds and parsley, stir, divide among plates and serve as a side dish.

Enjoy!
Nutrition:

- Calories 140
- Fat 3
- Fiber 2
- Carbs 12
- Protein 12.4

Delicious Pink Rice

It can't get easier than this!

Preparation time: 10 minutes
Cooking time: 5 minutes
Servings: 8
Ingredients:

- 1 teaspoon salt
- 2 and ½ cups water
- 2 cups pink rice

Directions:

1. Put the rice in your instant pot.
2. Add the water and salt, stir, cover and cook at High for 5 minutes.
3. Release the pressure naturally for 10 minutes, uncover the pot, fluff rice with a fork, divide among plates and serve.

Enjoy!
Nutrition:

- Calories 114
- Fat 1
- Fiber 2
- Carbs 13
- Protein 4

Mushroom Risotto

This is one of the best side dishes you've ever had.

Preparation time: 10 minutes
Cooking time: 15 minutes
Servings: 4
Ingredients:

- 2 cups risotto rice
- 4 cups chicken stock
- 2 garlic cloves, crushed
- 2 ounces extra virgin olive oil
- 1 yellow onion, chopped
- 8 ounces mushrooms, sliced
- 4 ounces heavy cream
- 4 ounces sherry vinegar
- 2 tablespoons parmesan cheese, grated
- 1-ounce basil, finely chopped

Directions:

1. Set your instant pot on Sauté mode, add the oil and heat it up.
2. Add onions, garlic and mushrooms, stir and cook for 3 minutes.
3. Add rice, stock and vinegar, stir, cover the pot and cook at High for 10 minutes.
4. Release the pressure, uncover the pot, add cream and parmesan and stir
5. Divide among plates, sprinkle basil and serve.

Enjoy!

Nutrition:

- Calories 340
- Fat 1
- Fiber 1
- Carbs 15
- Protein 4

Simple Pumpkin Risotto

A great risotto can only be made perfect if you use the right ingredients and of course, an instant pot.

Preparation time: 5 minutes
Cooking time: 10 minutes
Servings: 4
Ingredients:

- 2 ounces extra virgin olive oil
- 1 small yellow onion, chopped
- 2 garlic cloves, minced
- 12 ounces risotto rice
- 4 cups chicken stock
- 6 ounces pumpkin puree
- ½ teaspoon nutmeg
- 1 teaspoon thyme, chopped
- ½ teaspoon ginger, grated
- ½ teaspoon cinnamon
- ½ teaspoon allspice
- 4 ounces heavy cream

Directions:

1. Set your instant pot on Sauté mode, add oil and heat it up.
2. Add onion and garlic, stir and cook for 1-2 minutes.
3. Also add risotto, chicken stock, pumpkin puree, thyme, nutmeg, cinnamon, ginger and allspice and stir.
4. Cover the pot and cook at High for 10 minutes
5. Release the pressure, add cream, stir very well and serve as a side dish.

Enjoy!
Nutrition:

- Calories 263
- Fat 5
- Fiber 2
- Carbs 37
- Protein 6

Veggies And Rice Side Dish

Your steaks will taste so much better if you are serving them with a veggie and rice side dish made in your instant pot.

Preparation time: 6 minutes
Cooking time: 15 minutes
Servings: 4
Ingredients:

- 2 cups basmati rice
- 1 cup mixed frozen carrots, peas, corn, green beans
- 2 cups water
- ½ teaspoon green chili, minced
- ½ teaspoon ginger, grated
- 3 garlic cloves, minced
- 2 tablespoons butter
- 1 cinnamon stick
- 1 tablespoon cumin seeds
- 2 bay leaves
- 3 whole cloves
- 5 black peppercorns
- 2 whole cardamoms
- 1 tablespoon sugar
- Salt to the taste

Directions:

1. Put the water in your instant pot.
2. Add rice, mixed frozen veggies, green chili, grated ginger, garlic cloves, cinnamon stick, whole cloves and butter.
3. Also add cumin seeds, bay leaves, cardamoms, black peppercorns, salt and sugar.
4. Stir, cover and cook at High for 15 minutes
5. Release the pressure, divide among plates and serve with your favorite steaks.

Enjoy!

Nutrition:

- Calories 340
- Fat 6
- Fiber 5.5
- Carbs 40
- Protein 14.2

Flavored Mashed Potatoes

It goes perfectly with a turkey-based meal!

Preparation time: 10 minutes
Cooking time: 9 minutes
Servings: 8
Ingredients:

- 2 garlic cloves
- 3 pounds sweet potatoes, peeled and chopped
- Salt and black pepper to the taste
- ½ teaspoon parsley, dried
- ¼ teaspoon sage, dried
- ½ teaspoon rosemary, dried
- ½ teaspoon thyme dried
- 1 and ½ cups water
- ¼ cup milk
- ½ cup parmesan, grated
- 2 tablespoon butter

Directions:

1. Put potatoes and garlic in the steamer basket of your instant pot, add 1 and ½ cups water in the pot, cover and cook at High for 10 minutes.
2. Release the pressure quick, drain water, transfer the potatoes and garlic to a bowl and mash them using your kitchen mixer.
3. Add butter, parmesan, milk, salt, pepper, parsley, sage, rosemary and thyme and blend everything well.
4. Divide among plates and serve.

Enjoy!

Nutrition:

- Calories 240
- Fat 1
- Fiber 8.2
- Carbs 34
- Protein 4.5

Tasty Saffron Risotto

This risotto is better than everything you've had before!

Preparation time: 10 minutes
Cooking time: 10 minutes
Servings: 10
Ingredients:

- 2 tablespoons extra virgin olive oil
- ½ teaspoon saffron threads, crushed
- ½ cup onion, chopped
- 2 tablespoons hot milk
- 1 and ½ cups Arborio rice
- 3 and ½ cups veggie stock
- A pinch of salt
- 1 tablespoon honey
- 1 cinnamon stick
- 1/3 cup almonds, chopped
- 1/3 cup currants, dried

Directions:

1. In a bowl, mix hot milk with saffron, stir and leave aside.
2. Set your instant pot on Sauté mode, add oil and heat it up.
3. Add onions, stir and cook for 5 minutes.
4. Add rice, veggie stock, saffron and milk, honey, salt, almonds, cinnamon stick and currants.
5. Stir, cover the pot and cook at High for 5 minutes.
6. Release the pressure quick, fluff the rice a bit, discard cinnamon, divide it among plates and serve.

Enjoy!

Nutrition:

- Calories 260
- Fat 7
- Fiber 2
- Carbs 41
- Sugar 1.5
- Protein 3.9

Simple Farro Side Dish

Get ready to impress everyone with this special, yet simple side dish!

Preparation time: 10 minutes
Cooking time: 40 minutes
Servings: 6
Ingredients:

- 1 tablespoon apple cider vinegar
- 1 cup whole grain farro
- 1 teaspoon lemon juice
- Salt to the taste
- 3 cups water
- 1 tablespoon extra virgin olive oil
- ½ cup cherries, dried and chopped
- ¼ cup green onions, chopped
- 10 mint leaves, chopped
- 2 cups cherries, pitted and cut into halves

Directions:

1. Put the water in your instant pot, add rinsed farro, stir, cover and cook at High for 40 minutes.
2. Release the pressure quick, drain farro, transfer to a bowl and mix with salt, oil, lemon juice, vinegar, dried cherries, fresh cherries, green onions, and mint.
3. Stir well, divide among plates and serve,

Enjoy!

Nutrition:

- Calories 160
- Fat 1
- Fiber 2
- Carbs 12
- Protein 4

Herbed Polenta

This can be a side dish for a pork stew! Try it!

Preparation time: 15 minutes
Cooking time: 6 minutes
Servings: 6
Ingredients:

- 4 cups veggie stock
- 2 tablespoons extra virgin olive oil
- 2 teaspoons garlic, minced
- ½ cup yellow onion, chopped
- 1/3 cup sun-dried tomatoes, chopped
- Salt to the taste
- 1 cup polenta
- 1 bay leaf
- 2 teaspoons oregano, finely chopped
- 3 tablespoons basil, finely chopped
- 1 teaspoon rosemary, finely chopped
- 2 tablespoons parsley, finely chopped

Directions:

1. Set your instant pot on sauté mode, add the oil and heat it up.
2. Add onion, stir and cook for 1 minute.
3. Add garlic, stir again and cook for 1 minute.
4. Add stock, salt, tomatoes, bay leaf, rosemary, oregano, half of the basil, half of the parsley and polenta.
5. Do not stir, cover the pot, cook at High for 5 minutes and release pressure naturally for 10 minutes.
6. Uncover the pot, discard bay leaf, stir polenta gently, add the rest of the parsley, basil and more salt, stir, divide among plates and serve.

Enjoy!

Nutrition:

- Calories 150
- Fat 1.6
- Fiber 3.6
- Carbs 35
- Protein 3.7

Mexican Rice

Serve this as a side dish for some flavored burritos!

Preparation time: 10 minutes

Cooking time: 4 minutes

Servings: 8

Ingredients:

- 1 cup long grain rice
- 1 and ¼ cups veggie stock
- ½ cup cilantro, chopped
- ½ avocado, pitted, peeled and chopped
- Salt and black pepper to the taste
- ¼ cup green hot sauce

Directions:

1. Put the rice in your instant pot, add stock, stir, cover and cook at High for 4 minutes.
2. Release the pressure naturally for 10 minutes, uncover the pot, fluff it with a fork and transfer to a bowl.
3. Meanwhile, in your food processor, mix avocado with hot sauce and cilantro and blend well.
4. Pour this over rice, stir well, add salt and pepper to the taste, stir again, divide among plates and serve.

Enjoy!

Nutrition:

- Calories 100
- Fat 2
- Fiber 1
- Carbs 18
- Protein 2

Simple Cauliflower And Barley Risotto

You just have to learn how to make this incredible side dish!

Preparation time: 10 minutes
Cooking time: 1 hour
Servings: 4
Ingredients:

- 4 tablespoons extra virgin olive oil
- Salt and black pepper to the taste
- 1 cauliflower head, florets separated
- ½ cup parmesan, grated
- 2 garlic cloves, minced
- 1 cup pearl barley
- 1 yellow onion, chopped
- 3 cups chicken stock
- 2 thyme springs
- 2 tablespoons parsley, chopped
- 1 tablespoon butter

Directions:

1. Spread cauliflower florets on a lined baking dish, add 3 tablespoons oil, salt and pepper, toss to coat, introduce in the oven at 425 degrees F and bake for 20 minutes, turning them every 10 minutes.
2. Take cauliflower out of the oven, sprinkle ¼ cup parmesan and bake for 5 minutes more.
3. Meanwhile, set your instant pot on Sauté mode, add 1 tablespoon oil and heat it up.
4. Add onion, stir and cook for 5 minutes.
5. Add garlic, stir and cook for 1 minute.
6. Add stock, thyme, and barley, stir, cover the pot and cook at High for 25 minutes.
7. Release the pressure quickly, uncover, the pot, stir the barley, discard thyme, add butter, the rest of the parmesan, roasted cauliflower, salt, pepper to the taste and parsley.
8. Stir the risotto well, divide among plates and serve.

Enjoy!

Nutrition:

- Calories 350
- Fat 16
- Fiber 10
- Carbs 25
- Protein 14.6

Delightful Potatoes Side Dish

This is one of our favorites side dishes! It will soon be yours as well!

Preparation time: 10 minutes
Cooking time: 6 minutes
Servings: 4
Ingredients:

- 1 pound new potatoes, peeled and thinly sliced
- 1 cup water
- Salt and black pepper to the taste
- ¼ teaspoon rosemary, dried
- 1 tablespoon extra virgin olive oil
- 2 garlic cloves, minced

Directions:

1. Put the potatoes and the water in the steamer basket of your instant pot, cover and cook at High for 4 minutes.
2. In a heat proof dish, mix rosemary with oil and garlic, cover and microwave for 1 minute.
3. Release the pressure fro the pot, drain potatoes and spread them on a lined baking sheet.
4. Add heated oil mix, salt and pepper to the taste, toss to coat, divide among plates and serve as a side dish.

Enjoy!
Nutrition:

- Calories 94
- Fat 1
- Fiber 2.2
- Carbs 21
- Protein 2.5

Delicious Lemon Parmesan And Peas Risotto

It's a creamy, flavored side dish you must try!

Preparation time: 10 minutes
Cooking time: 17 minutes
Servings: 6
Ingredients:

- 1 and ½ cup rice
- 2 tablespoons butter
- 1 yellow onion, chopped
- 1 tablespoon extra virgin olive oil
- 2 tablespoons lemon juice
- 1 teaspoon lemon zest, grated
- 3 and ½ cups chicken stock
- 2 tablespoons parsley, finely chopped
- Salt and black pepper to the taste
- 1 and ½ cup peas
- 2 tablespoons parmesan, finely grated

Directions:

1. Set your instant pot on sauté mode, add 1 tablespoon butter and the oil and heat them up.
2. Add onions, stir and cook for 5 minutes.
3. Add rice, stir and cook for 3 more minutes.
4. Add 3 cups stock and the lemon juice, stir, cover and cook at High for 5 minutes.
5. Release the pressure quickly, set the pot on Simmer, add peas and the rest of the stock, stir and cook for 2 minutes.
6. Add parmesan, parsley, the rest of the butter, lemon zest, salt and pepper to the taste and stir.
7. Divide among plates and serve.

Enjoy!

Nutrition:

- Calories 140
- Fat 1.5
- Fiber 1
- Carbs 27
- Protein 5

Spinach And Goat Cheese Risotto

Don't worry! It's simply amazing!

Preparation time: 10 minutes
Cooking time: 10 minutes
Servings: 6
Ingredients:

- 2 garlic cloves, minced
- 2 tablespoons extra virgin olive oil
- ¾ cup yellow onion, chopped
- 1 and ½ cups Arborio rice
- ½ cup white wine
- 12 ounces spinach, chopped
- 3 and ½ cups hot veggie stock
- Salt and black pepper to the taste
- 4 ounces goat cheese, soft and crumbled
- 2 tablespoons lemon juice
- 1/3 cup pecans, toasted and chopped

Directions:

1. Set your instant pot on sauté mode, add the oil and heat it up.
2. Add garlic and onions, stir and cook for 5 minutes.
3. Add rice, stir and cook for 1 minute more.
4. Add wine, stir and cook until it's absorbed.
5. Add 3 cups stock, cover the pot and cook at High for 4 minutes.
6. Release the pressure quickly, uncover the pot, add spinach, stir and cook on Simmer mode for 3 minutes.
7. Add salt, pepper, the rest of the stock, lemon juice and goat cheese and stir.
8. Divide among plates, garnish with pecans and serve.

Enjoy!

Nutrition:

- Calories 340
- Fat 23
- Fiber 4.5
- Carbs 24
- Protein 18.9

Rice And Artichokes Side Dish

This is a traditional Italian side dish you can serve with your favorite meat!

Preparation time: 10 minutes
Cooking time: 20 minutes
Servings: 4
Ingredients:

- 1 tablespoon extra virgin olive oil
- 5 ounces Arborio rice
- 2 garlic cloves crushed
- 1 and ¼ cups chicken broth
- 1 tablespoon white wine
- 6 ounces graham cracker crumbs
- 1 and ¼ cups water
- 15 ounces canned artichoke hearts chopped
- 16 ounces cream cheese
- 1 tablespoon grated parmesan cheese
- 1 and ½ tablespoons thyme chopped
- Salt and black pepper to the taste

Directions:

1. Set your instant pot on Sauté mode, add the oil, heat up, add rice and cook for 2 minutes.
2. Add garlic, stir and cook for 1 minute.
3. Transfer this to a heat proof dish.
4. Add stock, crumbs, salt, pepper and wine, stir and cover the with tin foil.
5. Place the dish in the steamer basket of the pot, add water, cover and cook at High for 8 minutes
6. Release the pressure, take the dish out, uncover, add cream cheese, parmesan, artichoke hearts, and thyme.
7. Mix well and serve while it's hot!

Enjoy!

Nutrition:

- Calories 240
- Fat 7.2
- Fiber 5.1
- Carbs 34
- Protein 6

Potatoes Au Gratin

It's a fancy side dish you can serve on a special occasion but we can assure you it's very easy to make!

Preparation time: 10 minutes
Cooking time: 17 minutes
Servings: 6
Ingredients:

- 1 cup chicken stock
- ½ cup yellow onion, chopped
- 2 tablespoons butter
- 6 potatoes, peeled and sliced
- Salt and black pepper to the taste
- ½ cup sour cream
- 1 cup Monterey jack cheese, shredded

For the topping:
- 3 tablespoons melted butter
- 1 cup bread crumbs

Directions:

1. Set your instant pot on Sauté mode, add butter and melt it.
2. Add onion, stir and cook for 5 minutes.
3. Add stock, salt, pepper and put the steamer basket in the pot as well.
4. Add potatoes, cover the pot and cook at High for 5 minutes.
5. In a bowl, mix 3 tablespoons butter with bread crumbs and stir well.
6. Release pressure from the pot fast, take the steamer basket out and transfer potatoes to a baking dish.
7. Pour cream and cheese into instant pot and stir.
8. Add potatoes and stir gently.
9. Spread bread crumbs mix all over, introduce in preheated broiler and broil for 7 minutes.
10. Serve right away!

Enjoy!

Nutrition:

- Calories 340
- Fat 22
- Fiber 2
- Carbs 32
- Protein 11

Tasty Mashed Squash

Why don't you try this side dish today? It's really good!

Preparation time: 10 minutes
Cooking time: 20 minutes
Servings: 4
Ingredients:

- ½ cup water
- 2 acorn squash, cut into halves and seeded
- Salt and black pepper to the taste
- ¼ teaspoon baking soda
- 2 tablespoons butter
- ½ teaspoon nutmeg, grated
- 2 tablespoons brown sugar

Directions:

1. Sprinkle squash halves with salt, pepper and baking soda and place them in the steamer basket of your instant pot.
2. Add ½ cup water to the pot, cover and cook at High for 20 minutes.
3. Release the pressure quickly, take squash and leave aside on a plate to cool down.
4. Scrape flesh from the squash and put in a bowl.
5. Add salt, pepper to the taste, butter, sugar and nutmeg and mash everything with a potato mashes.
6. Stir well and serve.

Enjoy!

Nutrition:

- Calories 140
- Fat 1
- Fiber 0.5
- Carbs 10.5
- Protein 1.7

Delicious Potato Casserole

If you want to try something different as a side dish for a change, then this is what you need to make!

Preparation time: 15 minutes
Cooking time: 10 minutes
Servings: 4
Ingredients:

- 3 pounds sweet potatoes, scrubbed
- 1 cup water
- ¼ cup coconut milk
- 1/3 cup palm sugar
- ½ teaspoon nutmeg, ground
- 2 tablespoons coconut flour
- 1 teaspoon cinnamon
- ¼ teaspoon allspice
- Salt to the taste

- ½ cup walnuts, soaked, drained and ground
- ¼ cup pecans, soaked, drained and ground
- ¼ cup shredded coconut
- 1 tablespoon chia seeds
- ¼ cup palm sugar
- A pinch of salt
- 1 teaspoon cinnamon, ground
- 5 tablespoons salted butter

For the topping:

- ½ cup almond flour

Directions:

1. Prick potatoes with a fork, place them in the steamer basket of your instant pot, add 1 cup water to the pot, cover and cook at High for 20 minutes.
2. Meanwhile, in a bowl, mix almond flour with pecans, walnuts, ¼ cup coconut, ¼ cup palm sugar, chia seeds, 1 teaspoon cinnamon, a pinch of salt and the butter and stir everything.
3. Release the pressure naturally from the pot, take potatoes and peel them and add ½ cup water to the pot.
4. Chop potatoes and place them in a baking dish.
5. Add crumble mix you've made, stir everything, spread evenly in the dish, cover, place in the steamer basket, cover the pot again and cook at High for 10 minutes.
6. Release the pressure quickly, take the dish out of the pot, uncover, leave it to cool down, cut and serve as a side dish.

Enjoy!

Nutrition:

- Calories 150
- Fat 9
- Fiber 3

- Carbs 25
- Sugar 10
- Protein 4

Simple French Fries

This is probably the most popular side dish! Did you know you can make it in your instant pot?

Preparation time: 10 minutes
Cooking time: 10 minutes
Servings: 4
Ingredients:

- 8 medium potatoes, peeled, cut into medium matchsticks and pat dried
- 1 cup water
- Salt to the taste
- ¼ teaspoon baking soda
- Oil for frying

Directions:

1. Put the water in your instant pot, add salt and the baking soda and stir.
2. Put potatoes in the steamer basket and introduce it in the pot.
3. Cover and cook at High for 3 minutes.
4. Release the pressure naturally, take fries out of the pot and put them in a bowl.
5. Heat up a pan with enough oil over medium high heat, add fries, spread them and cook until they become golden.
6. Transfer fries to paper towels to drain excess grease and then put them in a bowl.
7. Add salt, toss to coat and serve.

Enjoy!

Nutrition:

- Calories 300
- Fat 10
- Fiber 3.7
- Carbs 41
- Protein 3.4

Green Beans And Mushrooms Side Dish

It's a very healthy side dish you can make for a special occasion!

Preparation time: 10 minutes
Cooking time: 6 minutes
Servings: 4
Ingredients:

- 1 pound fresh green beans, trimmed
- 1 small yellow onion, chopped
- 6 ounces bacon, chopped
- 1 garlic clove, minced
- 8 ounces mushrooms, sliced
- Salt and black pepper to the taste
- A splash of balsamic vinegar

Directions:

1. Put the beans in your instant pot, add water to cover them, cover the pot and cook at High for 3 minutes.
2. Release the pressure naturally, drain beans and leave them aside for now.
3. Set your instant pot on Sauté mode, add bacon and brown it for 1 or 2 minutes stirring often.
4. Add garlic and onion, stir and cook 2 more minutes.
5. Add mushrooms, stir and cook until they are soft.
6. Add drained beans, salt, pepper and a splash of vinegar, stir, take off heat, divide among plates and serve.

Enjoy!

Nutrition:

- Calories 120
- Fat 3.7
- Fiber 3.3
- Carbs 7.5
- Protein 2.4

Easy Refried Beans

This is a Mexican-style side dish you can serve with some tasty burritos or tacos! It's your choice!

Preparation time: 10 minutes
Cooking time: 20 minutes
Servings: 4
Ingredients:

- 3 cups pinto beans, soaked for 4 hours and drained
- 1 yellow onion, cut into halves
- 1 jalapeno, chopped
- 2 tablespoons garlic, minced
- Salt and black pepper to the taste
- 9 cups vegetable stock
- 1/8 teaspoon cumin, ground

Directions:

1. In your instant pot, mix beans with salt, pepper, stock, onion, jalapeno, garlic and cumin.
2. Stir, cover and cook at High for 20 minutes.
3. Release the pressure naturally, discard onion halves, strain beans, transfer them to your blender and reserve cooking liquid.
4. Blend very well adding some of the liquid, transfer to a bowl and serve them as a side dish.

Enjoy!

Nutrition:

- Calories 100
- Fat 2
- Fiber 5
- Carbs 15
- Protein 6

Three Beans Side Dish

It's is a very hearty side dish! It goes with a pork roast!

Preparation time: 10 minutes
Cooking time: 15 minutes
Servings: 4
Ingredients:

- 1 cup garbanzo beans, soaked overnight and drained
- 1 cup cranberry beans, soaked overnight and drained
- 1 and ½ cups green beans
- 4 cups water
- 1 garlic clove, crushed
- 1 bay leaf
- 2 celery stalks, chopped
- 1 bunch parsley, chopped
- 1 small red onion, chopped
- 1 tablespoon sugar
- 5 tablespoons apple cider vinegar
- 4 tablespoons extra virgin olive oil
- Salt and black pepper to the taste

Directions:

1. Put the water in your instant pot.
2. Add bay leaf, garlic and garbanzo beans.
3. Put the steamer basket in your pot as well and put cranberry beans in it.
4. Wrap green beans in tin foil and also place in the steamer basket.
5. Cover the pot and cook at High for 15 minutes.
6. Release the pressure naturally for 10 minutes, uncover the pot, drain beans, unwrap green beans and put them all in a bowl.
7. In another bowl, mix onion with vinegar and sugar, stir well and leave aside for a few minutes.
8. Add onions to beans and toss to coat.
9. Also add celery, olive oil, salt, pepper to the taste and parsley, toss to coat and divide among plates.
10. Serve right away as a side dish.

Enjoy!
Nutrition:

- Calories 200
- Fat 1
- Fiber 6
- Carbs 45
- Protein 4

Black Beans Side Dish

It's ready in not time!

Preparation time: 10 minutes
Cooking time: 5 minutes
Servings: 8
Ingredients:

- 1 cup black beans, soaked overnight, drained and rinsed
- 1 piece kombu seaweed
- 2/3 cup water
- Salt to the taste
- 1 spring epazote
- 2 garlic cloves, minced
- ½ teaspoon cumin seeds

Directions:

1. In your instant pot, mix beans with kombu, water, garlic, epazote, and cumin.
2. Stir, cover the pot and cook at High for 5 minutes.
3. Release the pressure quickly, discard kombu and epazote, divide beans among plates, season with salt and serve.

Enjoy!
Nutrition:

- Calories 330
- Fat 1
- Fiber 16
- Carbs 23
- Protein 21

Simple Pineapple And Cauliflower Rice

Don't hesitate! The combination is delicious!

Preparation time: 10 minutes
Cooking time: 20 minutes
Servings: 6
Ingredients:

- 2 cups rice
- 4 cups water
- 1 cauliflower, florets separated and chopped
- ½ pineapple, peeled and chopped
- Salt and black pepper to the taste
- 2 teaspoons extra virgin olive oil

Directions:

1. In your instant pot, mix rice with pineapple, cauliflower, water, oil, salt and pepper, stir, cover and cook for 20 minutes on Low.
2. Release the pressure naturally for 10 minutes, uncover the pot, fluff with a fork, add more salt and pepper to the taste, divide among plates and serve.

Enjoy!
Nutrition:

- Calories 100
- Fat 2.7
- Fiber 2.9
- Carbs 12
- Protein 4.9

Tasty Red Beans And Rice

It's a simple and very tasty combination! You'll see!

Preparation time: 20 minutes
Cooking time: 25 minutes
Servings: 6
Ingredients:

- 1 pound red kidney beans, soaked overnight and drained
- Salt to the taste
- 1 teaspoon vegetable oil
- 1 pound smoked sausage, cut into wedges
- 1 yellow onion, chopped
- 1 celery stalk, chopped
- 4 garlic cloves, chopped
- 1 green bell pepper, chopped
- 1 teaspoon thyme, dried
- 2 bay leaves
- 5 cups water
- Long grain rice already cooked
- 2 green onions, minced for serving
- 2 tablespoons parsley, minced for serving
- Hot sauce for serving

Directions:

1. Set your instant pot on Sauté mode, add the oil and heat it up.
2. Add sausage, onion, bell pepper, celery, garlic, thyme and salt to the taste, stir and cook for 8 minutes.
3. Add beans, bay leaves and the water, stir, cover the pot and cook at High for 15 minutes.
4. Release the pressure naturally for 20 minutes, discard bay leaves and put 2 cups of beans and some liquid in your blender.
5. Pulse them well and return to pot.
6. Divide the rice among plates, add beans, sausage, and veggies on top, sprinkle green onions and parsley and serve with hot sauce on top.

Enjoy!
Nutrition:

- Calories 160
- Fat 3.8
- Fiber 3.4
- Carbs 24
- Protein 4.6

Special Side Dish

It's a special side dish! Find out why!

Preparation time: 10 minutes
Cooking time: 20 minutes
Servings: 4
Ingredients:

- 1 and ½ cups water
- ½ cup butter
- 1 and ¼ cup turkey stock
- 1 bread loaf, cubed and toasted
- 1 cup celery, chopped
- 1 yellow onion, chopped
- Salt and black pepper to the taste
- 1 teaspoon sage
- 1 teaspoon poultry seasoning

Directions:

1. Set your instant pot on Sauté mode, add butter and melt it.
2. Add stock, onion, celery, salt, pepper, sage and poultry seasoning and stir well.
3. Add bread cubes, stir and cook for 1 minute.
4. Transfer this to a Bundt pan and cover it with tin foil.
5. Clean your instant pot, add the water and place the pan in the steamer basket, cover the pot and cook at High for 15 minutes.
6. Release the pressure quickly, uncover the pan, introduce it in the oven at 350 degrees F and bake for 5 minutes.
7. Serve hot.

Enjoy!

Nutrition:

- Calories 230
- Fat 3.4
- Fiber 3.2
- Carbs 23
- Protein 11

Delicious Parsnips And Onions

The taste is simply unbelievable!

Preparation time: 10 minutes
Cooking time: 30 minutes
Servings: 4
Ingredients:

- 2 and ½ pounds parsnips, chopped
- 4 tablespoons pastured lard
- Salt and black pepper to the taste
- 1 and ½ cups beef stock
- 1 thyme spring
- 1 yellow onion, thinly sliced

Directions:

1. Set your instant pot on Sauté mode, add 3 tablespoons lard and heat it up.
2. Add parsnips, stir and cook for 15 minutes.
3. Add stock and thyme, stir, cover and cook at High for 3 minutes.
4. Release the pressure, transfer the parsnips mix to your blender, add salt and pepper to the taste and pulse very well.
5. Set the pot on Sauté mode again, add the rest of the lard and heat it up.
6. Add onion, stir and cook for 10 minutes.
7. Transfer blended parsnips to plates, top with sautéed onions and serve.

Enjoy!

Nutrition:

- Calories 130
- Fat 2
- Fiber 3
- Carbs 6.7
- Protein 10.1

Delicious Cauliflower Mash

Even your kids will adore this side dish!

Preparation time: 10 minutes
Cooking time: 6 minutes
Servings: 4
Ingredients:

- 1 cauliflower, florets separated
- Salt and black pepper to the taste
- 1 and ½ cups water
- ½ teaspoon turmeric
- 1 tablespoon butter
- 3 chives, finely chopped

Directions:

1. Put the water in your instant pot, place cauliflower in the steamer basket, cover the pot and cook at High for 6 minutes.
2. Release the pressure naturally for 2 minutes and then release the rest quick.
3. Transfer cauliflower to a bowl and mash it with a potato masher.
4. Add salt, pepper, butter and turmeric, stir, transfer to a blender and pulse well.
5. Serve with chives sprinkled on top.

Enjoy!

Nutrition:

- Calories 70
- Fat 5
- Fiber 2
- Carbs 5
- Protein 2

Mashed Turnips Side Dish

You will start loving turnips from now on!

Preparation time: 10 minutes
Cooking time: 5 minutes
Servings: 4
Ingredients:

- 4 turnips, peeled and chopped
- Salt and black pepper to the taste
- 1 yellow onion, chopped
- ¼ cup sour cream
- ½ cup chicken stock

Directions:

1. In your instant pot, mix turnips with stock and onion.
2. Stir, cover and cook at High for 5 minutes.
3. Release the pressure naturally, drain turnips and transfer them to a bowl.
4. Puree them using your mixer and add salt, pepper to the taste and sour cream.
5. Blend again and serve right away.

Enjoy!
Nutrition:

- Calories 70
- Fat 1
- Fiber 4.6
- Carbs 11.2
- Protein 1.6

Sweet Carrot Puree

It's perfect for a meat-based main course!

Preparation time: 5 minutes
Cooking time: 5 minutes
Servings: 4
Ingredients:

- 1 and ½ pounds carrots, peeled and chopped
- 1 tablespoon soft butter
- Salt to the taste
- 1 cup water
- 1 tablespoon honey
- 1 teaspoon brown sugar

Directions:

1. Put carrots in your instant pot, add the water, cover and cook at High for 4 minutes.
2. Release the pressure naturally, drain carrots and place them in a bowl.
3. Mash them using a hand blender, add butter salt and honey.
4. Blend again well, add sugar on top and serve right away.

Enjoy!
Nutrition:

- Calories 50
- Fat 1
- Fiber 3
- Carbs 11
- Protein 1

Butternut And Apple Mash

You can try this for your holiday feast!

Preparation time: 10 minutes
Cooking time: 15 minutes
Servings: 4
Ingredients:

- 1 cup water
- 1 butternut squash, peeled and cut into medium chunks
- 2 apples, sliced
- 2 tablespoons brown butter
- 1 yellow onion, thinly sliced
- ½ teaspoon apple pie spice
- Salt to the taste

Directions:

1. Put squash, onion and apple pieces in the steamer basket of your instant pot, put the water in the pot, cover and cook at High for 8 minutes.
2. Release the pressure quickly and transfer squash, onion and apple pieces to a bowl.
3. Mash using a potato masher, add salt, apple pie spice and brown butter, stir well and serve warm.

Enjoy!

Nutrition:

- Calories 140
- Fat 2.3
- Fiber 6.5
- Carbs 24
- Protein 2.5

Glazed Carrots

This side dish goes with a pork roast!

Preparation time: 10 minutes
Cooking time; 6 minutes
Servings: 4
Ingredients:

- ½ cup water
- 1 pound baby carrots
- ½ cup honey
- 1 teaspoon thyme, dried
- 1 teaspoon dill, dried
- Salt to the taste
- 2 tablespoons butter

Directions:

1. Put the water in your instant pot, place carrots in the steamer basket, cover and cook at High for 3 minutes.
2. Release the pressure, drain carrots and put them in a bowl.
3. Set your instant pot on Sauté mode, add butter and melt it.
4. Add dill, thyme, honey and salt and stir well.
5. Add carrots, toss to coat, cook for 1 minute, transfer them to plates and serve hot as a side dish.

Enjoy!

Nutrition:

- Calories 200
- Fat 11
- Fiber 4
- Carbs 12
- Protein 1.4

Special Brussels Sprouts Side Dish

It can be one of the most surprising side dishes you'll ever have!

Preparation time: 10 minutes
Cooking time: 4 minutes
Servings: 8
Ingredients:

- 2 pounds Brussels sprouts
- Salt and black pepper to the taste
- ¼ cup orange juice
- 1 teaspoon orange zest, grated
- 1 tablespoon buttery spread
- 2 tablespoons maple syrup

Directions:

1. In your instant pot, mix Brussels sprouts with orange juice, orange zest, buttery spread, maple syrup, salt and pepper to the taste, stir, cover and cook at High for 4 minutes.
2. Release the pressure naturally, transfer sprouts mix to plates and serve them.

Enjoy!
Nutrition:

- Calories 65
- Fat 2
- Fiber 3
- Carbs 12
- Protein 3

Broccoli side dish

Your friends and your loved ones will be so happy to taste this dish! It only takes a few minutes to prepare this recipe!

Preparation time: 5 minutes
Cooking time: 15 minutes
Servings: 6
Ingredients:

- 31 oz broccoli, florets separated
- 1 cup water
- 5 lemon slices
- Salt and black pepper to the taste

Directions:

1. Pour the water in your instant pot
2. Season broccoli with salt and pepper to the taste and add it to the pot
3. Also, add lemon slices and stir gently.
4. Cover the pot and cook at High for 15 minutes.
5. Release the pressure and divide broccoli among plates.
6. Serve with a tasty meat-based the main course!

Enjoy!
Nutrition:

- Calories 55
- Fat 0.5
- Fiber 5
- Carbs 11
- Protein 3.4

Garlic And Parmesan Asparagus

This side dish will make everyone admire your cooking skills!

Preparation time: 5 minutes
Cooking time: 8 minutes
Servings: 4
Ingredients:

- 3 garlic cloves, minced
- 1 bunch asparagus, trimmed
- 1 cup water
- 3 tablespoons butter
- 3 tablespoons parmesan cheese, grated

Directions:

1. Put the water in your instant pot.
2. Place asparagus on a tin foil, add garlic and butter and curve the edges of the foil.
3. Place this in your pot, cover it and cook at High for 8 minutes.
4. Release the pressure quickly, arrange asparagus on plates, sprinkle parmesan and serve.

Enjoy!

Nutrition:

- Calories 70
- Fat 5.2
- Fiber 1.8
- Carbs 3.8
- Protein 4

Tasty Poached Fennel

This will make you love fennel forever!

Preparation time: 5 minutes
Cooking time: 6 minutes
Servings: 3
Ingredients:

- 2 big fennel bulbs, sliced
- 2 tablespoons butter
- 1 tablespoon white flour
- 2 cups milk
- A pinch of nutmeg, ground
- Salt to the taste

Directions:

1. Set your instant pot on Sauté mode, add butter and melt it.
2. Add fennel slices, stir and cook until they brown a bit.
3. Add flour, salt, pepper, nutmeg and milk, stir, cover and cook on Low for 6 minutes.
4. Release pressure quick, transfer fennel to plates and serve.

Enjoy!

Nutrition:

- Calories 140
- Fat 5
- Fiber 4.7
- Carbs 12
- Protein 4.4

Tasty "Drunken "Peas Side Dish

You'll soon understand why they are called like this!

Preparation time: 10 minutes
Cooking time: 7 minutes
Servings: 4
Ingredients:

- 4 ounces smoked pancetta, chopped
- 1 pound fresh peas
- 1 green onion, sliced
- 1 tablespoon mint, chopped
- ¼ cup beer
- 1 tablespoon butter
- Salt and black pepper to the taste
- 2 cups water

Directions:

1. Put the water in your instant pot, place the steamer basket inside as well and leave aside.
2. In a heat proof pan, mix pancetta with half of the onion and spread on the bottom.
3. Heat this up on the stove over medium high heat for 3 minutes, add beer, peas, and salt, stir and take off heat.
4. Cover this pan with some tin foil, place in the steamer basket, cover the pot and cook at High for 1 minute.
5. Release the pressure quickly, uncover the pan, add more salt, pepper, mint and butter, stir, divide among plates and serve with the rest of the onions sprinkled on top.

Enjoy!
Nutrition:

- Calories 134
- Fat 2
- Fiber 2.5
- Carbs 10
- Protein 4.3

Easy Artichokes Side Dish

It can't get any easier that this!

Preparation time: 10 minutes
Cooking time: 25 minutes
Servings: 4
Ingredients:

- 1 cup water
- 2 medium artichokes, trimmed
- 1 lemon wedges
- Salt to the taste

Directions:

1. Rub artichokes with the lemon wedges, place them in the steamer basket of your instant pot, add the water in the pot, cover and cook at High for 20 minutes.
2. Release the pressure for 10 minutes, divide artichokes among plates add salt on top and serve them with a dipping sauce and with a steak on the side.

Enjoy!
Nutrition:

- Calories 78
- Fat 0.4
- Fiber 3
- Carbs 2
- Protein 4

Veggies Side Dish

This is a very popular side dish also knows as "peperonata." Try it soon!

Preparation time: 10 minutes
Cooking time: 6 minutes
Servings: 4
Ingredients:

- 2 yellow bell peppers, thinly sliced
- 1 green bell pepper, thinly sliced
- 2 red bell peppers, thinly sliced
- 2 tomatoes, chopped
- 2 garlic cloves, minced
- 1 red onion, thinly sliced
- Salt and black pepper to the taste
- 1 bunch parsley, finely chopped
- A drizzle of extra virgin olive oil

Directions:

1. Set your instant pot on Sauté mode, add a drizzle of oil and heat it up.
2. Add onions, stir and cook for 3 minutes.
3. Add red, yellow and green peppers, stir and cook for 5 minutes.
4. Add tomatoes, salt and pepper, stir, cover and cook at High for 6 minutes.
5. Release the pressure quickly, uncover the pot, transfer peppers and tomatoes to a bowl, add more salt and pepper if needed, chopped garlic, parsley and a drizzle of oil.
6. Toss to coat and serve as a side dish!

Enjoy!

Nutrition:

- Calories 146
- Fat 2.2
- Fiber 8.1
- Carbs 28.1
- Protein 4.5

Tasty Eggplant Side Dish

This is another Italian-style side dish you will love!

Preparation time: 10 minutes
Cooking time: 13 minutes
Servings: 4
Ingredients:

- 2 eggplants, cubed
- Salt and black pepper to the taste
- 2 tablespoons extra virgin olive oil
- 1 garlic clove, crushed
- A pinch of hot pepper flakes
- 1 bunch oregano, chopped
- ½ cup water
- 2 anchovies, chopped

Directions:

1. Sprinkle eggplant pieces with salt, place them in a strainer, press them with a plate and then drain them.
2. Set your instant pot on Sauté mode, add the oil and the garlic and heat it up.
3. Add anchovies, oregano and pepper flakes, stir and cook for 5 minutes.
4. Discard the garlic, add eggplants, salt and pepper, toss to coat and cook for 5 minutes.
5. Add the water, stir, cover the pot and cook at High for 3 minutes.
6. Release the pressure quick, transfer eggplant mix to plates and serve.

Enjoy!
Nutrition:

- Calories 130
- Fat 5
- Fiber 10
- Carbs 12
- Protein 15

Calamari And Tomato Side Dish

Italians use this both as a main course and as a side dish for different rice-based main courses!

Preparation time: 10 minutes
Cooking time: 32 minutes
Servings: 4
Ingredients:

- 1 and ½ pounds calamari, washed, tentacles separated and cut into strips
- Salt and black pepper to the taste
- 14 ounces canned tomatoes, chopped
- 1 bunch parsley, chopped
- 1 garlic clove, crushed
- ½ cup white wine
- 1 cup water
- 2 anchovies
- Juice of 1 lemon
- 2 tablespoons extra virgin olive oil
- A pinch of red pepper flakes

Directions:

1. Set your instant pot on Sauté mode, add oil, pepper flakes, garlic and anchovies, stir and cook for 3 minutes.
2. Add calamari, stir and cook for 5 minutes.
3. Add wine, stir and cook 3 minutes.
4. Add tomatoes, 1 cup water, half of the parsley, salt, and pepper.
5. Stir, cover the pot and cook at High for 20 minutes.
6. Release the pressure quick, add the rest of the parsley, the lemon juice, salt, and pepper, stir, divide among plates and serve with rice.

Enjoy!

Nutrition:

- Calories 230
- Fat 6.5
- Fiber 1.2
- Carbs 11
- Protein 24

Simple Cauliflower And Citrus Side Dish

This is a very fresh and tasty side dish everyone will enjoy!

Preparation time: 10 minutes
Cooking time: 6 minutes
Servings: 4
Ingredients:

- 1 cauliflower, florets separated
- 1 pound broccoli, florets separated
- 1 romanesco cauliflower, florets separated
- 2 oranges, peeled and sliced
- Zest from 1 orange
- Juice from 1 orange
- A pinch of hot pepper flakes
- 4 anchovies
- 1 tablespoon capers, chopped
- Salt and black pepper to the taste
- 4 tablespoons extra virgin olive oil
- 1 cup water

Directions:

1. In a bowl, mix orange zest with orange juice, pepper flakes, anchovies, capers salt, pepper and olive oil, stir well and leave aside for now.
2. Place cauliflower and broccoli florets in the steamer basket of you instant pot, add 1 cup water to the pot, cover and cook on Low for 6 minutes.
3. Release the pressure quickly, uncover the pot, transfer florets to a bowl and mix with orange slices.
4. Add the orange vinaigrette you've made earlier, toss to coat and divide among plates.
5. Serve with some chicken!

Enjoy!

Nutrition:

- Calories 260
- Fat 2.9
- Fiber 6.5
- Carbs 33
- Protein 4.2

Beet And Garlic Side Dish

Get all the right ingredients, and you will obtain a divine side dish!

Preparation time: 10 minutes
Cooking time: 15 minutes
Servings: 4
Ingredients:

- 3 beets, greens cut off and washed
- Water to cover
- 1 tablespoon extra virgin olive oil
- Salt to the taste
- 2 garlic cloves, minced
- 1 teaspoon lemon juice

Directions:

1. Put beets in your instant pot, add water to cover, also add salt to the taste, cover the pot and cook at High for 15 minutes.
2. Release the pressure naturally for 10 minutes, strain beets, peel them and roughly chop.
3. Heat up a pan with the oil over medium high heat, add beets, stir and cook for 3 minutes.
4. Add garlic, lemon juice, and more salt, stir, take off heat and divide among plates.

Enjoy!
Nutrition:

- Calories 70
- Fat 1
- Fiber 3.8
- Carbs 13
- Protein 2.2

Fava Bean Sauté

We give you the ultimate side dish!

Preparation time: 10 minutes
Cooking time: 7 minutes
Servings: 4
Ingredients:

- 3 pounds fava beans, shelled
- 1 teaspoon extra virgin olive oil
- Salt and black pepper to the taste
- 4 ounces bacon, chopped
- ½ cup white wine
- 3 parsley springs, chopped
- ¾ cup water

Directions:

1. Set your instant pot on Sauté mode, add the oil and heat up.
2. Add bacon, stir and cook until it browns.
3. Add wine, stir and cook for 2 minutes.
4. Add water and fava beans, stir, cover and cook at High for 7 minutes.
5. Release pressure quick, transfer beans to plates, add parsley, salt and pepper, stir and serve.

Enjoy!
Nutrition:

- Calories 140
- Fat 3
- Fiber 1
- Carbs 23
- Protein 13

Green Bean Side Dish

It's a tasty and simple combination you should try!

Preparation time: 10 minutes
Cooking time: 5 minutes
Servings: 4
Ingredients:

- 2 cups tomatoes, chopped
- 1 tablespoon extra virgin olive oil
- 1 garlic clove crushed
- 1 pound green beans, trimmed
- 1 teaspoon extra virgin olive oil
- Salt to the taste
- 1 basil spring

Directions:

1. Set your instant pot on Sauté mode, add 1 tablespoon oil and heat it up.
2. Add garlic, stir and cook for 1 minute.
3. Add tomatoes, stir and cook for 1minute.
4. Place green beans in the steamer basket and introduce it in the pot.
5. Add salt to the taste, cover the pot and cook at High for 5 minutes.
6. Release the pressure quick, transfer green beans from the basket into the pot and toss to coat.
7. Transfer to plates, sprinkle with basil and drizzle 1 teaspoon oil over them.

Enjoy!
Nutrition:

- Calories 55
- Fat 3.2
- Fiber 2.6
- Carbs 1.6
- Protein 1.6

Tasty Bok Choy Side Dish

This is very simple and of course, tasty!

Preparation time: 10 minutes
Cooking time: 10 minutes
Servings: 4
Ingredients:

- 5 bok choy bunches, end cut off
- 5 cups water
- 2 garlic cloves, minced
-
- 1 teaspoon ginger, grated
- 1 tablespoon coconut oil
- Salt to the taste

Directions:

1. Put bok choy in your instant pot, add the water, cover the pot and cook at High for 7 minutes.
2. Release the pressure, drain bok choy, chop it and put them in a bowl.
3. Heat up a pan with the oil over medium heat, add bok choy, stir and cook for 3 minutes.
4. Add more salt to the taste, garlic and ginger, stir and cook for 2 more minutes.
5. Divide among plates and serve with your favorite meat.

Enjoy!

Nutrition:

- Calories 60
- Fat 0.4
- Fiber 1.3
- Carbs 6.5
- Protein 2.4

Israeli Couscous Side Dish

Get ready to taste the best couscous in your life!

Preparation time: 10 minutes
Cooking time: 5 minutes
Servings: 10
Ingredients:

- 16 ounces harvest grains blend
- Salt and black pepper to the taste
- 2 and ½ cups chicken stock
- 2 tablespoons butter
- Parsley leaves, chopped for serving

Directions:

1. Set your instant pot on Sauté mode, add butter and melt it.
2. Add grains and stock and stir.
3. Cover the pot and cook at High for 5 minutes.
4. Release pressure quick, fluff couscous with a fork, season with salt and pepper to the taste, divide among plates, sprinkle parsley on top and serve.

Enjoy!

Nutrition:

- Calories 190
- Fat 1
- Fiber 2
- Carbs 34
- Protein 6

Tasty Red Cabbage Side Dish

Transform cabbage into a very special side dish!

Preparation time: 10 minutes
Cooking time: 10 minutes
Servings: 4
Ingredients:

- 4 garlic cloves, minced
- ½ cup yellow onion, chopped
- 1 tablespoon vegetable oil
- 6 cups red cabbage, chopped
- 1 cup water
- 1 tablespoon apple cider vinegar
- 1 cup applesauce
- Salt and black pepper to the taste

Directions:

1. Set your instant pot on Sauté mode, add the oil and heat it up.
2. Add onions, stir and cook for 4 minutes.
3. Add garlic, stir and cook for 1 minute.
4. Add cabbage, water, applesauce, vinegar, salt and pepper, stir, cover and cook at High for 10 minutes.
5. Release the pressure quickly, uncover the pot, stir cabbage mix again, add more vinegar, salt, and pepper if needed, divide among plates and serve right away as a side dish for a pork based main course.

Enjoy!

Nutrition:

- Calories 160
- Fat 12
- Fiber 2.2
- Crabs 10.2
- Protein 5.6

Instant Pot Poultry Recipes

Delicious Lemongrass Chicken

It's so flavored! You need to make it right away!

Preparation time: 10 minutes
Cooking time: 20 minutes
Servings: 5
Ingredients:

- 1 bunch lemongrass, rough bottom removed and trimmed
- 1 inch piece ginger root, chopped
- 4 garlic cloves, crushed
- 2 tablespoons fish sauce
- 3 tablespoons coconut aminos
- 1 teaspoon Chinese five spice
- 10 chicken drumsticks
- 1 cup coconut milk
- Salt and black pepper to the taste
- 1 teaspoon ghee
- ¼ cup cilantro, finely chopped
- 1 yellow onion, chopped
- 1 tablespoon lime juice

Directions:

1. In your food processor, mix lemongrass with ginger, garlic, aminos, fish sauce and five spice and pulse well.
2. Add coconut milk and pulse again.
3. Set your instant pot on Sauté mode, add ghee and melt it.
4. Add onion, stir and cook for 5 minutes.
5. Add chicken pieces, salt and pepper, stir and cook for 1 minute.
6. Add coconut milk and lemongrass mix, stir, cover, set "poultry" mode and cook for 15 minutes sat High.
7. Release the pressure quickly, uncover, add more salt and pepper and lime juice, stir, divide among plates and serve with cilantro sprinkled on top.

Enjoy!

Nutrition:

- Calories 400
- Fat 18
- Fiber 2
- Carbs 6
- Protein 20

Easy Salsa Chicken Dish

Have this for dinner tonight!

Preparation time: 10 minutes
Cooking time: 25 minutes
Servings: 5
Ingredients:

- 1 pound chicken breast, skinless and boneless
- ¾ teaspoon cumin
- Salt and black pepper to the taste
- A pinch of oregano
- 1 cup chunky salsa

Directions:

1. Season chicken with salt and pepper to the taste and add it to your instant pot.
2. Add oregano, cumin and the chunky salsa, stir, cover, set the pot on "poultry" mode and cook for 25 minutes.
3. Release the pressure quick, transfer chicken and salsa to a bowl, shred meat with a fork and serve with some tortillas on the side.

Enjoy!

Nutrition:

- Calories 125
- Fat 3
- Fiber 1
- Carbs 3
- Protein 22

Chicken And Potatoes Dish

It's so rich and textured! It's great!

Preparation time: 15 minutes
Cooking time: 15 minutes
Servings: 4
Ingredients:

- 2 tablespoons extra virgin olive oil
- 2 pounds chicken thighs, skinless and boneless
- ¾ cup chicken stock
- ¼ cup lemon juice
- 2 pounds red potatoes, peeled and cut into quarters
- 3 tablespoons Dijon mustard
- 2 tablespoons Italian seasoning
- Salt and black pepper to the taste

Directions:

1. Set your instant pot on sauté mode, add the oil and heat it up.
2. Add chicken thighs, salt, and pepper, stir and brown for 2 minutes.
3. In a bowl, mix stock with mustard, Italian seasoning, and lemon juice and stir well.
4. Pour this over chicken, add potatoes, stir, cover the pot and cook at High for 15 minutes.
5. Release the pressure quickly, uncover the pot, stir chicken, divide among plates and serve.

Enjoy!

Nutrition:

- Calories 190
- Fat 6
- Fiber 3.3
- Carbs 23
- Protein 18

Tasty Chicken Sandwiches

This could be your lunch tomorrow!

Preparation time: 10 minutes
Cooking time: 15 minutes
Servings: 8
Ingredients:

- 6 chicken breasts, skinless and boneless
- 12 ounces canned orange juice
- 2 tablespoons lemon juice
- 15 ounces canned peaches and their juice
- 1 teaspoon soy sauce
- 20 ounces canned pineapple and its juice, chopped
- 1 tablespoon cornstarch
- ¼ cup brown sugar
- 8 hamburger buns
- 8 grilled pineapple slices, for serving

Directions:

1. In a bowl, mix orange juice with soy sauce, lemon juice, canned pineapples pieces, peaches and sugar and stir well.
2. Pour half of this mix in your instant pot, add chicken and pour the rest of the sauce over meat.
3. Cover the pot and cook at High for 12 minutes.
4. Release the pressure quick, take the chicken and put on a cutting board.
5. Shred meat and leave aside for now.
6. In a bowl, mix cornstarch with 1 tablespoon cooking juice and stir well.
7. Transfer the sauce to a pot, add cornstarch mix and chicken, stir and cook for a few more minutes.
8. Divide this chicken mix on hamburger buns, top with grilled pineapple pieces and serve.

Enjoy!

Nutrition:

- Calories 240
- Fat 4.6
- Fiber 4
- Carbs 21
- Protein 14

Moroccan Chicken

It's a special and exotic chicken dish!

Preparation time: 10 minutes
Cooking time: 25 minutes
Servings: 4
Ingredients:

- 6 chicken thighs
- 2 tablespoons extra virgin olive oil
- 10 cardamom pods
- 2 bay leaves
- ½ teaspoon coriander
- 1 teaspoon cloves
- ½ teaspoon cumin
- ½ teaspoon ginger
- ½ teaspoon turmeric
- ½ teaspoon cinnamon, ground
- 1 teaspoon paprika
- 2 yellow onions, chopped
- 2 tablespoons tomato paste
- 5 garlic cloves, chopped
- ¼ cup white wine
- 1 cup green olives
- 1 cup chicken stock
- ¼ cup cranberries, dried
- Juice of 1 lemon
- ½ cup parsley, finely chopped

Directions:

1. In a bowl, mix bay leaf with cardamom, cloves, coriander, ginger, cumin, cinnamon, turmeric and paprika and stir.
2. Set your instant pot on Sauté mode, add the oil and heat up.
3. Add chicken thighs, brown for a few minutes and transfer to a plate.
4. Add onion to the pot, stir and cook for 4 minutes.
5. Add garlic, stir and cook for 1 minute.
6. Add wine, tomato paste, spices from the bowl, stock and chicken.
7. Stir, cover and cook at High for 15 minutes.
8. Release the pressure quick, discard bay leaf, cardamom, and cloves, add olives, cranberries, lemon juice and parsley, stir, divide chicken mix among plates and serve.

Enjoy!

Nutrition:

- Calories 381
- Fat 10.2
- Fiber 7.8
- Carbs 4
- Fiber 32

Tasty Cacciatore Chicken

It's ready in only 30 minutes! Why don't you try it today for lunch?

Preparation time: 10 minutes
Cooking time: 15 minutes
Servings: 4
Ingredients:

- 1 cup chicken stock
- Salt to the taste
- 8 chicken drumsticks, bone-in
- 1 bay leaf
- 1 teaspoon garlic powder
- 1 yellow onion, chopped
- 28 ounces canned tomatoes and juice, crushed
- 1 teaspoon oregano, dried
- ½ cup black olives, pitted and sliced

Directions:

1. Set your instant pot on Sauté mode, add stock, bay leaf and salt and stir.
2. Add chicken, garlic powder, onion, oregano, and tomatoes, stir, cover the pot and cook at High for 15 minutes.
3. Release the pressure naturally, uncover the pot, discard bay leaf, divide cacciatore chicken among plates, drizzle cooking liquid all over, sprinkle olives and serve.

Enjoy!

Nutrition:

- Calories 210
- Fat 2.9
- Fiber 2.4
- Carbs 9.5
- Protein 25.9

Honey Bbq Chicken

Pay attention and learn how to make the best chicken dish!

Preparation time: 10 minutes
Cooking time: 25 minutes
Servings: 4
Ingredients:

- 2 pounds chicken wings
- Salt and black pepper to the taste
- ¾ cup honey Bbq sauce
- A pinch of cayenne pepper
- ½ cup apple juice
- 1 teaspoon red pepper, crushed
- 2 teaspoons paprika
- ½ cup water
- ½ teaspoon basil, dried
- ½ cup brown sugar

Directions:

1. Put chicken wings in your instant pot.
2. Add BBQ sauce, apple juice, salt, pepper, red pepper, paprika, basil, sugar, and water.
3. Stir, cover and cook at High for 10 minutes.
4. Release the pressure quickly, uncover the pot, transfer chicken to a baking sheet, add sauce all over, introduce in preheated broiler, broil for 7 minutes, flip chicken wings, broil for 7 more minutes, divide among plates and serve.

Enjoy!

Nutrition:

- Calories 147.5
- Fat 2.2
- Fiber 1
- Carbs 8
- Protein 21.8

Thai Chicken Dish

It's flavored and exotic! It's the best combination!

Preparation time: 10 minutes
Cooking time: 10 minutes
Servings: 4
Ingredients:

- 2 pounds chicken thighs, boneless and skinless
- ½ cup fish sauce
- 1 cup lime juice
- 2 tablespoons coconut nectar
- ¼ cup extra virgin olive oil
- 1 teaspoon ginger, grated
- 2 teaspoons cilantro, finely chopped
- 1 teaspoon mint, chopped

Directions:

1. Put chicken thighs in your instant pot.
2. In a bowl, mix lime juice with fish sauce, olive oil, coconut nectar, ginger, mint and cilantro and whisk well.
3. Pour this over chicken, cover the pot and cook at High for 10 minutes.
4. Release the pressure quick, divide Thai chicken among plates and serve.

Enjoy!

Nutrition:

- Calories 300
- Fat 5
- Fiber 4
- Carbs 23
- Protein 32

Tasty Turkey Chili

Did you ever try a turkey chili? If not, this is the time to do it!

Preparation time: 10 minutes
Cooking time: 10 minutes
Servings: 4
Ingredients:

- 1 pound turkey meat, ground
- Salt and black pepper to the taste
- 5 ounces water
- 15 ounces chickpeas, already cooked
- 1 yellow onion, chopped
- 1 yellow bell pepper, chopped
- 3 garlic cloves, chopped
- 2 and ½ tablespoons chili powder
- 1 and ½ teaspoons cumin
- A pinch of cayenne pepper
- 12 ounces veggies stock

Directions:

1. Put turkey meat in your instant pot.
2. Add water, stir, cover and cook at High for 5 minutes.
3. Release the pressure quickly, uncover the pot and add chickpeas, bell pepper, onion, garlic, chili powder, cumin, salt, pepper, cayenne and veggie stock.
4. Stir, cover the pot and cook at High for 5 minutes.
5. Release the pressure for 10 minutes, uncover the pot again, stir chili, divide it among plates and serve.

Enjoy!

Nutrition:

- Calories 224
- Fat 7.7
- Fiber 6.1
- Carbs 18
- Protein 19.7

Special Chicken Romano

It's simple to make a special chicken dish for your loved ones!

Preparation time: 10 minutes
Cooking time: 15 minutes
Servings: 4
Ingredients:

- 6 chicken things, boneless and skinless and cut into medium chunks
- Salt and black pepper to the taste
- ½ cup white flour
- 2 tablespoons vegetable oil
- 10 ounces tomato sauce
- 1 teaspoon white wine vinegar
- 4 ounces mushrooms, sliced
- 1 tablespoon sugar
- 1 tablespoon oregano, dried
- 1 teaspoon garlic, minced
- 1 teaspoon basil, dried
- 1 teaspoon chicken bouillon granules
- 1 yellow onion, chopped
- 1 cup Romano cheese, grated

Directions:

1. Set your instant pot on Sauté mode, add oil and heat it up.
2. Add chicken pieces, stir and brown them for 2 minutes.
3. Add onion and garlic, stir and cook for 3 minutes more.
4. Add salt, pepper, flour and stir very well.
5. Add tomato sauce, vinegar, mushrooms, sugar, oregano, basil and bouillon granules, stir cover and cook at High for 10 minutes.
6. Release the pressure for 10 minutes, uncover the pot, add cheese, stir, divide among plates and serve.

Enjoy!
Nutrition:

- Calories 450
- Fat 11
- Fiber 1
- Carbs 24.2
- Protein 61.2

Filipino Chicken

You simply need to make this superb, yet so simple dish!

Preparation time: 10 minutes
Cooking time: 15 minutes
Servings: 4
Ingredients:

- 5 pounds chicken thighs
- Salt and black pepper to the taste
- ½ cup white vinegar
- 1 teaspoon black peppercorns
- 4 garlic cloves, minced
- 3 bay leaves
- ½ cup soy sauce

Directions:

1. Set your instant pot on Poultry mode, add chicken, vinegar, soy sauce, salt, pepper, garlic, peppercorns and bay leaves, stir, cover and cook for 15 minutes.
2. Release the pressure for 10 minutes, uncover the pot, discard bay leaves, stir, divide chicken between plates and serve.

Enjoy!

Nutrition:

- Calories 430
- Fat 19.2
- Fiber 1
- Carbs 2.4
- Protein 76

Chicken In Tomatillo Sauce

This is a Mexican style chicken dish, very popular all over the world!

Preparation time: 10 minutes
Cooking time: 15 minutes
Servings: 6
Ingredients:

- 1 pound chicken thighs, skinless and boneless
- 2 tablespoons extra virgin olive oil
- 1 yellow onion, thinly sliced
- 1 garlic clove, crushed
- 4 ounces canned green chilies, chopped
- 1 handful cilantro, finely chopped
- Salt and black pepper to the taste
- 15 ounces canned tomatillos, chopped
- 5 ounces canned garbanzo beans, drained
- 15 ounces rice, already cooked
- 5 ounces tomatoes, chopped
- 15 ounces cheddar cheese, grated
- 4 ounces black olives, pitted and chopped

Directions:

1. Set your instant pot on Sauté mode, add oil and heat it up.
2. Add onions, stir and cook for 5 minutes.
3. Add garlic, stir and cook 15 more seconds.
4. Add chicken, chilies, salt, pepper, cilantro, and tomatillos, stir, cover the pot and cook on Poultry mode for 8 minutes.
5. Release the pressure quickly, uncover the pot, take the chicken out and shred it.
6. Return chicken to pot, add rice, beans, set the instant pot on Sauté mode again and cook for 1 minute.
7. Add cheese, tomatoes, and olives, stir, cook for 2 minutes more, divide among plates and serve.

Enjoy!

Nutrition:

- Calories 245
- Fat 11.4
- Fiber 1.3
- Carbs 14.2
- Protein 20

Braised Duck And Potatoes

It's the best, an easy and tasty combination of ingredients!

Preparation time: 10 minutes
Cooking time: 20 minutes
Servings: 4
Ingredients:

- 1 duck, cut into small chunks
- Black pepper to the taste
- 1 potato, cut into cubes
- 1 inch ginger root, sliced
- 4 garlic cloves, minced
- 4 tablespoons sugar
- 4 tablespoons soy sauce
- 2 green onions, roughly chopped
- 4 tablespoons sherry wine
- A pinch of salt
- ¼ cup water

Directions:

1. Set your instant pot on Sauté mode, add duck pieces, stir and brown them for a few minutes.
2. Add garlic, ginger, green onions, soy sauce, sugar, wine, a pinch of salt, black pepper and water, stir, cover, set the pot to Poultry mode and cook for 18 minutes.
3. Release the pressure quickly, uncover the pot, add potatoes, stir, cover and cook at High for 5 minutes.
4. Release the pressure quick, divide braised duck among plates and serve.

Enjoy!
Nutrition:

- Calories 238
- Fat 18
- Fiber 0
- Carbs 1
- Protein 19

Tasty Duck And Veggies

It's great for lunch!

Preparation time: 10 minutes
Cooking time: 40 minutes
Servings: 8
Ingredients:

- 1 duck, chopped into medium pieces
- 1 cucumber, chopped
- 1 tablespoon wine
- 2 carrots, chopped
- 2 cups water
- Salt and black pepper to the taste
- 1 inch ginger pieces, chopped

Directions:

1. Put duck pieces in your instant pot.
2. Add cucumber, carrots, wine, water, ginger, salt and pepper, stir, cover and cook on Poultry mode for 40 minutes.
3. Release the pressure, divide the mix among plates and serve.

Enjoy!
Nutrition:

- Calories 189
- Fat 2
- Fiber 1
- Carbs 4
- Protein 22

Delicious Turkey Meatballs

Your guests will ask for more once they try this dish!

Preparation time: 10 minutes
Cooking time: 40 minutes
Servings: 8
Ingredients:

- 1 pound turkey meat, ground
- 1 yellow onion, minced
- ¼ cup parmesan cheese, grated
- ½ cup panko bread crumbs
- 4 garlic cloves, minced
- ¼ cup parsley, chopped
- Salt and black pepper to the taste
- 1 teaspoon oregano, dried
- 1 egg, whisked
- ¼ cup milk
- 2 teaspoons soy sauce
- 1 teaspoon fish sauce
- 12 cremini mushrooms, chopped
- 3 dried shiitake mushrooms, soaked in water, drained and chopped
- 1 cup chicken stock
- 2 tablespoons extra virgin olive oil
- 2 tablespoons butter
- A splash of sherry wine
- 2 tablespoons cornstarch mixed with 2 tablespoons water

Directions:

1. In a bowl, mix turkey meat with parmesan cheese, salt, pepper to the taste, yellow onion, garlic, bread crumbs, parsley, oregano, egg, milk, 1 teaspoon soy sauce and 1 teaspoon fish sauce, stir very well and shape 16 meatballs.
2. Heat up a pan with 1 tablespoon oil over medium high heat, add meatballs, brown them for 1 minutes on each side and transfer them to a plate.
3. Pour chicken stock into the pan, stir and take off heat.
4. Set your instant pot on Sauté mode, add 1 tablespoon oil and 2 tablespoons butter and heat them up.
5. Add cremini mushrooms, salt, and pepper, stir and cook for 10 minutes.
6. Add dried mushrooms, sherry wine and the rest of the soy sauce and stir well.
7. Add meatballs, cover the pot and cook at High for 6 minutes.
8. Release the pressure quickly, uncover the pot, add cornstarch mix, stir well, divide everything between plates and serve.

Enjoy!
Nutrition:

- Calories 330
- Fat 16
- Fiber 3
- Carbs 21
- Protein 28

Delicious Turkey Mix And Mashed Potatoes

It's a 100% rich and flavored dish for you and your loved ones!

Preparation time: 10 minutes
Cooking time: 50 minutes
Servings: 3
Ingredients:

- 2 turkey quarters
- 1 yellow onion, chopped
- 1 carrot, chopped
- 3 garlic cloves, minced
- 1 celery stalk, chopped
- 1 cup chicken stock
- Salt and black pepper to the taste
- A splash of white wine
- 2 tablespoons extra virgin olive oil
- A pinch of rosemary, dried
- 2 bay leaves
- A pinch of sage, dried
- A pinch of thyme, dried
- 3 tablespoons cornstarch mixed with 2 tablespoons water
- 5 gold potatoes, cut into halves
- 2 tablespoons parmesan cheese, grated
- 3.5 ounces cream
- 2 tablespoons butter

Directions:

1. Season turkey with salt and pepper.
2. Put 1 tablespoon oil in your instant pot, set the pot on Sauté mode and heat it up.
3. Add turkey, brown pieces for 4 minutes, transfer them to a plate and leave aside for now.
4. Add ½ cup stock to the pot and stir well.
5. Add 1 tablespoon oil and heat it up.
6. Add onion, stir and cook for 1 minute.
7. Add garlic, stir and cook for 20 seconds.
8. Add salt and pepper, carrot and celery, stir and cook for 7 minutes.
9. Add 2 bay leaves, thyme, sage, and rosemary, stir and cook everything 1 minute.
10. Add wine, turkey and the rest of the stock.
11. Put potatoes in the steamer basket and also introduce it in the pot, cover and cook for 20 minutes at High.
12. Release the pressure for 10 minutes, uncover the pot, transfer potatoes to a bowl and mash them.
13. Add salt, pepper, butter, parmesan and cream and stir well.
14. Divide turkey quarters to plates and set your instant pot on Sauté mode again.
15. Add cornstarch mix to pot, stir well and cook for 2-3 minutes.
16. Drizzle sauce over turkey, add mashed potatoes on the side and serve.

Enjoy

Nutrition:

- Calories 200
- Fat 5
- Fiber 4
- Carbs 19
- Protein 18

Stuffed Chicken Breast

Did you know you can make a stuffed chicken breast in your instant pot?

Preparation time: 10 minutes
Cooking time: 30 minutes
Servings: 2
Ingredients:

- 2 chicken breasts, skinless and boneless and butterflied
- 1 piece ham, halved and cooked
- 6 asparagus spears
- 16 bacon strips
- 4 mozzarella cheese slices
- Salt and black pepper to the taste
- 2 cup water

Directions:

1. In a bowl, mix chicken breasts with salt and 1 cup water, stir, cover and keep in the fridge for 30 minutes.
2. Pat dry chicken breasts and place them on a working surface.
3. Add 2 slices of mozzarella, 1 piece ham and 3 asparagus pieces on each.
4. Add salt and pepper and roll up each chicken breast.
5. Place 8 bacon strips on a working surface, add chicken and wrap it in bacon.
6. Repeat this with the rest of the bacon strips and the other chicken breast.
7. Put rolls in the steamer basket of the pot, add 1 cup water in the pot, cover and cook at High for 10 minutes.
8. Release the pressure quick, pat dry rolls with paper towels and leave them on a plate.
9. Set your instant pot on Sauté mode, add chicken rolls and brown them for a few minutes.
10. Divide among plates and serve.

Enjoy!

Nutrition:

- Calories 270
- Fat 11
- Fiber 1
- Carbs 6
- Protein 37

Simple Chicken Salad

This is so simple, tasty and extremely healthy and light! It's great!

Preparation time: 55 minutes
Cooking time: 10 minutes
Servings: 2
Ingredients:

- 1 chicken breast, skinless and boneless
- 3 cups water
- Salt and black pepper to the taste
- 1 tablespoon mustard
- 3 garlic cloves, minced
- 1 tablespoon balsamic vinegar
- 1 tablespoon honey
- 3 tablespoons extra virgin olive oil
- Mixed salad greens
- A handful cherry tomatoes, cut into halves

Directions:

1. In a bowl, mix 2 cups water with salt to the taste.
2. Add chicken to this mix, stir and keep in the fridge for 45 minutes.
3. Add 1 cup water to your instant pot, place chicken breast in the steamer basket of the pot, cover and cook at High for 5 minutes.
4. Release the pressure naturally, leave chicken breast on a plate for 8 minutes and cut into thin strips.
5. In a bowl, mix garlic with salt and pepper to the taste, mustard, honey, vinegar and olive oil and whisk very well.
6. In a salad bowl, mix chicken strips with salad greens and tomatoes.
7. Drizzle the vinaigrette on top and serve.

Enjoy!

Nutrition:

- Calories 140
- Fat 2.5
- Fiber 4
- Carbs 11
- Protein 19

Delicious Chicken And Rice

It's so tender and moist, and it's very flavored!

Preparation time: 15 minutes
Cooking time: 35 minutes
Servings: 2
Ingredients:

- 3 chicken quarters cut into small pieces
- 2 carrots, cut into chunks
- 2 potatoes, cut into quarters
- 1 shallot, sliced
- 1 yellow onion, sliced
- 3 garlic cloves, minced
- Salt and black pepper to the taste
- 1 green bell pepper, chopped
- 7 ounces coconut milk
- 2 bay leaves
- 1 tablespoon soy sauce
- 1 tablespoon peanut oil
- 1 and ½ teaspoon turmeric powder
- 1 teaspoon cumin, ground
- 1 and ½ tablespoons cornstarch mixed with 2 tablespoons water

For the marinade:

- 1 tablespoon soy sauce
- ½ teaspoon sugar
- 1 tablespoon white wine
- A pinch of white pepper
- 1 and ½ cups water
- 1 and ½ cups rice

Directions:

1. In a bowl, mix chicken with sugar, white pepper, 1 tablespoon soy sauce and 1 tablespoon white wine, stir and keep in the fridge for 20 minutes.
2. Set your instant pot on Sauté mode, add peanut oil and heat it up.
3. Add onion and shallot, stir and cook for 3 minutes.
4. Add garlic, salt, and pepper, stir and cook for 2 minutes more.
5. Add chicken, stir and brown for 2 minutes.
6. Add turmeric and cumin, stir and cook for 1 minute.
7. Add bay leaves, carrots, potatoes, bell pepper, coconut milk and 1 tablespoon soy sauce.
8. Stir everything, place steamer basket in the pot, place the rice in a bowl and the basket,
9. Add 1 and ½ cups water in the bowl, cover the pot and cook at High for 4 minutes.
10. Release the pressure naturally, take the rice out of the pot and divide among plates, add cornstarch to pot and stir.
11. Add chicken next to rice and serve.

Enjoy!

Nutrition:

- Calories 200
- Fat 9
- Fiber 1
- Carbs 22
- Protein 26

Crispy Chicken

This is great for a movie night!

Preparation time: 10 minutes
Cooking time: 40 minutes
Servings: 4
Ingredients:

- 4 garlic cloves, chopped
- 6 chicken thighs
- 1 yellow onion, thinly sliced
- A pinch of rosemary, dried
- 1 cup cold water
- 1 tablespoon soy sauce
- Salt and black pepper to the taste
- 2 tablespoons cornstarch mixed with 2 and ½ tablespoons water
- 1 and ½ cups panko breadcrumbs
- 2 tablespoons extra virgin olive oil
- 2 tablespoons butter
- 1 cup white flour
- 2 eggs, whisked

Directions:

1. In your instant pot, mix garlic with onion, rosemary and 1 cup water.
2. Place chicken things in the steamer basket and introduce in the pot.
3. Cover and cook at High for 9 minutes.
4. Release the pressure naturally for 10 minutes and uncover the pot.
5. Heat up a pan with the butter and oil over medium high heat.
6. Add 1 and ½ cups breadcrumbs, stir, toast them and take them off heat.
7. Remove chicken thighs from the pot; pat dry them, season with salt and pepper to the taste, coat them with the flour, dip them in whisked egg and then coat them in toasted breadcrumbs.
8. Place chicken thighs on a lined baking sheet, introduce in the oven at 300 degrees F and bake for 10 minutes.
9. Meanwhile, set your instant pot on Sauté mode and heat up the cooking liquid.
10. Add 1 tablespoon soy sauce, salt, pepper and cornstarch, stir and transfer to a bowl.
11. Take chicken thighs out of the oven, divide them between plates and serve with the sauce from the pot on the side.

Enjoy!

Nutrition:

- Calories 360
- Fat 7
- Fiber 4
- Carbs 18
- Protein 15

Tasty Braised Quail

Get all the ingredients and make this recipe today!

Preparation time: 10 minutes
Cooking time: 15 minutes
Servings: 2
Ingredients:

- 2 quails, cleaned and emptied
- 3.5 ounces smoked pancetta, chopped
- ½ cup champagne
- 2 scallions, chopped
- ½ bunch thyme, chopped
- ½ bunch thyme
- 1 bay leaf
- Salt and black pepper to the taste
- ½ bunch rosemary, chopped
- ½ bunch rosemary
- ½ fennel bulb, cut into matchsticks
- 4 carrots, cut into thin matchsticks
- A handful arugula
- Lemon juice of 1 lemon
- A drizzle of olive oil

Directions:

1. Put fennel and carrot in the steamer basket of your instant pot, add 2 cups water to the pot, cover, cook at High for 1 minute, release the pressure, rinse veggies with cold water, transfer them to a bowl and also keep the cooking liquid in a separate bowl.
2. Set your instant pot on Sauté mode, add shallots, pancetta, chopped rosemary, chopped thyme and bay leaf, salt and pepper, stir and cook for 4 minutes.
3. Stuff quail with whole rosemary and thyme and add to pot.
4. Brown on all sides, add champagne, stir and cook for 2 minutes.
5. Add cooking liquid from veggies, stir, cover and cook at High for 9 minutes.
6. Release the pressure, take quail out of the pot and leave aside.
7. Strain liquid from the pot into a pan, heat up over medium heat and simmer until it reduces to half.
8. Arrange arugula on a platter, add steamed fennel and carrots, a drizzle of oil, lemon juice and top with quail.
9. Drizzle the sauce from the pan all over and serve.

Enjoy!

Nutrition:

- Calories 300
- Fat 17
- Fiber 0.2
- Carbs 0.2
- Protein 40

Braised Turkey Wings

This recipe fascinates us!

Preparation time: 10 minutes
Cooking time: 20 minutes
Servings: 4
Ingredients:

- 4 turkey wings
- 2 tablespoons butter
- 2 tablespoons vegetable oil
- 1 and ½ cups cranberries
- Salt and black pepper to the taste

- 1 yellow onions, sliced
- 1 cup walnuts
- 1 cup orange juice
- 1 bunch thyme, roughly chopped

Directions:

1. Set your instant pot on Sauté mode, add butter and oil and heat up.
2. Add turkey wings, salt and pepper and brown them on all sides.
3. Take wings out of the pot, add onion, walnuts, cranberries and thyme, stir and cook for 2 minutes.
4. Add orange juice and return turkey wings to pot, stir, cover and cook at High for 20 minutes.
5. Release the pressure naturally, uncover the pot and divide turkey wings among plates.
6. Transfer cranberry mix to a pan, heat up over medium heat and simmer for 5 minutes.
7. Drizzle sauce over turkey wings and serve.

Enjoy!

Nutrition:

- Calories 320
- Fat 15.3
- Fiber 2.1

- Carbs 16.4
- Protein 29

Easy Chicken Dish

It's the best way to cook a whole chicken!

Preparation time: 10 minutes
Cooking time: 35 minutes
Servings: 8
Ingredients:

- 1 whole chicken
- 1 tablespoon extra virgin olive oil
- 1 and ½ tablespoons lemon zest
- 1 cup chicken stock
- 1 tablespoon thyme leaves
- ½ teaspoon cinnamon powder
- Salt and black pepper to the taste
- 1 tablespoon cumin powder
- 2 teaspoons garlic powder
- 1 tablespoon coriander powder

Directions:

1. In a bowl, mix cinnamon with cumin, garlic, coriander, salt, pepper and lemon zest and stir well.
2. Rub chicken with half of the oil, then rub it inside and out with spices mix.
3. Set your instant pot on Sauté mode, add the rest of the oil and heat it up.
4. Add chicken and brown it on all sides for 5 minutes.
5. Add stock and thyme, stir, cover and cook at High for 25 minutes.
6. Release the pressure naturally and transfer chicken to a platter.
7. Add cooking liquid over it and serve.

Enjoy!
Nutrition:

- Calories 260
- Fat 3.1
- Fiber 1
- Carbs 4
- Protein 26.7

Party Chicken Wings

This is the perfect dish for your next party!

Preparation time: 10 minutes
Cooking time: 25 minutes
Servings: 6
Ingredients:

- 12 chicken wings, cut into 24 pieces
- 1 pound celery, cut into thin matchsticks
- ¼ cup honey
- 4 tablespoons hot sauce
- Salt to the taste
- 1 cup water
- ¼ cup tomato puree
- 1 cup yogurt
- 1 tablespoon parsley, finely chopped

Directions:

1. Put 1 cup water into your instant pot.
2. Place chicken wings in the steamer basket of your pot, cover and cook at High for 19 minutes.
3. Meanwhile, in a bowl, mix tomato puree with hot sauce, salt and honey and stir very well.
4. Release the pressure from the pot, add chicken wings to honey mix and toss them to coat.
5. Arrange chicken wings on a lined baking sheet and introduce in preheated broiler for 5 minutes.
6. Arrange celery sticks on a platter and add chicken wings next to it.
7. In a bowl, mix yogurt with parsley, stir well and place next to the platter.
8. Serve right away.

Enjoy!

Nutrition:

- Calories 300
- Fat 3.1
- Fiber 2
- Carbs 14
- Protein 33

Chicken Delight

There are many chicken based recipes but today, we recommend you this one!

Preparation time: 10 minutes
Cooking time: 37 minutes
Servings: 4
Ingredients:

- 6 chicken thighs
- 1 teaspoon vegetable oil
- Salt and black pepper to the taste
- 1 yellow onion, chopped
- 1 celery stalk, chopped
- ¼ pound baby carrots, cut into halves
- ½ teaspoon thyme, dried
- 2 tablespoons tomato paste
- ½ cup white wine
- 15 ounces canned tomatoes, chopped
- 2 cups chicken stock
- 1 and ½ pounds potatoes, chopped

Directions:

1. Set your instant pot on Sauté mode, add oil and heat it up.
2. Add chicken pieces, salt and pepper to the taste and brown them for 4 minutes on each side.
3. Take chicken out of the pot and leave on a plate for now.
4. Add onion, carrots, celery, thyme and tomato paste to the pot, stir and cook for 5 minutes.
5. Add white wine and salt, stir and cook for 3 minutes.
6. Add chicken stock, chicken pieces and chopped tomatoes and stir.
7. Place the steamer basket in the pot, add potatoes in it, cover the pot and cook at High for 30 minutes.
8. Release the pressure, take potatoes out of the pot and also take chicken pieces out.
9. Shred chicken meat and return to pot.
10. Also return potatoes, more salt and pepper, stir, divide among plates and serve.

Enjoy!

Nutrition:

- Calories 237
- Fat 12
- Fiber 0
- Carbs 1
- Protein 30

Chicken Gumbo

It's a quick gumbo recipe for you to enjoy!

Preparation time: 10 minutes
Cooking time: 45 minutes
Servings: 4
Ingredients:

- 1 pound smoky sausage, sliced
- 1 tablespoon vegetable oil
- 1 pound chicken thighs, cut into halves
- Salt and black pepper to the taste

For the roux:

- ½ cup flour
- ¼ cup vegetable oil
- 1 teaspoon Cajun spice

Aromatics:

- 1 bell pepper, chopped

- 1 yellow onion, chopped
- 1 celery stalk, chopped
- Salt to the taste
- 4 garlic cloves, minced
- 2 quarts chicken stock
- 15 ounces canned tomatoes, chopped
- ½ pound okra
- A dash of Tabasco sauce

For serving:

- White rice, already cooked
- ½ cup parsley, chopped

Directions:

1. Set your instant pot on Sauté mode, add 1 tablespoon oil and heat it up.
2. Add sausage, stir, brown for 4 minutes and transfer to a plate.
3. Add chicken pieces, stir, brown for 6 minutes and transfer next to the sausage.
4. Add ¼ cup vegetable oil to your pot and heat it up.
5. Add Cajun spice, stir and cook for 5 minutes.
6. Add bell pepper, onion, garlic, celery, salt and pepper, stir and cook for 5 minutes more.
7. Return chicken and sausage to the pot and stir.
8. Add stock, tomatoes and stir everything.
9. Cover the pot and cook at High for 10 minutes.
10. Release the pressure naturally for 15 minutes, uncover the pot, add okra, set the pot to Simmer mode and cook for 10 minutes.
11. Add more salt and pepper and the Tabasco sauce, stir and divide gumbo among plates.
12. Serve with rice on the side and with parsley sprinkled on top.

Enjoy!

Nutrition:

- Calories 208
- Fat 15
- Fiber 1

- Carbs 8
- Protein 10

Duck Chili

Have you ever tried a duck chili before? Well, today is the best day to give it a chance!

Preparation time: 10 minutes
Cooking time: 1 hour
Servings: 4
Ingredients:

- 1 pound northern beans, soaked and rinsed
- 1 yellow onion, cut into half
- 1 garlic heat, top trimmed off
- Salt to the taste
- 2 cloves
- 1 bay leaf
- 6 cups water

For the duck:

- 1 pound duck, ground
- 1 tablespoon vegetable oil
- 1 yellow onion, minced
- 2 carrots, chopped
- Salt and black pepper to the taste
- 4 ounces canned green chilies and their juice
- 1 teaspoon brown sugar
- 15 ounces canned tomatoes and their juices, chopped
- A handful cilantro, chopped

Directions:

1. Put the beans in your instant pot.
2. Add whole onion, garlic head, cloves, bay leaf, the water and salt to the taste, stir, cover and cook at High for 25 minutes.
3. Release the pressure, uncover the pot, discard solids and transfer beans to a bowl.
4. Heat up a pan with the oil over medium high heat, add carrots and chopped onion, season with salt and pepper to the taste, stir and cook for 5 minuets.
5. Add duck, stir and cook for 5 minutes.
6. Add chilies and tomatoes, bring to a simmer and take off heat.
7. Pour this into your instant pot, cover and cook at High for 5 minutes.
8. Release pressure naturally for 15 minutes, uncover the pot, add more salt and pepper, beans and brown sugar, stir and divide among plates.
9. Serve with cilantro on top.

Enjoy!

Nutrition:

- Calories 270
- Fat 13
- Fiber 26
- Carbs 15
- Protein 25

Coca-Cola Chicken

Have you ever heard of such a combination? We are sure you haven't!

Preparation time: 10 minutes
Cooking time: 10 minutes
Servings: 4
Ingredients:

- 1 yellow onion, minced
- 4 chicken drumsticks
- 1 tablespoon balsamic vinegar
- 1 chili pepper, chopped
- 15 ounces coca cola
- Salt and black pepper to the taste
- 2 tablespoons extra virgin olive oil

Directions:

1. Set your instant pot on Sauté mode, add the oil and heat it up.
2. Add chicken pieces, stir and brown them on all sides and then transfer them to a plate.
3. Add vinegar, coca cola and chili to the pot, stir and simmer for 2 minutes.
4. Return chicken, add salt and pepper to the taste, stir, cover and cook at High for 10 minutes.
5. Release the pressure quickly, uncover the pot, divide chicken among plates and serve.

Enjoy!

Nutrition:

- Calories 410
- Fat 23
- Fiber 1
- Carbs 24
- Sugar 21
- Protein 27

Delicious Chicken Curry

It's flavored and super tasty!

Preparation time: 10 minutes
Cooking time: 20 minutes
Servings: 4
Ingredients:

- 15 ounces chicken breast, chopped
- 1 tablespoon extra virgin olive oil
- 1 yellow onion, thinly sliced
- 6 potatoes, cut into halves
- 5 ounces canned coconut cream
- 1 bag chicken curry base
- ½ bunch coriander, chopped

Directions:

1. Set your instant pot on Sauté mode, add the oil and heat it up.
2. Add chicken, stir and brown for 2 minutes.
3. Add onion, stir and cook for 1 minute.
4. In a bowl, mix curry base with coconut cream and stir.
5. Pour this over chicken, also add potatoes, stir, cover and cook at High for 15 minutes.
6. Release pressure fast, uncover the pot, divide curry among plates and serve with chopped coriander on top.

Enjoy!

Nutrition:

- Calories 120
- Fat 8.6
- Fiber 1.2
- Carbs 6.11
- Protein 14.8

Coq Au Vin

This is a very famous recipe all over the world! Try making it in your instant pot!

Preparation time: 10 minutes
Cooking time: 50 minutes
Servings: 4
Ingredients:

- 2 pounds chicken pieces
- 4 ounces bacon, chopped
- ¼ cup peanut oil
- 2 brown onions, sliced
- 2 garlic cloves, crushed
- 14 ounces red wine
- 1 bay leaf
- 2 tablespoons flour
- 7 ounces white mushrooms, sliced
- 1 cup parsley, finely chopped
- Salt and black pepper to the taste
- 12 small potatoes, cut into halves
- 2 tablespoons cognac

Directions:

1. Set your instant pot on Sauté mode, add the oil and heat it up.
2. Add chicken pieces, brown them on all sides and transfer them to a bowl.
3. Add bacon and onions to the pot, stir and cook for 5 minutes.
4. Add garlic, stir and cook for 1 minute
5. Return chicken to pot, add flour and cognac, stir and cook for 1 minute.
6. Add salt, pepper, bay leaf and red wine, stir, bring to a boil, cover pot and cook at High for 30 minutes.
7. Release the pressure quick, add mushrooms to the pot, add potatoes in the steamer basket, cover the pot again and cook everything for 15 minutes.
8. Release the pressure again, take potatoes and divide them among plates.
9. Add chicken on top, sprinkle parsley and serve.

Enjoy!

Nutrition:

- Calories 281
- Fat 12.4
- Fiber 2.2
- Carbs 15
- Protein 23

Italian Chicken

It's a very rich and healthy poultry dish that you can make in your instant pot!

Preparation time: 10 minutes
Cooking time: 20 minutes
Servings: 6

Ingredients:

- 1 tablespoon extra virgin olive oil
- 2 pounds chicken breasts, skinless and boneless
- Salt and black pepper to the taste
- ¾ cup yellow onion, diced
- ½ cup green bell pepper, chopped
- ½ cup red bell pepper, chopped
- ¾ cup marinara sauce
- 2 tablespoons pesto
- ¾ cup mushrooms, sliced
- Cheddar cheese, shredded for serving

Directions:

1. Set your instant pot on Sauté mode, add the oil and heat it up.
2. Add onion, red and green bell pepper, salt and pepper to the taste, stir and cook for 4 minutes.
3. Add pesto, marinara sauce and chicken, stir, cover and cook at High for 12 minutes.
4. Release the pressure, uncover the pot, remove chicken, place on a cutting board and shred,
5. Discard 2/3 cup cooking liquid, add mushrooms to the pot, set it on Sauté mode again and cook them for 3 minutes.
6. Return chicken, stir, divide among plates and serve with shredded cheese on top.

Enjoy!

Nutrition:

- Calories 340
- Fat 15
- Fiber 3.5
- Carbs 10.1
- Protein 34

Teriyaki Chicken

You can serve this with some rice, and that's it!

Preparation time: 10 minutes
Cooking time: 12 minutes
Servings: 6
Ingredients:

- 2 pounds chicken breasts, skinless and boneless
- 2/3 cup teriyaki sauce
- 1 tablespoon honey
- ½ cup chicken stock
- Salt and black pepper to the taste
- A handful green onions, chopped

Directions:

1. Set your instant pot on Sauté mode, add teriyaki sauce and honey, stir and simmer for 1 minute.
2. Add stock, chicken, salt and pepper, stir, cover and cook at High for 12 minutes.
3. Release the pressure quick, take chicken breasts, place them on a cutting board and shred with 2 forks.
4. Remove ½ cup of cooking liquid, return shredded chicken to pot, add green onions, stir, divide among plates and serve.

Enjoy!
Nutrition:

- Calories 240
- Fat 13
- Fiber 1
- Carbs 8
- Protein 34

Creamy Chicken

It's a very creamy chicken dish!

Preparation time: 10 minutes
Cooking time: 20 minutes
Servings: 6
Ingredients:

- 2 slices bacon, chopped
- 1 cup chicken stock
- 4 ounces cream cheese
- 1 ounce ranch seasoning
- 2 pounds chicken breasts, skinless and boneless
- Green onions, chopped for serving

Directions:

1. Set your instant pot on Sauté mode, add bacon and cook for 4 minutes.
2. Add chicken, stock and seasoning, stir, cover and cook at High for 12 minutes.
3. Release the pressure, uncover the pot, transfer chicken to a cutting board and shred it.
4. Remove 2/3 cup liquid from the pot, add cream cheese, set the pot to Sauté mode again and cook for 3 minutes.
5. Return chicken to pot, stir, add green onions, divide among plates and serve.

Enjoy!

Nutrition:

- Calories 300
- Fat 7
- Fiber 3
- Carbs 23
- Protein 22

Buffalo Chicken

Get creative! Try something new each day!

Preparation time: 10 minutes
Cooking time: 15 minutes
Servings: 6
Ingredients:

- 2 pounds chicken breasts, skinless, boneless and cut into thin strips
- ½ cup celery, chopped
- 1 small yellow onion, chopped
- ½ cup buffalo sauce
- ½ cup chicken stock
- ¼ cup bleu cheese, crumbled

Directions:

1. In your instant pot, mix onion with celery, buffalo sauce, stock and chicken, stir, cover and cook at High for 12 minutes.
2. Release the pressure, uncover the pot, discard 2/3 cup of cooking liquid, add crumbled cheese, stir very well, divide among plates and serve.

Enjoy!

Nutrition:

- Calories 190
- Fat 9
- Fiber 1
- Carbs 20
- Protein 14

Colombian Chicken Dish

You only need 5 ingredients to create a hypnotizing dish!

Preparation time: 10 minutes
Cooking time: 25 minutes
Servings: 4
Ingredients:

- 4 gold potatoes, cut into medium chunks
- 1 yellow onion, thinly sliced
- 4 big tomatoes, cut into medium chunks
- 1 chicken, cut into 8 pieces
- Salt and black pepper to the taste
- 2 bay leaves
- Salt and black pepper to the taste

Directions:

1. In your instant pot, mix potatoes with onion, chicken, tomato, bay leaves, salt, and pepper, stir well, cover and cook at High for 25 minutes.
2. Release the pressure naturally, uncover the pot, add more salt and pepper, discard bay leaves, divide chicken among plates and serve.

Enjoy!

Nutrition:

- Calories 270
- Fat 12
- Fiber 1
- Carbs 23
- Protein 14

Chicken And Lentils Dish

Get ready to eat something super tasty in only 30 minutes!

Preparation time: 10 minutes
Cooking time: 25 minutes
Servings: 4
Ingredients:

- 8 ounces bacon, chopped
- 2 tablespoons extra virgin olive oil
- A drizzle of olive oil for serving
- 1 cup yellow onion, chopped
- 8 ounces lentils, dried
- 2 carrots, chopped
- 12 parsley springs, chopped
- Salt and black pepper to the taste
- 2 bay leaves
- 2 and ½ pounds chicken pieces
- 1-quart chicken stock
- 2 teaspoons sherry vinegar

Directions:

1. Set your instant pot on Sauté mode, add the oil and heat it up.
2. Add bacon, stir and cook for 1 minute.
3. Add onions, stir and cook 2 minutes.
4. Add lentils, carrots, chicken pieces, parsley, bay leaves, stock, salt and pepper to the taste, stir, cover and cook at High for 20 minutes.
5. Release pressure, take chicken pieces and place them on a cutting board.
6. Discard skin and bones, shred chicken and return to pot.
7. Set the pot on Sauté mode again and cook everything for 7 minutes.
8. Add more salt and pepper and the vinegar, stir and divide among plates.
9. Drizzle some olive oil over the whole mix and serve.

Enjoy!

Nutrition:

- Calories 340
- Fat 3.3
- Fiber 23
- Carbs 30
- Protein 29

Chicken Curry With Eggplant And Squash

The flavors will make you want more and more!

Preparation time: 10 minutes
Cooking time: 25 minutes
Servings: 4
Ingredients:

- 3 garlic cloves, crushed
- 2 tablespoons vegetable oil
- 3 bird's eye chilies, cut into halves
- 1 inch piece ginger, sliced
- 2 tablespoons green curry paste
- 1/8 teaspoon cumin, ground
- ¼ teaspoon coriander, ground
- 14 ounces canned coconut milk
- 6 cups quash, cubed

- 8 chicken pieces
- 1 eggplant, cubed
- Salt and black pepper to the taste
- 1 tablespoon fish sauce
- 4 cups spinach, chopped
- ½ cup cilantro, chopped
- ½ cup basil, chopped
- Cooked barley for serving
- Lime wedges, for serving

Directions:

1. Set your instant pot on Sauté mode, add oil and heat it up.
2. Add garlic, ginger, chilies, cumin and coriander, stir and cook for 1 minute.
3. Add curry paste, stir and cook 3 minutes.
4. Add coconut milk, stir and simmer for 1 minute.
5. Add chicken, squash, eggplant, salt, and pepper, stir, cover and cook at High for 20 minutes.
6. Release the pressure, uncover the pot, add spinach, fish sauce, more salt and pepper, basil and cilantro, stir and divide among plates.
7. Serve with cooked barley on the side and lime wedges.

Enjoy!
Nutrition:

- Calories 160
- Fat 8.2
- Fiber 4.1

- Carbs 13.2
- Protein 6

Chicken And Chickpea Masala

You need something to impress your guests? We offer you this amazing recipe!

Preparation time: 10 minutes
Cooking time: 25 minutes
Servings: 4
Ingredients:

- 1 yellow onion, finely chopped
- 2 tablespoons butter
- 4 garlic cloves, minced
- 1 tablespoon ginger, grated
- 1 and ½ teaspoon paprika
- 1 tablespoon cumin, ground
- 1 and ½ teaspoons coriander, ground
- 1 teaspoon turmeric, ground
- Salt and black pepper to the taste
- A pinch of cayenne pepper
- 15 ounces canned tomatoes, crushed
- ¼ cup lemon juice
- 1 pound spinach, chopped
- 3 pounds chicken drumsticks and thighs
- ½ cup cilantro, chopped
- ½ cup chicken stock
- 15 ounces canned chickpeas, drained
- ½ cup heavy cream

Directions:

1. Set your instant pot on Sauté mode, add butter and melt it.
2. Add ginger, onion, and garlic, stir and cook for 5 minutes.
3. Add paprika, cumin, coriander, cayenne, turmeric, salt, and pepper, stir and cook for 30 seconds.
4. Add tomatoes and spinach, stir and cook for 2 minutes.
5. Add half of the cilantro, chicken pieces, and stock, stir, cover the pot and cook at High for 15 minutes.
6. Release the pressure, uncover the pot, add heavy cream, chickpeas, lemon juice, more salt, and pepper, stir, set the pot on Sauté mode again and simmer for 3 minutes.
7. Sprinkle the rest of the cilantro on top, stir, divide among plates and serve.

Enjoy!

Nutrition:

- Calories 270
- Fat 8
- Fiber 7.6
- Carbs 30
- Protein 31

Sesame Chicken

It's an easy chicken recipe with such a great taste!

Preparation time: 10 minutes
Cooking time: 8 minutes
Servings: 4
Ingredients:

- 2 pounds chicken breasts, skinless, boneless and chopped
- ½ cup yellow onion, chopped
- Salt and black pepper to the taste
- 1 tablespoon vegetable oil
- 2 garlic cloves, minced
- ½ cup soy sauce
- ¼ cup ketchup
- 2 teaspoons sesame oil
- ½ cup honey
- 2 tablespoons cornstarch
- ¼ teaspoon red pepper flakes
- 3 tablespoons water
- 2 green onions, chopped
- 1 tablespoons sesame seeds, toasted

Directions:

1. Set your instant pot on Sauté mode, add the oil and heat it up.
2. Add garlic, onion, chicken, salt and pepper, stir and cook for 3 minutes.
3. Add pepper flakes, soy sauce and ketchup, stir, cover and cook at High for 3 minutes.
4. Release pressure quick, uncover the pot, add sesame oil and honey and stir.
5. In a bowl, mix cornstarch with water and stir well.
6. Add this to the pot, also add green onions and sesame seeds, stir well, divide among plates and serve.

Enjoy!

Nutrition:

- Calories 170
- Fat 3.5
- Fiber 2.9
- Carbs 16
- Protein 7

Chicken With Duck Sauce

Is this amazing or what?

Preparation time: 10 minutes
Cooking time: 20 minutes
Servings: 4
Ingredients:

- 1 chicken, cut into medium pieces
- Salt and black pepper to the taste
- 1 tablespoon extra virgin olive oil
- ½ teaspoon paprika
- ¼ cup white wine
- ½ teaspoon marjoram, dried
- ¼ cup chicken stock

For the duck sauce:

- 2 tablespoons white vinegar
- ¼ cup apricot preserves
- 1 and ½ teaspoon ginger root, grated
- 2 tablespoons honey

Directions:

1. Set your instant pot on Sauté mode, add oil and heat it up.
2. Add chicken pieces, brown them on all sides and transfer to a bowl.
3. Season them with salt, pepper, marjoram and paprika and toss to coat.
4. Drain fat from pot, add stock and wine, stir and simmer for 2 minutes.
5. Return chicken, cover the pot and cook at High for 9 minutes.
6. Release the pressure, transfer chicken to servings dishes and leave aside for now.
7. Add apricot preserves to pot, ginger, vinegar, and honey, set pot to Sauté mode again, stir and simmer sauce for 10 minutes.
8. Drizzle over chicken and serve.

Enjoy!

Nutrition:

- Calories 170
- Fat 4
- Fiber 3
- Carbs 9
- Protein 23

Chicken And Dumplings

These chicken and dumplings are worth trying!

Preparation time: 10 minutes
Cooking time: 20 minutes
Servings: 6
Ingredients:

- 2 pounds chicken breasts, skinless and bone-in
- 4 carrots, chopped
- 1 yellow onion, chopped
- 3 celery stalks, chopped
- ¾ cup chicken stock
- Salt and black pepper to the taste
- ½ teaspoon thyme, dried
- 2 eggs
- 2/3 cup milk
- 1 tablespoon baking powder
- 2 cups flour
- 1 tablespoon chives

Directions:

1. In your instant pot, add chicken, onion, carrots, celery, stock, thyme, salt and pepper, stir, cover and cook on Low for 15 minutes.
2. Release the pressure quick, transfer chicken to a bowl and keep warm for now.
3. In a bowl, mix eggs with salt, milk and baking powder and stir.
4. Add flour gradually and stir very well.
5. Set instant pot to Simmer mode and bring the liquid inside to a boil.
6. Shape dumplings from eggs mix, drop them into stock, cover the pot and cook at High for 7 minutes.
7. Shred chicken and add to the pot after you've released the pressure, stir, divide everything among plates and serve with chives sprinkled on top.

Enjoy!

Nutrition:

- Calories 380
- Fat 4.2
- Fiber 2.9
- Carbs 40
- Protein 43

Tasty Chicken And Noodles

It's a delicious casserole, perfect for lunch!

Preparation time: 10 minutes
Cooking time: 20 minutes
Servings: 6
Ingredients:

- 8 chicken thighs, skinless and boneless
- 3 carrots, chopped
- 2 garlic cloves, minced
- 1 yellow onion, chopped
- 3 celery stalks, chopped
- 6 cups chicken stock
- 1 bay leaf
- 2 sage springs
- 1 rosemary spring
- 5 thyme springs
- Salt and black pepper to the taste
- 1 teaspoon chicken seasoning
- 1 pound egg noodles
- 2 tablespoons cornstarch
- 3 tablespoons water
- 1 cup peas, frozen
- Juice of 1 lemon
- ¼ cup parsley, chopped

Directions:

1. Set your instant pot on Sauté mode, add onion, garlic, and celery, stir and brown for 4 minutes.
2. Add carrot, chicken, stock, bay leaf, thyme, rosemary, sage, chicken seasoning, salt and pepper to the taste, stir, cover the pot and cook on Low for 10 minutes.
3. Release the pressure naturally, uncover the pot, add egg noodles, cornstarch mixed with water, peas, lemon juice, parsley and more salt and pepper if needed.
4. Discard herbs springs, stir everything, divide among plates and serve.

Enjoy!

Nutrition:

- Calories 560
- Fat 11.2
- Fiber 5.2
- Carbs 77
- Protein 39

Chicken And Pomegranate

Here is how you can make a simple and tasty meal in your instant pot!

Preparation time: 10 minutes
Cooking time: 15 minutes
Servings: 6
Ingredients:

- 10 chicken pieces
- 2 cups walnuts
- Salt and black pepper to the taste
- 3 tablespoons extra virgin olive oil
- 1 yellow onion, chopped
- ¼ teaspoon cardamom, ground
- ½ teaspoon cinnamon, ground
- 2/3 cup pomegranate molasses
- ¾ cup water
- 2 tablespoons sugar
- Juice of ½ lemon
- Pomegranate seeds for serving

Directions:

1. Heat up a pan over medium high heat, add walnuts, stir and toast for 5 minutes.
2. Transfer them to your food processor, blend well, transfer to a bowl and leave aside.
3. Set your instant pot on Sauté mode, add 2 tablespoons oil and heat it up.
4. Add chicken pieces, salt and pepper, brown them on all sides and transfer them to a plate.
5. Add the rest of the oil to the pot, add onion, stir and cook for 3 minutes.
6. Add cardamom and cinnamon, stir and cook for 1 minute.
7. Add ground walnuts, pomegranate molasses, lemon juice, chicken and sugar, stir, cover and cook at High for 7 minutes.
8. Release the pressure, uncover the pot, add more salt and pepper, stir, divide among plates and serve with the sauce from the pot and with pomegranate seeds on top.

Enjoy!
Nutrition:

- Calories 200
- Fat 1
- Fiber 4
- Carbs 27
- Protein 17

Delicious Goose

It's so tender and delicious!

Preparation time: 10 minutes
Cooking time: 1 hour
Servings: 5
Ingredients:

- 1 goose breast, fat trimmed off and cut into pieces
- 1 goose leg, skinless
- 1 goose thigh, skinless
- Salt and black pepper to the taste
- 3 and ½ cups water
- 2 teaspoons garlic, minced
- 1 yellow onion, chopped
- 12 ounces canned mushroom cream

Directions:

1. Put goose meat in your instant pot.
2. Add onion, salt, pepper, water and garlic, stir, cover and cook on Low for 1 hour.
3. Release the pressure, uncover the pot, add mushroom cream, set the pot on Simmer mode and cook everything for 5 minutes.
4. Divide into bowls and serve with toasted bread on the side.

Enjoy!

Nutrition:

- Calories 345
- Fat 7.8
- Fiber 1
- Carbs 1
- Protein 28.4

Goose And Chili Sauce

The combination between the goose and the sweet sauce is amazing!

Preparation time: 10 minutes
Cooking time: 15 minutes
Servings: 4
Ingredients:

- 1 goose breast half, skinless, boneless and cut into thin slices
- ¼ cup extra virgin olive oil
- 1 sweet onion, chopped
- 2 teaspoons garlic, chopped
- Salt and black pepper to the taste
- ¼ cup sweet chili sauce

Directions:

1. Set your instant pot on Sauté mode, add the oil and heat it up.
2. Add onion and garlic, stir and cook for 2 minutes.
3. Add goose breast slices, salt and pepper to the taste, stir and cook for 2 minutes on each side.
4. Add chili sauce, stir, cover and cook at High for 5 minutes.
5. Release pressure quick, divide among plates and serve.

Enjoy!

Nutrition:

- Calories 190
- Fat 8
- Fiber 1
- Carbs 1
- Protein 29

Tasty Chicken And Shrimp

This is wonderful!

Preparation time: 10 minutes
Cooking time: 15 minutes
Servings: 4
Ingredients:

- 8 ounces shrimp, peeled and deveined
- 8 ounces sausages, sliced
- 8 ounces chicken breasts, skinless, boneless and chopped
- 2 tablespoons extra virgin olive oil
- 1 teaspoon Creole seasoning
- 2 teaspoons thyme, dried
- A pinch of cayenne pepper
- 2 teaspoons Worcestershire sauce
- 1 dash Tabasco sauce
- 3 garlic cloves, minced
- 1 yellow onion, chopped
- 1 green bell pepper, chopped
- 3 celery stalks, chopped
- 1 cup white rice
- 1 cup chicken stock
- 2 cups canned tomatoes, chopped
- 3 tablespoons parsley, chopped

Directions:

1. In a bowl, mix Creole seasoning with thyme and cayenne and stir.
2. Set your instant pot on Sauté mode, add the oil and heat it up.
3. Add chicken and brown for a few minutes.
4. Add sausage slices, stir and cook for 3 minutes.
5. Add shrimp and half of the seasoning mix, stir and cook for 2 minutes.
6. Transfer everything to a bowl and leave aside for now.
7. Add garlic, onions, celery and bell peppers to your instant pot.
8. Add the rest of the seasoning mix, stir and cook for 10 minutes.
9. Add rice, stock, tomatoes, Tabasco sauce and Worcestershire sauce, stir, cover and cook on High for 8 minutes.
10. Release the pressure, return chicken, sausage and shrimp, stir, cover and leave instant pot aside for 5 minutes.
11. Divide everything among plates and serve.

Enjoy!

Nutrition:

- Calories 269
- Fat 5.9
- Fiber 2.4
- Carbs 23.5
- Protein 28.4

Indian Butter Chicken

This is a classic Indian meal! Now it will become your new favorite Sunday meal!

Preparation time: 10 minutes
Cooking time: 15 minutes
Servings: 6
Ingredients:

- 10 chicken thighs, skinless and boneless
- 2 jalapeno peppers, chopped
- 28 ounces canned tomatoes and their juice, chopped
- 2 teaspoons cumin, ground
- 2 tablespoons ginger, chopped
- ½ cup butter
- Salt and black pepper to the taste
- ¾ cup heavy cream
- 2 teaspoons garam masala
- ¾ cup Greek yogurt
- 2 teaspoons cumin seeds, toasted and ground
- 2 tablespoons cornstarch
- 2 tablespoons water
- ¼ cup cilantro, chopped

Directions:

1. In your food processor, mix tomatoes with ginger and jalapenos and blend well.
2. Set your instant pot on Sauté mode, add butter and melt it.
3. Add chicken, stir and brown for 3 minutes on each side.
4. Transfer chicken pieces to a bowl and leave aside.
5. Add paprika and ground cumin to your pot, stir and cook for 10 seconds.
6. Add tomato mix, salt, pepper, yogurt, heavy cream and chicken pieces, stir, cover and cook at High for 5 minutes.
7. Release the pressure naturally for 15 minutes, uncover the pot, add cornstarch mixed with the water, garam masala and cumin seeds and stir well.
8. Add cilantro, stir, divide among plates and serve with naan bread.

Enjoy!

Nutrition:

- Calories 380
- Fat 29
- Fiber 2
- Carbs 8
- Sugar 2
- Protein 24

Chicken And Broccoli

Do you want something healthy and tasty at the same time? Then maybe you should try this recipe!

Preparation time: 10 minutes
Cooking time: 15 minutes
Servings: 6
Ingredients:

- 2 chicken breasts, skinless and boneless
- 1 tablespoon butter
- 1 tablespoon extra virgin olive oil
- ½ cup yellow onion, chopped
- 14 ounces canned chicken stock
- Salt and black pepper to the taste
- A pinch of red pepper flakes
- 1 tablespoon parsley, dried
- 2 tablespoons water
- 2 tablespoons cornstarch
- 3 cups broccoli, steamed and chopped
- 1 cup cheddar cheese, shredded
- 4 ounces cream cheese, cubed

Directions:

1. Set your instant pot on Sauté mode, add butter and oil and heat up.
2. Add chicken breasts, salt and pepper, brown on all sides and transfer to a bowl.
3. Add onion to the pot, stir and cook for 5 minutes.
4. Add more salt, pepper, stock, parsley, pepper flakes and return chicken breasts as well.
5. Stir, cover the pot and cook at High for 5 minutes.
6. Release the pressure quick, transfer chicken to a cutting board, chop it and return to pot.
7. Add cornstarch mixed with the water, shredded cheese and cream cheese and stir until all cheese dissolves.
8. Add broccoli, stir, set the pot on Simmer mode and cook for 5 minutes.
9. Divide among plates and serve.

Enjoy!

Nutrition:

- Calories 280
- Fat 13
- Fiber 4
- Carbs 23
- Protein 30

Simple Chicken And Corn Mix

We think you will like this combination as soon as you try it!

Preparation time: 10 minutes
Cooking time: 25 minutes
Servings: 4
Ingredients:

- 8 chicken drumsticks
- Salt and black pepper to the taste
- 1 teaspoon extra virgin olive oil
- ½ teaspoon garlic powder
- 3 scallions, chopped
- ½ yellow onion, chopped
- 1 tomato, chopped
- ¼ cup cilantro, chopped
- 1 garlic clove, minced
- 2 cups water
- 8 ounces tomato sauce
- 1 tablespoon chicken bouillon
- 2 corn on the cob, husked and cut into halves
- ½ teaspoon cumin, ground

Directions:

1. Set your instant pot on Sauté mode, add oil and heat up.
2. Add onions, tomato, scallions, and garlic, stir and cook for 3 minutes.
3. Add cilantro, stir and cook for 1 minute.
4. Add tomato sauce, water, bouillon, cumin, garlic powder, chicken, salt, pepper and top with the corn.
5. Cover the pot and cook at High for 20 minutes.
6. Release the pressure quickly, uncover the pot, add more salt and pepper if needed, divide chicken and corn among plates and serve.

Enjoy!

Nutrition:

- Calories 320
- Fat 10
- Fiber 3
- Carbs 18
- Protein 42

Delicious Chicken And Cabbage

It's a quick and extremely easy dinner idea!

Preparation time: 10 minutes
Cooking time: 30 minutes
Servings: 3
Ingredients:

- 1 and ½ pounds chicken thighs, boneless
- 1 green cabbage, roughly chopped
- 1 tablespoon vegetable oil
- Salt and black pepper to the taste
- 2 chili peppers, chopped
- 1 yellow onion, chopped
- 4 garlic cloves, chopped
- 3 tablespoons curry paste
- A pinch of cayenne pepper
- ½ cup white wine
- 10 ounces coconut milk
- 1 tablespoon fish sauce

Directions:

1. Set your instant pot on Sauté mode, add oil and heat it up.
2. Add chicken, season with salt and pepper, stir, brown for a few minutes and transfer to a bowl.
3. Add garlic, chili peppers and onions to the pot, stir and cook for 4 minutes.
4. Add curry paste, stir and cook for 2 minutes more.
5. Add wine, cabbage, coconut milk, cayenne, fish sauce, chicken pieces, salt and pepper, stir, cover and cook at High for 20 minutes.
6. Release the pressure naturally, uncover the pot, stir your mix, divide it among plates and serve.

Enjoy!

Nutrition:

- Calories 260
- Fat 5.5
- Fiber 4.9
- Carbs 15.2
- Protein 30.2

Instant Pot Meat Recipes

Simple Corned Beef

It's an excellent choice for you and your kids!

Preparation time: 10 minutes
Cooking time: 60 minutes
Servings: 6
Ingredients:

- 4 pounds beef brisket
- 2 oranges, sliced
- 2 garlic cloves, minced
- 2 yellow onions, thinly sliced
- 11 ounces celery, thinly sliced
- 1 tablespoon dill, dried
- 3 bay leaves
- 4 cinnamon sticks, cut into halves
- Salt and black pepper to the taste
- 17 ounces water

Directions:

1. Put the beef in a bowl, add some water to cover, leave aside to soak for a few hours, drain and transfer to your instant pot.
2. Add celery, orange slices, onions, garlic, bay leaves, dill, cinnamon, dill, salt and pepper and 17 ounces water.
3. Stir, cover the pot and cook at High for 50 minutes.
4. Release the pressure, leave beef aside to cool down for 5 minutes, transfer to a cutting board, slice and divide among plates.
5. Drizzle the juice and veggies from the pot over beef and serve.

Enjoy!

Nutrition:

- Calories 251
- Fat 3.14
- Fiber 0
- Carbs 1
- Protein 7

Tasty Beef Bourguignon

It will simply melt in your mouth! Try it and see!

Preparation time: 15 minutes
Cooking time: 30 minutes
Servings: 6
Ingredients:

- 10 pounds round steak, cut into small cubes
- 2 carrots, sliced
- ½ cup beef stock
- 1 cup dry red wine
- 3 bacon slices, chopped
- 8 ounces mushrooms, cut into quarters
- 2 tablespoons white flour
- 12 pearl onions
- 2 garlic cloves, minced
- ¼ teaspoon basil, dried
- Salt and black pepper to the taste

Directions:

1. Set your instant pot on Sauté mode, add bacon and brown it for 2 minutes.
2. Add beef pieces, stir and brown for 5 minutes.
3. Add flour and stir very well.
4. Add salt, pepper, wine, stock, onions, garlic and basil, stir, cover and cook at High for 20 minutes.
5. Release the pressure quickly, uncover your pot, add mushrooms and carrots, cover the pot again and cook at High for 5 minutes more.
6. Release the pressure again, divide beef bourguignon among plates and serve.

Enjoy!

Nutrition:

- Calories 442
- Fat 17.2
- Fiber 3
- Carbs 16
- Protein 39

Tasty Beef Curry

This is the best recipe for a family gathering!

Preparation time: 10 minutes
Cooking time: 20 minutes
Servings: 4
Ingredients:

- 2 pounds beef steak, cubed
- 2 tablespoons extra virgin olive oil
- 3 potatoes, diced
- 1 tablespoon wine mustard
- 2 and ½ tablespoons curry powder
- 2 yellow onions, chopped
- 2 garlic cloves, minced
- 10 ounces canned coconut milk
- 2 tablespoons tomato sauce
- Salt and black pepper to the taste

Directions:

1. Set your instant pot on Sauté mode, add the oil and heat it up.
2. Add onions and garlic, stir and cook for 4 minutes.
3. Add potatoes and mustard, stir and cook for 1 minute.
4. Add beef, stir and brown on all sides.
5. Add curry powder, salt and pepper, stir and cook for 2 minutes.
6. Add coconut milk and tomato sauce, stir, cover the pot and cook at High for 10 minutes.
7. Release the pressure, uncover the pot, divide curry among plates and serve.

Enjoy!

Nutrition:

- Calories 434
- Fat 20
- Fiber 2.9
- Carbs 14
- Protein 27.5

Beef Stroganoff

This is a Russian comfort food, very popular all over the world!

Preparation time: 10 minutes
Cooking time: 25 minutes
Servings: 4
Ingredients:

- 10 pounds beef, cut into small cubes
- 1 yellow onion, chopped
- 2 and ½ tablespoons vegetable oil
- 1 and ½ tablespoons white flour
- 2 garlic cloves, minced
- 4 ounces mushrooms, sliced
- 1 and ½ tablespoon tomato paste
- Salt and black pepper to the taste
- 3 tablespoons Worcestershire sauce
- 13 ounces beef stock
- 8 ounces sour cream
- Egg noodles, already cooked for serving

Directions:

1. Put beef, salt, pepper and flour in a bowl and toss to coat.
2. Set your instant pot on Sauté mode, add oil and heat it up.
3. Add meat and brown it on all sides.
4. Add onion, garlic, mushrooms, Worcestershire sauce, stock and tomato paste, stir well, cover the pot and cook at High for 20 minutes.
5. Release the pressure, uncover the pot, add sour cream, more salt and pepper, stir well and divide among plates on top of egg noodles.

Enjoy!

Nutrition:

- Calories 335
- Fat 18.4
- Fiber 1.3
- Carbs 22.5
- Protein 20.1

Beef Chili

It's so hearty and delicious! It's a must!

Preparation time: 10 minutes
Cooking time: 40 minutes
Servings: 6
Ingredients:

- 1 and ½ pounds beef, ground
- 1 sweet onion, chopped
- Salt and black pepper to the taste
- 16 ounces mixed beans, soaked overnight and drained
- 28 ounces canned tomatoes, chopped
- 17 ounces beef stock
- 12 ounces pale ale
- 6 garlic cloves, chopped
- 7 jalapeno peppers, diced
- 2 tablespoons vegetable oil
- 4 carrots, chopped
- 3 tablespoons chili powder
- 1 bay leaf
- 1 teaspoon chipotle powder

Directions:

1. Set your instant pot on Sauté mode, add half of the oil and heat it up.
2. Add beef, stir, brown for 8 minutes and transfer to a bowl.
3. Add the rest of the oil to the pot and heat it up.
4. Add carrots, onion, jalapenos and garlic, stir and sauté for 4 minutes.
5. Add ale and tomatoes and stir.
6. Also add beans, bay leaf, stock, chili powder, chipotle powder, salt and pepper and the beef, stir, cover and cook at High for 25 minutes.
7. Release the pressure naturally, uncover the pot, stir chili, transfer to bowls and serve.

Enjoy!

Nutrition:

- Calories 272
- Fat 5
- Fiber 0
- Carbs 32
- Protein 25

Chili Con Carne

Are you in the mood for a Mexican style dish today? Well, here is an option for you!

Preparation time: 10 minutes
Cooking time: 30 minutes
Servings: 4
Ingredients:

- 1 pound beef, ground
- 1 yellow onion, chopped
- 4 tablespoons extra virgin olive oil
- Salt and black pepper to the taste
- 2 garlic cloves, minced
- 1 bay leaf
- 4 ounces kidney beans, soaked overnight and drained
- 1 teaspoon tomato paste
- 8 ounces canned tomatoes, chopped
- 1 tablespoon chili powder
- ½ teaspoon cumin, ground
- 5 ounces water

Directions:

1. Set your instant pot on Sauté mode, add 1 tablespoon oil and heat it up.
2. Add meat, brown for a few minutes and transfer to a bowl.
3. Add the rest of the oil to the pot and also heat it up.
4. Add onion and garlic, stir and cook for 3 minutes.
5. Return beef to pot, add bay leaf, beans, tomato paste, tomatoes, chili powder, cumin, salt, pepper and water, stir, cover and cook on High for 18 minutes.
6. Release the pressure, uncover the pot, discard bay leaf, divide chili among bowls and serve.

Enjoy!

Nutrition:

- Calories 256
- Fat 8
- Fiber 1
- Carbs 22
- Protein 25

Beef Pot Roast

It's delicious, and you can make it tonight for dinner!

Preparation time: 10 minutes
Cooking time: 1 hour
Servings: 6
Ingredients:

- 3 pounds beef roast
- Salt and black pepper to the taste
- 17 ounces beef stock
- 3 ounces red wine
- ½ teaspoon chicken salt
- ½ teaspoon smoked paprika
- 1 yellow onion, chopped
- 4 garlic cloves, minced
- 3 carrots, chopped
- 5 potatoes, chopped

Directions:

1. In a bowl, mix salt, pepper, chicken salt and paprika and stir.
2. Rub beef with this mix and put it in your instant pot.
3. Add onion, garlic, stock, and wine, toss to coat, cover the pot and cook on High for 50 minutes.
4. Release the pressure quickly, uncover the pot, add carrots and potatoes, cover again and cook at High for 10 minutes.
5. Release the pressure again, uncover the pot, transfer roast to a platter, drizzle cooking juices all over and serve with veggies on the side.

Enjoy!

Nutrition:

- Calories 290
- Fat 20
- Fiber 0
- Carbs 2
- Protein 25

Beef Dish

It's a rich and textured dish! It's delightful!

Preparation time: 10 minutes
Cooking time: 30 minutes
Servings: 4
Ingredients:

- 2 tablespoons extra virgin olive oil
- 1 and ½ pounds beef stew meat, cubed
- 4 tablespoons white flour
- 1 yellow onion, chopped
- 2 tablespoons red wine
- 2 garlic cloves, minced
- 2 cups water
- 2 cups beef stock
- Salt and black pepper to the taste
- 1 bay leaf
- ½ teaspoon thyme, dried
- 2 celery stalks, chopped
- 2 carrots, chopped
- 4 potatoes, chopped
- ½ bunch parsley, chopped

Directions:

1. Season beef with salt and pepper and mix with half of the flour.
2. Set your instant pot on Sauté mode, add oil and heat it up.
3. Add beef, brown for 2 minutes and transfer to a bowl.
4. Add onion to your pot, stir and cook for 3 minutes.
5. Add garlic, stir and cook for 1 minute.
6. Add wine, stir well and cook for 15 seconds.
7. Add the rest of the flour and stir well for 2 minutes.
8. Return meat to pot, add stock, water, bay leaf and thyme, stir, cover and cook on High for 12 minutes.
9. Release the pressure quickly, uncover your pot, add carrots, celery and potatoes, stir, cover pot again and cook at High for 5 minutes.
10. Release the pressure naturally for 10 minutes, uncover the pot, divide among plates and serve with parsley sprinkled on top.

Enjoy!

Nutrition:

- Calories 221
- Fat 5.3
- Fiber 1
- Carbs 20.2
- Protein 22.7

Special Veal Dish

It's perfect for a winter meal! It's hearty and super tasty!

Preparation time: 10 minutes
Cooking time: 35 minutes
Servings: 4
Ingredients:

- 3.5 ounces button mushrooms, sliced
- 3.5 ounces shiitake mushrooms, sliced
- 2 pounds veal shoulder, cut into medium chunks
- 17 ounces potatoes, chopped
- 16 ounces shallots, chopped
- 9 ounces beef stock
- 2 ounces white wine
- 1 tablespoon white flour
- 2 garlic cloves, minced
- 2 tablespoons chives, chopped
- 1 teaspoon sage, dried
- 1/8 teaspoon thyme, dried
- Salt and black pepper to the taste
- 3 and ½ tablespoons extra virgin olive oil

Directions:

1. Set your instant pot on Sauté mode, add 1 and ½ tablespoons oil and heat it up.
2. Add veal, season with salt and pepper, stir, brown for 5 minutes and transfer to a bowl.
3. Add the rest of the oil to the pot and heat it up.
4. Add all mushrooms, stir and cook for 3 minutes.
5. Add garlic, stir, cook for 1 minute and transfer everything to a bowl.
6. Add wine and flour to the pot, stir and cook for 1 minute.
7. Add stock, sage, thyme and return meat to pot as well.
8. Stir, cover and cook at High for 20 minutes.
9. Release pressure, uncover the pot, return mushrooms and garlic and stir.
10. Also add potatoes and shallots, stir, cover and cook at High for 4 minutes.
11. Release the pressure again, uncover your instant pot, add more salt and pepper if needed, also add chives, stir, divide among bowls and serve.

Enjoy!

Nutrition:

- Calories 395
- Fat 18
- Fiber 1.4
- Carbs 7.1
- Protein 47.8

Beef And Pasta Casserole

This is a casserole everyone will love!

Preparation time: 10 minutes
Cooking time: 20 minutes
Servings: 4
Ingredients:

- 17 ounces pasta
- 1 pound beef, ground
- 13 ounces mozzarella cheese, shredded
- 16 ounces tomato puree
- 1 celery stalk, chopped
- 1 yellow onion, chopped
- 1 carrot, chopped
- 1 tablespoon red wine
- 2 tablespoons butter
- Salt and black pepper to the taste

Directions:

1. Set your instant pot on Sauté mode, add the butter and melt it.
2. Add carrot, onion, and celery, stir and cook for 5 minutes.
3. Add beef, salt and pepper and cook for 10 minutes.
4. Add wine, stir and cook for 1 minute more.
5. Add pasta, tomato puree and water to cover pasta, stir, cover and cook at High for 6 minutes.
6. Release the pressure, uncover the pot, add cheese, stir, divide everything among plates and serve.

Enjoy!

Nutrition:

- Calories 182
- Fat 1
- Fiber 1.4
- Carbs 31
- Protein 12

Korean Beef Dish

Are you planning a special meal? Then this is the recipe you need to try!

Preparation time: 10 minutes
Cooking time: 25 minutes
Servings: 6
Ingredients:

- ¼ cup Korean soybean paste
- 1 cup chicken stock
- 2 pounds beefsteak, cut into thin strips
- ¼ teaspoon red pepper flakes
- Salt and black pepper to the taste
- 1 yellow onion, thinly sliced
- 1 zucchini, cubed
- 1-ounce shiitake mushroom caps, cut into quarters
- 12 ounces extra firm tofu, cubed
- 1 chili pepper, sliced
- 1 scallion, chopped

Directions:

1. Set your instant pot on Sauté mode, add stock and soybean paste, stir and simmer for 2 minutes.
2. Add beef, salt, pepper, and pepper flakes stir, cover the pot and cook at High for 15 minutes.
3. Release the pressure quickly, add tofu, onion, zucchini and mushrooms, stir, bring to a boil, cover the pot and cook at High for 4 minutes more.
4. Release the pressure again, uncover the pot, add more salt and pepper to the taste, add chili and scallion, stir, divide into bowls and serve.

Enjoy!

Nutrition:

- Calories 310
- Fat 9.3
- Fiber 0.2
- Carbs 18.4
- Protein 35.3

Beef And Broccoli

This is another exotic option for you! It's a Chinese style dish!

Preparation time: 10 minutes
Cooking time: 10 minutes
Servings: 4
Ingredients:

- 3 pounds chuck roast, cut into thin strips
- 1 tablespoon peanut oil
- 1 yellow onion, chopped
- ½ cup beef stock
- 1 pound broccoli florets
- 2 teaspoons toasted sesame oil
- 2 tablespoons potato starch

For the marinade:

- ½ cup soy sauce
- ½ cup black soy sauce

- 1 tablespoon sesame oil
- 2 tablespoons fish sauce
- 5 garlic cloves, minced
- 3 red peppers, dried and crushed
- ½ teaspoon Chinese five spice
- White rice, already cooked for servings
- Toasted sesame seeds for serving

Directions:

1. In a bowl, mix black soy sauce with soy sauce, fish sauce, 1 tablespoon sesame oil, 5 garlic cloves, five spice and crushed red peppers and stir well.
2. Add beef strips, toss to coat and leave aside for 10 minutes.
3. Set your instant pot on Sauté mode, add peanut oil and heat it up.
4. Add onions, stir and cook for 4 minutes.
5. Add beef and marinade, stir and cook for 2 minutes.
6. Add stock, stir, cover the pot and cook at High for 5 minutes.
7. Release the pressure naturally for 10 minutes, uncover the pot, add cornstarch after you've mixed it with ¼ cup liquid from the pot, add broccoli to the steamer basket, cover pot again and cook for 3 minutes at High.
8. Release the pressure again, uncover the pot, divide beef into bowls on top of rice, add broccoli on the side, drizzle toasted sesame oil, sprinkle sesame seeds and serve.

Enjoy!
Nutrition:

- Calories 338
- Fat 18
- Fiber 5

- Carbs 50
- Protein 20

Tasty Beef And Cabbage

Today we want to share our best instant pot recipes with you! Here is another delicious one!

Preparation time: 10 minutes
Cooking time: 1 hour and 20 minutes
Servings: 6
Ingredients:

- 2 and ½ pounds beef brisket
- 4 cups water
- 2 bay leaves
- 3 garlic cloves, chopped
- 4 carrots, chopped
- 1 cabbage heat, cut into 6 wedges
- 6 potatoes, cut into quarters
- Salt and black pepper to the taste
- 3 turnips, cut into quarters
- Horseradish sauce for serving

Directions:

1. Put beef brisket and water in your instant pot, add salt, pepper, garlic and bay leaves, cover the pot and cook at High for 1 hour and 15 minutes.
2. Release the pressure quickly, uncover the pot, add carrots, cabbage, potatoes, and turnips, stir, cover the pot again and cook at High for 6 minutes.
3. Release the pressure naturally, uncover your pot again, divide among plates and serve with horseradish sauce on top.

Enjoy!

Nutrition:

- Calories 340
- Fat 24
- Fiber 1
- Carbs 14
- Protein 26

Special Lamb Shanks

It's tender and has such a special taste! Try it now!

Preparation time: 10 minutes
Cooking time: 45 minutes
Servings: 4
Ingredients:

- 4 lamb shanks
- 2 tablespoons extra virgin olive oil
- 2 tablespoons white flour
- 1 yellow onion, finely chopped
- 3 carrots, roughly chopped
- 2 garlic cloves, minced
- 2 tablespoons tomato paste
- 1 teaspoon oregano, dried
- 1 tomato, roughly chopped
- 2 tablespoons water
- 4 ounces red wine
- Salt and black pepper to the taste
- 1 beef bouillon cube

Directions:

1. In a bowl, mix flour with salt and pepper.
2. Add lamb shanks and toss to coat.
3. Set your instant pot on Sauté mode, add oil and heat it up.
4. Add lamb, brown on all sides and transfer to a bowl.
5. Add onion, oregano, carrots and garlic to the pot, stir and cook for 5 minutes.
6. Add tomato, tomato paste, water, wine and bouillon cube, stir and bring to a boil.
7. Return lamb to pot, stir, cover and cook on High for 25 minutes.
8. Release the pressure, uncover the pot, divide lamb among plates, pour cooking sauce all over and serve.

Enjoy!

Nutrition:

- Calories 430
- Fat 17
- Fiber 2.5
- Carbs 11.3
- Protein 50

Special Lamb Dish

It's a really flavored dish you can serve during the holidays!

Preparation time: 15 minutes
Cooking time: 20 minutes
Servings: 8
Ingredients:

- 8 lamb ribs
- 4 garlic cloves, minced
- 2 carrots, chopped
- 13 ounces veggie stock
- 4 rosemary springs
- 2 tablespoons extra virgin olive oil
- Salt and black pepper to the taste
- 3 tablespoons white flour

Directions:

1. Set your instant pot on Sauté mode, add the oil and heat it up.
2. Add lamb, garlic, salt and pepper and brown it on all sides.
3. Add flour, stock, rosemary and carrots, stir well, cover the pot and cook at High for 20 minutes.
4. Release pressure quickly, uncover the pot, discard rosemary, divide lamb on plates and serve with the cooking liquid drizzled on top.

Enjoy!

Nutrition:

- Calories 234
- Fat 8.4
- Fiber 1
- Carbs 3
- Protein 35

Mediterranean Lamb

Do you need a good idea for a tasty meal? Well, today you've got one!

Preparation time: 15 minutes
Cooking time: 60 minutes
Servings: 4
Ingredients:

- 6-pound lamb leg, boneless
- 2 tablespoons extra virgin olive oil
- Salt and black pepper to the taste
- 1 bay leaf
- 1 teaspoon marjoram
- 1 teaspoon sage, dried
- 1 teaspoon ginger, grated
- 3 garlic cloves, minced
- 1 teaspoon thyme, dried
- 2 cups veggie stock
- 3 pounds potatoes, chopped
- 3 tablespoons arrowroot powder mixed with 1/3 cup water

Directions:

1. Set your instant pot on Sauté mode, add the oil and heat it up.
2. Add lamb leg and brown on all sides.
3. Add salt, pepper, bay leaf, marjoram, sage, ginger, garlic, thyme and stock, stir, cover the pot and cook at High for 50 minutes.
4. Release the pressure quickly, add potatoes, arrowroot mix, more salt and pepper if needed, stir, cover again and cook on High for 10 minutes.
5. Release the pressure again, uncover the pot, divide Mediterranean lamb among plates and serve.

Enjoy!
Nutrition:

- Calories 238
- Fat 5
- Fiber 4
- Carbs 17
- Protein 7.3

Lamb Curry

It's a very healthy curry recipe you should try soon!

Preparation time: 10 minutes
Cooking time: 25 minutes
Servings: 6
Ingredients:

- 1 and ½ pounds lamb shoulder, cut into medium chunks
- 2 ounces coconut milk
- 3 ounces dry white wine
- 3 tablespoons pure cream
- 3 tablespoons curry powder
- 2 tablespoons vegetable oil
- 3 tablespoons water
- 1 yellow onion, chopped
- 1 tablespoon parsley, chopped
- Salt and black pepper to the taste

Directions:

1. In a bowl, mix half of the curry powder with salt, pepper and coconut milk and stir well.
2. Set your instant pot on Sauté mode, add oil and heat it up.
3. Add onion, stir and cook for 4 minutes.
4. Add the rest of the curry powder, stir and cook for 1 minute.
5. Add lamb pieces, brown them for 3 minutes and mix with water, salt, pepper and wine.
6. Stir, cover the pot and cook at High for 20 minutes.
7. Release the pressure quickly, set the pot to Simmer mode, add coconut milk mix, stir and boil for 5 minutes.
8. Divide among plates, sprinkle parsley on top and serve.

Enjoy!

Nutrition:

- Calories 378
- Fat 8
- Fiber 3
- Carbs 18
- Protein 22

Simple Lamb Dish

You will make this dish very often from now on!

Preparation time: 15 minutes
Cooking time: 35 minutes
Servings: 6
Ingredients:

- 3 pounds lamb chops
- Salt and black pepper to the taste
- 2 tablespoons flour
- 2 tablespoons extra virgin olive oil
- 2 yellow onions, chopped
- 3 ounces red wine
- 2 garlic cloves, crushed
- 2 carrots, sliced
- 2 celery sticks, chopped
- 2 tablespoons tomato sauce
- 2 bay leaves
- 1 cup green peas
- 14 ounces canned tomatoes, chopped
- 4 ounces green beans
- 2 tablespoons parsley, finely chopped
- Beef stock for the pot

Directions:

1. Put flour in a bowl and mix with salt and pepper.
2. Add lamb chops and toss to coat.
3. Set your instant pot on Sauté mode, add the oil and heat it up.
4. Add lamb, stir, brown for 3 minutes on all sides and transfer to a plate.
5. Add garlic and onion to the taste, stir and cook for 2 minutes.
6. Add wine and cook for 2 minutes.
7. Add bay leaves, carrots, celery and return lamb to pot.
8. Also add tomato sauce, tomatoes, green beans and peas and stir.
9. Add stock to cover everything, cover the pot and cook at High for 20 minutes.
10. Release the pressure, uncover the pot, add parsley, more salt and pepper if needed, divide among plates and serve.

Enjoy!

Nutrition:

- Calories 435
- Fat 31
- Fiber 4
- Carbs 6
- Protein 22

Moroccan Lamb

Such a dish is worth trying as soon as possible! Enjoy some intense and rich tastes!

Preparation time: 10 minutes
Cooking time: 25 minutes
Servings: 8
Ingredients:

- 2 and ½ pounds lamb shoulder, chopped
- 3 tablespoons honey
- 3 ounces almonds, peeled and chopped
- 9 ounces prunes, pitted
- 8 ounces vegetable stock
- 2 yellow onions, chopped
- 2 garlic cloves, minced
- 1 bay leaf
- Salt and black pepper to the tastes
- 1 cinnamon stick
- 1 teaspoon cumin powder
- 1 teaspoon turmeric powder
- 1 teaspoon ginger powder
- 1 teaspoon cinnamon powder
- Sesame seeds for servings
- 3 tablespoons extra virgin olive oil

Directions:

1. In a bowl, mix the cinnamon powder with ginger, cumin, turmeric, garlic and 2 tablespoons olive oil and stir well.
2. Add meat and toss to coat.
3. Put prunes in a bowl, cover them with hot water and leave aside.
4. Set your instant pot on Sauté mode, add the rest of the oil and heat it up.
5. Add onions, stir, cook for 3 minutes, transfer to a bowl and leave aside.
6. Add meat to your pot and brown it for 10 minutes.
7. Add stock, cinnamon stick, bay leaf and return onions, stir, cover the pot and cook at High for 25 minutes.
8. Release the pressure naturally, uncover the pot, add drained prunes, salt, pepper, honey and stir.
9. Set the pot on Simmer mode, cook everything for 5 minutes and discard bay leaf and cinnamon stick.
10. Divide among plates and serve with almonds and sesame seeds on top.

Enjoy!

Nutrition:

- Calories 434
- Fat 21
- Fiber 4
- Carbs 41
- Protein 20
- Sugar 9

Delicious And Simple Lamb Ragout

It's one of the most delicious and simple lamb recipes you'll ever try!

Preparation time: 15 minutes
Cooking time: 1 hour
Servings: 8
Ingredients:

- 1 and ½ pounds mutton, bone-in
- 2 carrots, sliced
- ½ pounds mushrooms, sliced
- 4 tomatoes, chopped
- 1 small yellow onion, chopped
- 6 garlic cloves, minced
- 2 tablespoons tomato paste
- 1 teaspoon vegetable oil
- Salt and black pepper to the taste
- 1 teaspoon oregano, dried
- A handful parsley, finely chopped

Directions:

1. Set your instant pot on Sauté mode, add oil and heat it up.
2. Add meat and brown it on all sides.
3. Add tomato paste, tomatoes, onion, garlic, mushrooms, oregano, carrots and water to cover everything.
4. Add salt, pepper, stir, cover the pot and cook at High for 1 hour.
5. Release the pressure, take meat out of the pot, discard bones and shred it.
6. Return meat to pot, add parsley and stir.
7. Add more salt and pepper if needed and serve right away.

Enjoy!

Nutrition:

- Calories 360
- Fat 14
- Fiber 3
- Carbs 15.1
- Protein 30

Lamb And Barley Dish

It's a real comfort dish!

Preparation time: 15 minutes
Cooking time: 45 minutes
Servings: 4
Ingredients:

- 6 ounces barley
- 5 ounces peas
- 1 lamb leg, already cooked, boneless and chopped
- 3 yellow onions, chopped
- 5 carrots, chopped
- 6 ounces beef stock
- 12 ounces water
- Salt and black pepper to the taste

Directions:

1. In your instant pot, mix stock with water and barley, cover and cook at High for 20 minutes.
2. Release the pressure, uncover the pot, add onions, peas and carrots, stir, cover again and cook at High for 10 minutes.
3. Release the pressure again, add meat, salt and pepper to the taste, stir, divide into bowls and serve.

Enjoy!

Nutrition:

- Calories 324
- Fat 9
- Fiber 4
- Carbs 21
- Protein 15

Lamb And White Beans Dish

The combination is really good!

Preparation time: 10 minutes
Cooking time: 40 minutes
Servings: 4
Ingredients:

- 4 lamb chops
- 1 and ½ cups white beans, soaked overnight and drained
- 1 cup onion, chopped
- 2 cups canned tomatoes, chopped
- 1 cup leek, chopped
- 2 tablespoons garlic, minced
- 1 teaspoon herbs de Provence
- Salt and black pepper to the taste
- 3 cups water
- 2 teaspoons Worcestershire sauce

Directions:

1. Put lamb chops in your instant pot.
2. Add beans, onion, tomatoes, leek, garlic, salt, pepper, herbs de Provence, Worcestershire sauce and water.
3. Stir, cover and cook at High for 40 minutes.
4. Release the pressure, uncover the pot, divide among plates and serve.

Enjoy!

Nutrition:

- Calories 520
- Fat 17
- Fiber 7
- Carbs 35
- Protein 56

Mexican Style Lamb

Every once in a while you need to make a special dish for your loved ones! Try this one today!

Preparation time: 10 minutes
Cooking time: 50 minutes
Servings: 4
Ingredients:

- 3 pounds lamb shoulder, cubed
- 19 ounces enchilada sauce
- 3 garlic cloves, minced
- 1 yellow onion, chopped
- 2 tablespoons extra virgin olive oil
- Salt to the taste
- ½ bunch cilantro, finely chopped
- corn tortillas, warm for serving
- lime wedges for serving
- refried beans for serving

Directions:

1. Put enchilada sauce in a bowl, add lamb meat and marinade for 24 hours.
2. Set your instant pot on Sauté mode, add the oil and heat it up.
3. Add onions and garlic, stir and cook for 5 minutes.
4. Add lamb, salt and its marinade, stir, bring to a boil, cover the pot and cook at High for 45 minutes.
5. Release the pressure, take meat and put on a cutting board and leave aside to cool down for a few minutes.
6. Shred meat and put in a bowl.
7. Add cooking sauce to it and stir.
8. Divide meat on tortillas, sprinkle cilantro on each, add beans, squeeze lime juice, roll and serve.

Enjoy!
Nutrition:

- Calories 484
- Fat 19
- Fiber 9
- Carbs 28
- Protein 44

Delicious Goat Mix

It's a fulfilling and delicious dish!!

Preparation time: 10 minutes
Cooking time: 60 minutes
Servings: 4
Ingredients:

- 17 ounces goat meat, cubed
- 1 carrot, chopped
- 1 celery rib, chopped
- 4 ounces tomato paste
- 1 yellow onion, chopped
- 3 garlic cloves, crushed
- A dash of sherry wine
- ½ cup water
- Salt and black pepper to the taste
- 1 cup chicken stock
- 2 tablespoons extra virgin olive oil
- 1 tablespoon cumin seeds, ground
- A pinch of rosemary, dried
- 2 roasted tomatoes, chopped

Directions:

1. Set your instant pot on Sauté mode, add 1 tablespoon oil and heat it up.
2. Add goat meat, salt and pepper and brown for a few minutes on each side.
3. Add cumin seeds, rosemary, stir, cook for 2 minutes and transfer to a bowl.
4. Add the rest of the oil to the pot and heat it up.
5. Add onion, garlic, salt and pepper, stir and cook for 1 minute.
6. Add carrot and celery, stir and cook 2 minutes.
7. Add sherry wine, stock, water, goat meat, tomato paste, more salt and pepper, stir, cover and cook on High for 40 minutes.
8. Release the pressure naturally, uncover the pot, add tomatoes, stir, divide among plates and serve.

Enjoy!

Nutrition:

- Calories 340
- Fat 3.8
- Fiber 4.1
- Carbs 30
- Protein 12.6

Goat And Potatoes

It's a very consistent and spicy dish you can serve with some rice!

Preparation time: 10 minutes
Cooking time: 50 minutes
Servings: 5
Ingredients:

- 2 and ½ pounds goat meat, cut into small cubes
- Salt and black pepper to the taste
- 5 tablespoons vegetable oil
- 3 teaspoons turmeric powder
- 3 potatoes, cut into halves
- 1 teaspoon sugar
- 4 cloves
- 3 cardamom pods
- 3 onions, chopped
- 2-inch cinnamon stick
- A small piece of ginger, grated
- 2 tomatoes, chopped
- 4 garlic cloves, minced
- 2 green chilies, chopped
- ¾ teaspoon chili powder
- 2 and ½ cups water
- 1 teaspoon coriander, chopped

Directions:

1. Put goat cubes in a bowl, add salt, pepper and turmeric, toss to coat and leave aside for 10 minutes.
2. Set your instant pot on Sauté mode, add the oil and half of the sugar, stir and heat up.
3. Add potatoes, fry them a bit and transfer to a bowl.
4. Add cloves, cinnamon stick and cardamom to pot and stir.
5. Also add ginger, onion, chilies and garlic, stir and cook for 3 minutes.
6. Add tomatoes and chili powder, stir and cook for 5 minutes.
7. Add meat, stir and cook for 10 minutes.
8. Add 2 cups water, stir, cover and cook at High for 15 minutes.
9. Release the pressure, uncover the pot, add more salt and pepper, the rest of the sugar, potatoes and ½ cup water, cover and cook at High for 5 minutes.
10. Release the pressure again, uncover the pot, divide among plates, sprinkle coriander on top and serve.

Enjoy!

Nutrition:

- Calories 300
- Fat 17
- Fiber 1
- Carbs 5
- Protein 30

Tasty Apple Cider Pork

This dish can be served on a special occasion!

Preparation time: 10 minutes
Cooking time: 25 minutes
Servings: 4
Ingredients:

- 2 pounds pork loin
- 2 cups apple cider
- 2 tablespoons extra virgin olive oil
- Salt and black pepper to the taste
- 1 yellow onion, chopped
- 2 apples, chopped
- 1 tablespoon dry onion, minced

Directions:

1. Set your instant pot on Sauté mode, add the oil and heat it up.
2. Add pork loin, salt, pepper and dried onion, stir and brown meat on all sides and transfer to a plate.
3. Add onion to pot, stir and cook for 2 minutes.
4. Return meat to pot, add cider, apples, more salt and pepper, stir, cover and cook on High for 20 minutes.
5. Release the pressure, uncover the pot, transfer pork to a cutting board, slice it and divide among plates.
6. Add sauce and mix from the pot on the side and serve.

Enjoy!

Nutrition:

- Calories 450
- Fat 22
- Fiber 2.2
- Carbs 29
- Protein 37.2

Delicious Pork Chops

It's so tasty and easy to make!

Preparation time: 10 minutes
Cooking time: 15 minutes
Servings: 4
Ingredients:

- 4 pork chops
- 2 tablespoons parsley, chopped
- 1 garlic clove, minced
- 2 tablespoons lime juice
- 2 tablespoons extra virgin olive oil
- 1 pound onions, sliced
- ½ cup milk
- Salt and black pepper to the taste
- 2 tablespoons butter
- 2 tablespoons cornstarch mixed with 3 tablespoons water
- 1 tablespoon white flour
- ½ cup white wine

Directions:

1. Set your instant pot on Sauté mode, add the oil and butter and heat it up.
2. Add pork chops, salt and pepper, brown on all sides and transfer to a bowl.
3. Add garlic and onion to pot, stir and cook for 2 minutes.
4. Add wine, lime juice, milk, parsley and return pork chops to pot.
5. Stir, cover and cook at High for 15 minutes.
6. Release the pressure, uncover the pot, add cornstarch and flour, stir well and cook on Simmer mode for 3 minutes.
7. Divide pork chops and onions on plates, drizzle cooking sauce all over and serve.

Enjoy!

Nutrition:

- Calories 222
- Fat 7
- Fiber 3
- Carbs 9
- Protein 22.2

Creamy Pork Chops

It's a very succulent and tender meal!

Preparation time: 10 minutes
Cooking time: 20 minutes
Servings: 4
Ingredients:

- 4 pork chops, boneless
- 1 cup water
- 2 tablespoons extra virgin olive oil
- 2 teaspoons chicken bouillon powder
- 10 ounces canned cream of mushroom soup
- 1 cup sour cream
- Salt and black pepper to the taste
- ½ small bunch parsley, chopped

Directions:

1. Set your instant pot on Sauté mode, add oil and heat it up.
2. Add pork chops, salt and pepper, brown them on all sides, transfer to a plate and leave aside for now.
3. Add water and chicken bouillon powder to the pot and stir well.
4. Return pork chops, stir, cover and cook at High for 9 minutes.
5. Release the pressure naturally, transfer pork chops to a platter and leave aside.
6. Set the pot on Simmer mode and heat up the cooking liquid.
7. Add mushroom soup, stir, cook for 2 minutes and take off heat.
8. Add parsley and sour cream, stir and pour over pork chops.

Enjoy!

Nutrition:

- Calories 284
- Fat 16
- Fiber 1
- Carbs 10.5
- Protein 23.2

Tasty Pulled Pork

You get to try something tasty today!

Preparation time: 10 minutes
Cooking time: 1 hour and 20 minutes
Servings: 6
Ingredients:

- 3 pounds pork shoulder, halves
- 11 ounces beer
- 8 ounces water
- 3 ounces sugar
- Salt to the taste
- 2 teaspoons dried mustard
- 2 teaspoons smoked paprika
- 4 ounces hot water
- 12 ounces apple cider vinegar
- 2 tablespoons brown sugar
- Salt and black pepper to the taste
- A pinch of cayenne pepper
- 2 teaspoons dry mustard

For the sauce:

Directions:

1. In a bowl, mix 3 ounces sugar with smoked paprika, 2 teaspoons dry mustard and salt to the taste.
2. Rub pork meat with this mix and put pieces in your instant pot.
3. Add beer and 3 ounces water, stir, cover the pot and cook at High for 75 minutes.
4. Release the pressure quickly, uncover the pot, transfer pork to a cutting board, shred with 2 forks and leave aside for now.
5. Discard half of the cooking liquid from the pot.
6. In a bowl, mix brown sugar with 4 ounces hot water, vinegar, cayenne, salt, pepper and 2 teaspoons dry mustard and stir well.
7. Pour this over cooking sauce from the pot, stir, cover and cook at High for 3 minutes.
8. Release the pressure, divide pork among plates, drizzle the sauce all over and serve.

Enjoy!

Nutrition:

- Calories 440
- Fat 12
- Fiber 4
- Carbs 40
- Protein 32

Pork Roast With Fennel

The fennel gives this dish a very special taste!

Preparation time: 10 minutes
Cooking time: 1 hour and 20 minutes
Servings: 4
Ingredients:

- 2 pounds pork meat, boneless
- 2 tablespoons extra virgin olive oil
- Salt and black pepper to the taste
- 2 garlic cloves, minced
- 1 yellow onion, chopped
- 5 ounces white wine
- 5 ounces chicken stock
- 1 pound fennel bulbs, sliced

Directions:

1. Set your instant pot on Sauté mode, add oil and heat it up.
2. Add pork, salt and pepper, stir, brown on all sides and transfer to a plate.
3. Add garlic, wine and stock to the pot, stir and cook for 2 minutes.
4. Return pork to pot, cover and cook at High for 40 minutes.
5. Release the pressure, uncover the pot, add onion and fennels, stir, cover and cook at High for 15 minutes.
6. Release the pressure again, stir your mix, transfer pork to a cutting board, slice and divide among plates.
7. Serve with onion and fennel on the side and with cooking sauce all over.

Enjoy!

Nutrition:

- Calories 428
- Fat 16
- Fiber 1.1
- Carbs 29
- Protein 38

Chinese BBQ Pork

You will fall in love with this dish in no time!

Preparation time: 10 minutes
Cooking time: 50 minutes
Servings: 6
Ingredients:

- 2 pounds pork belly
- 4 tablespoons soy sauce
- 2 tablespoons dry sherry
- 1-quart chicken stock
- 8 tablespoons char siu sauce
- 2 teaspoons sesame oil
- 2 tablespoons honey
- 1 teaspoon peanut oil

Directions:

1. Set your instant pot on Simmer mode, add sherry, stock, soy sauce and half of char siu sauce, stir and cook for 8 minutes.
2. Add pork, stir, cover and cook at High for 30 minutes.
3. Release the pressure naturally, transfer pork to a cutting board, leave aside to cool down and chop into small pieces.
4. Heat up a pan with the peanut oil over medium high heat, add pork, stir and cook for a few minutes.
5. Meanwhile, in a bowl, mix sesame oil with the rest of the char siu sauce and honey.
6. Brush pork from the pan with this mix, stir and cook for 10 minutes.
7. Heat up another pan over medium high heat, add cooking liquid from the instant pot and bring to a boil.
8. Simmer for 3 minutes and take off heat.
9. Divide pork on plates, drizzle the sauce over it and serve.

Enjoy!

Nutrition:

- Calories 400
- Fat 23
- Fiber 1
- Carbs 15
- Sugar 14
- Protein 41

Braised Pork

You don't need any special skills to make this tasty dish!

Preparation time: 10 minutes
Cooking time: 75 minutes
Servings: 6
Ingredients:

- 4 pounds pork butt, chopped
- 16 ounces chicken stock
- 16 ounces red wine
- 4 ounces lemon juice
- 2 tablespoons extra virgin olive oil
- ¼ cup onion, chopped
- ¼ cup garlic powder
- 1 tablespoon paprika
- Salt and black pepper to the taste

Directions:

1. In your instant pot, mix pork with stock, wine, lemon juice, onion, garlic powder, oil, paprika, salt and pepper, stir, cover and cook on High for 45 minuets.
2. Leave the pot aside for 15 minutes, release the pressure quickly, stir braised pork, divide into bowls and serve.

Enjoy!

Nutrition:

- Calories 454
- Fat 45
- Fiber 1
- Carbs 2
- Protein 8

Pork Chops And Brown Rice

This is so easy and tasty! It's full of amazing flavors!

Preparation time: 10 minutes
Cooking time: 25 minutes
Servings: 6
Ingredients:

- 2 cups water
- 1/3 cup brown sugar
- 1/3 cup salt
- 2 cups ice
- 2 hot peppers, crushed
- 1 tablespoon peppercorns
- 4 garlic cloves, crushed
- 2 bay leaves
- 2 pounds pork chops
- 2 cups brown rice
- 1 cup onion, chopped
- 3 tablespoons butter
- 2 and ½ cups beef stock
- Salt and black pepper to the taste

Directions:

1. Heat up a pan over medium high heat with the water.
2. Add salt and brown sugar, stir until it dissolves, take off heat and add ice.
3. Add hot peppers, garlic, peppercorns and bay leaves and stir.
4. Add pork chops, toss to coat, cover and keep in the fridge for 4 hours.
5. Rinse pork chops and pat dry them with paper towels.
6. Set your instant pot on Sauté mode, add butter and melt it.
7. Add pork chops, brown them on all sides, transfer to a plate and leave aside for now.
8. Add onion to your instant pot and cook for 2 minutes.
9. Add rice, stir and cook for 1 minute.
10. Add stock, pork chops, cover the pot and cook at High for 22 minutes.
11. Release the pressure naturally for 10 minutes, uncover the pot, add salt and pepper, divide pork chops and rice among plates and serve.

Enjoy!

Nutrition:

- Calories 430
- Fat 12.3
- Fiber 4.3
- Carbs 53
- Protein 30

Pork Chops And Smashed Potatoes

You can make this for dinner! Your family will like this dish very much!

Preparation time: 15 minutes
Cooking time: 20 minutes
Servings: 6
Ingredients:

- 6 pork chops, boneless
- 2 pounds potatoes, cut into chunks
- 2 cups chicken stock
- 3 garlic cloves, chopped
- 1 yellow onion, cut into chunks
- 1 bunch mixed rosemary, sage, oregano and thyme
- Salt and black pepper to the taste
- 2 tablespoons butter
- 1 teaspoon smoked paprika
- 2 tablespoons white flour

Directions:

1. Put the potatoes in your instant pot.
2. Add garlic and half of the onion.
3. Add herbs and stock.
4. Place pork chops on top, add salt, pepper, and paprika.
5. Cover and cook at High for 15 minutes.
6. Meanwhile, heat up a pan over medium heat, add butter and heat it up.
7. Add flour, stir very well, cook for 2 minutes and take off heat.
8. Release the pressure quick, transfer pork to a platter and discard herbs.
9. Transfer potatoes to a bowl, add some of the cooking liquid, add salt, pepper, and stir using your hand mixer.
10. Set your instant pot on Simmer mode and cook the cooking liquid for 2 minutes.
11. Add butter mix and stir until it thickens.
12. Divide pork chops on plates, add mashed potatoes on the side and drizzle the gravy from the pot all over.

Enjoy!

Nutrition:

- Calories 510
- Fat 22
- Fiber 5.7
- Carbs 47
- Protein 30.2

Special Ribs

It's a special dish!

Preparation time: 2 hours
Cooking time: 20 minutes
Servings: 8
Ingredients:

- 5 pounds country style ribs, boneless

For the brine:

- ½ cup brown sugar
- ½ cup salt
- 4 cups water
- 2 tablespoons liquid smoke
- 3 garlic cloves, crushed

For the ribs:

- 2 tablespoons butter
- ½ tablespoons water
- 1 cup onion, chopped
- 1 pound apples, peeled and sliced
- ½ teaspoon cinnamon

- 1 teaspoon chili powder
- A pinch of cayenne pepper

For the sauce:

- 1 tablespoons liquid smoke
- 2 tablespoons yellow mustard
- 2 tablespoons Dijon mustard
- 2 tablespoons brown sugar
- 1 teaspoon hot chili sauce
- 1 tablespoon Worcestershire sauce
- 1 tablespoon soy sauce
- ¼ cup honey
- 2 tablespoons water
- 2 tablespoons cornstarch

Directions:

1. In a bowl, mix 4 cups water with ½ cup salt, ½ cup sugar, 2 tablespoons liquid smoke and garlic.
2. Stir, add pork ribs and keep in the fridge for 2 hours.
3. Set your instant pot on Sauté mode, add 2 tablespoons butter and melt it.
4. Add ribs, brown them on all sides and transfer to a plate.
5. Add onions and ½ tablespoon water, stir and cook for 2 minutes.
6. Add cinnamon, cayenne, chili powder, and apples.
7. Return ribs, cover the pot and cook at High for 15 minutes.
8. Release the pressure quick, transfer ribs to a plate and leave aside.
9. Puree onions and apples using a hand blender and set the pot on Sauté mode again.
10. Add mustard, Dijon mustard, 1 tablespoon liquid smoke, 2 tablespoons sugar, Worcestershire sauce, hot chili sauce, soy sauce and honey and stir well.
11. Add cornstarch mixed with 2 tablespoons water, stir and cook for 2 minutes.
12. Divide ribs on plates, drizzle the gravy all over and serve.

Enjoy!
Nutrition:

- Calories 470
- Fat 34
- Fiber 3

- Carbs 11
- Protein 29

Tasty Ribs And Coleslaw

Make sure you get all the ingredients to make this wonderful dish!

Preparation time: 15 minutes
Cooking time: 35 minutes
Servings: 4
Ingredients:

- 2 and ½ pounds baby back ribs
- Salt and black pepper to the taste
- 1 teaspoon onion powder
- ½ teaspoon paprika
- ½ teaspoon dry mustard
- ½ teaspoon chili powder
- ½ teaspoon garlic powder

For the sauce:

- 1 small yellow onion, chopped
- 2 bacon slices, chopped
- 6 ounces tomato paste
- ¾ cup tomato sauce
- 2 garlic cloves, minced
- Salt and black pepper to the taste
- ¼ cup coconut aminos
- ½ teaspoon smoked paprika
- A pinch of cayenne pepper
- 1/3 cup apple cider vinegar
- 1 tablespoon cooking fat
- ½ cup apple juice

For the coleslaw:

- 1 cup red cabbage, shredded
- 3 cups green cabbage, shredded
- 1 cup raisins
- 2 and ½ teaspoons caraway seeds
- ¼ cup apple cider vinegar
- ¾ cup mayonnaise
- Salt and black pepper to the taste
- 2 carrots, grated
- 2 green onions,, chopped

Directions:

1. In a salad bowl, mix red and green cabbage with green onions, carrots, and raisins.
2. In a small bowl, mix caraway seeds with mayo, salt, pepper and ¼ cup vinegar and stir well.
3. Pour this over salad, toss to coat and keep in the fridge until you serve it.
4. In a bowl, mix onion powder with paprika, salt, pepper, dry mustard, garlic powder, chili powder.
5. Rub ribs with this mix and place them in your instant pot, add some water, cover the pot and cook at High for 15 minutes.
6. Meanwhile, heat up a pan with cooking fat over medium heat, add bacon and cook for 2 minutes.
7. Add onion and garlic, stir and cook for 5 minutes.
8. Add tomato sauce and tomato paste, apple juice, coconut aminos, 1/3 cup vinegar, smoked paprika, a pinch of cayenne pepper, salt and pepper to the taste, stir and cook for 10 minutes.
9. Release the pressure from the pot, uncover and transfer ribs to a plate.
10. Add some of the sauce on the bottom of the pot, add a layer of ribs, then a layer of sauce, then another layer of ribs and so on.
11. Cover the pot again and cook at High for 10 minutes.
12. Release the pressure again, divide ribs and sauce among plates and serve with the coleslaw you've made at the beginning.

Enjoy!

Nutrition:

- Calories 360
- Fat 15
- Fiber 1
- Carbs 4
- Sugar 3
- Protein 17

Asian Short Ribs

It's perfect for a weekend meal!

Preparation time: 10 minutes
Cooking time: 60 minutes
Servings: 4
Ingredients:

- 2 green onions, chopped
- 1 teaspoon vegetable oil
- 3 garlic cloves, minced
- 3 ginger slices
- 4 pounds short ribs
- ½ cup water
- ½ cup soy sauce
- ¼ cup rice wine
- ¼ cup pear juice
- 2 teaspoons sesame oil

Directions:

1. Set your instant pot on Sauté mode, add the oil and heat it up.
2. Add green onions, ginger and garlic, stir and cook for 1 minute.
3. Add ribs, water, wine, soy sauce, sesame oil and pear juice, stir and cook for 2-3 minutes.
4. Cover the pot and cook at High for 45 minutes.
5. Release the pressure naturally for 15 minutes, uncover the pot and transfer the ribs to a plate.
6. Strain liquid from the pot, divide ribs among plates and drizzle the sauce all over.

Enjoy!

Nutrition:

- Calories 300
- Fat 11
- Fiber 1
- Carbs 5
- Protein 10

Short Ribs And Beer

It's the best combination ever!

Preparation time: 15 minutes
Cooking time: 60 minutes
Servings: 6
Ingredients:

- 4 pounds short ribs, cut into small pieces
- 1 teaspoon vegetable oil
- 1 yellow onion, chopped
- Salt and black pepper to the taste
- ¼ cup tomato paste
- 1 cup dark beer
- 1 cup chicken stock
- 1 bay leaf
- 6 thyme springs
- 1 Portobello mushroom, dried

Directions:

1. Set your instant pot on Sauté mode, add the oil and heat it up.
2. Add ribs, salt, and pepper, brown for 3 minutes on each side and transfer to a bowl.
3. Add tomato paste and onion to the pot, stir and cook for 5 minutes.
4. Add stock and beer, stir and cook 30 seconds more.
5. Add mushroom, bay leaves, thyme, and ribs, stir, cover the pot and cook at High for 35 minutes.
6. Release the pressure naturally for 15 minutes, uncover the pot, discard thyme, mushroom and bay leaves and strain sauce.
7. Divide ribs among plates and serve with beer sauce drizzled all over.

Enjoy!
Nutrition:

- Calories 240
- Fat 8.1
- Fiber 1
- Carbs 11
- Protein 24

Pork Carnitas

This is a great dish you can serve at a casual party!!

Preparation time: 10 minutes
Cooking time: 1 hour and 10 minutes
Servings: 8
Ingredients:

- 2 tablespoons extra virgin olive oil
- 3 pounds pork shoulder, chopped
- Salt and black pepper to the taste
- 1 jalapeno pepper, chopped
- 1 poblano pepper, chopped
- 1 green bell pepper, chopped
- 3 garlic cloves, minced
- 1 yellow onion, chopped
- 1 pound tomatillos, cut into quarters
- 1 teaspoon oregano
- 1 teaspoon cumin
- 2 cups chicken stock
- 2 bay leaves
- Flour tortillas for serving
- 1 red onion, chopped for serving
- Shredded cheddar cheese, for serving

Directions:

1. Set your instant pot on Sauté mode, add oil and heat it up.
2. Add pork pieces, salt and pepper and brown them for 3 minutes.
3. Add green bell pepper, jalapeno, poblano pepper, tomatillos, onion, garlic, oregano, cumin, bay leaves and stock.
4. Stir, cover and cook at High for 55 minutes.
5. Release the pressure naturally, for 10 minutes, uncover and transfer meat to a cutting board.
6. Puree the mix from the pot using a hand blender.
7. Shred meat with a fork and mix with the puree.
8. Divide this on flour tortillas, add red onion and cheese and serve.

Enjoy!
Nutrition:

- Calories 355
- Fat 23
- Fiber 1
- Carbs 10
- Protein 23

Pork With Orange And Honey

It's a simple and tasty dish!

Preparation time: 10 minutes
Cooking time: 1 hour
Servings: 4
Ingredients:

- 1 and ½ pounds pork shoulder, chopped
- 3 garlic cloves, minced
- 1 cinnamon stick
- Juice from 1 orange
- Salt and black pepper to the taste
- 1 yellow onion, sliced
- 1 tablespoon ginger, sliced
- 2 cloves
- ½ cup water
- 1 teaspoon rosemary, dried
- 1 tablespoon maple syrup
- 2 tablespoons soy sauce
- 1 tablespoon grape seed oil
- 1 tablespoon honey
- 1 tablespoon water
- 1 and ½ tablespoons cornstarch

Directions:

1. Set your instant pot on Sauté mode, add grape seed oil and heat it up.
2. Add pork, salt and pepper, stir, brown for 5 minutes on each side and transfer to a plate.
3. Add onions, ginger, salt and pepper to the pot, stir and cook for 1 minute.
4. Add garlic and cook for 30 seconds,
5. Add orange juice, water, soy sauce, honey, maple syrup, cinnamon, cloves, rosemary and pork pieces.
6. Cover the pot, cook at High for 50 minutes and release the pressure naturally.
7. Uncover the pot, discard cinnamon and cloves, add cornstarch mixed with water, stir, set the pot on Sauté mode again and cook until the sauce thickens.
8. Divide pork and sauce among plates and serve.

Enjoy!

Nutrition:

- Calories 300
- Fat 7.4
- Fiber 1
- Carbs 33
- Protein 20

Pork Tamales

Have you ever tried this recipe? Then, it's time you did!

Preparation time: 10 minutes
Cooking time: 1 hour and 35 minutes
Servings: 24 pieces

Ingredients:

- 8 ounces dried corn husks, soaked for 1 day and drained
- 4 cups water
- 3 pounds pork shoulder, boneless and chopped
- 1 yellow onion, chopped
- 2 garlic cloves, crushed
- 1 tablespoon chipotle chili powder
- 2 tablespoons chili powder
- Salt and black pepper to the taste
- 1 teaspoon cumin
- 4 cups masa
- ¼ cup corn oil
- ¼ cup shortening
- 1 teaspoon baking powder

Directions:

1. In your instant pot, mix 2 cups water with salt, pepper, onion, garlic, chipotle powder, chili powder, and cumin.
2. Add pork, stir, cover the pot and cook at High for 75 minutes.
3. Release the pressure naturally for 10 minutes, uncover the pot, transfer meat to a cutting board and shred it with 2 forks.
4. Put pork meat in a bowl, add 1 tablespoon of cooking liquid, more salt and pepper, stir and leave aside.
5. In a bowl, mix masa with salt, pepper, baking powder, shortening and oil and stir using a mixer.
6. Add cooking liquid from the instant pot and blend again well.
7. Add 2 cups of water to your instant pot and place the steamer basket inside.
8. Unfold 2 corn husks, place them on a work surface, add ¼ cup masa mix near the top of the husk, press into a square and leaves 2 inches at the bottom.
9. Add 1 tablespoon pork in the center of the masa, wrap the husk around the dough and place standing up in the steamer basket.
10. Repeat with the rest of the husks, cover the pot and cook at High for 20 minutes.
11. Release the pressure for 15 minutes, uncover the pot, transfer tamales to plates and serve.

Enjoy!

Nutrition:

- Calories 150
- Fat 7.2
- Fiber 2
- Carbs 11
- Protein 7

Pork Tostadas

This is tasty, and they look great too! Try them!

Preparation time: 10 minutes
Cooking time: 30 minutes
Servings: 4
Ingredients:

- 4 pounds pork shoulder, boneless and cubed
- Salt and black pepper to the taste
- 2 cups coke
- 1/3 cup brown sugar
- ½ cup picante sauce
- 2 teaspoons chili powder
- 2 tablespoons tomato paste
- ¼ teaspoon cumin
- 1 cup enchilada sauce
- Corn tortillas
- Mexican cheese, shredded for serving
- Shredded lettuce, for serving
- Salsa
- Guacamole for serving

Directions:

1. In your instant pot, mix 1 cup coke with picante sauce, salsa, sugar, tomato paste, chili powder and cumin and stir.
2. Add pork pieces, stir, cover and cook for 25 minutes.
3. Release the pressure for 15 minutes, uncover the pot, drain juice from the pot, transfer meat to a cutting board and shred it.
4. Return meat to instant pot, add the rest of the coke and enchilada sauce, stir, set the pot on Sauté mode and heat everything up.
5. Brown tortillas in the oven at 350 degrees F for 5 minutes and place them on a working surface.
6. Add lettuce leaves, cheese and guacamole, fold and serve.

Enjoy!

Nutrition:

- Calories 160
- Fat 3
- Fiber 3
- Carbs 13
- Protein 9

Hominy Dish

It's a special and very hearty comfort food!

Preparation time: 10 minutes
Cooking time: 30 minutes
Servings: 6
Ingredients:

- 1 and ¼ pounds pork shoulder, boneless and cut into medium pieces
- 2 tablespoons vegetable oil
- Salt and black pepper to the taste
- 2 tablespoons chili powder
- 1 white onion, chopped
- 4 garlic cloves, minced
- 30 ounces hominy, drained
- 4 cups chicken stock
- Avocado slices for serving
- Lime wedges for serving
- ¼ cup water
- 2 tablespoons cornstarch

Directions:

1. Set your instant pot on Sauté mode, add 1 tablespoon oil and heat it up.
2. Add pork, salt, and pepper, brown on all sides and transfer to a bowl.
3. Add the rest of the oil to the pot and heat it up.
4. Add garlic, onion and chili powder, stir and sauté for 4 minutes.
5. Add half of the stock, stir and cook for 1 minute.
6. Add the rest of the stock and return pork to pot, stir, cover and cook at High for 30 minutes.
7. Release the pressure naturally for 10 minutes, transfer pork to a cutting board and shred with 2 forks.
8. Add cornstarch mixed with water to the pot and set on Sauté mode again.
9. Add hominy, more salt and pepper and shredded pork, stir and cook for 2 minutes.
10. Divide among bowls and serve with avocado slices on top and lime wedges on the side.

Enjoy!

Nutrition:

- Calories 250
- Fat 8.7
- Fiber 7.7
- Carbs 29
- Protein 12

Kalua Pork

Do you want to try an exotic pork dish today? Then check this out!

Preparation time: 10 minutes
Cooking time: 90 minutes
Servings: 5
Ingredients:

- 4 pounds pork shoulder, cut into half
- ½ cup water
- 2 tablespoons vegetable oil
- Salt and black pepper to the taste
- 1 tablespoon liquid smoke
- Steamed green beans for serving

Directions:

1. Set your instant pot on Sauté mode, add the oil and heat it up.
2. Add pork, salt and pepper, brown for 3 minutes on each side and transfer to a plate.
3. Add water and liquid smoke to the pot and stir.
4. Return meat, stir, cover pot and cook at High for 90 minutes.
5. Release the pressure for 15 minutes, transfer meat to a cutting board and shred it with 2 forks.
6. Divide pork on plates, add some of the sauce on top and serve with steamed green beans on the side.

Enjoy!

Nutrition:

- Calories 243
- Fat 15
- Fiber 1
- Carbs 1
- Protein 26

Sausage And Red Beans Dish

It's going to make you fell full all day once you try this dish!

Preparation time: 15 minutes
Cooking time: 30 minutes
Servings: 8
Ingredients:

- 1 pound smoked sausage, sliced
- 1 pound red beans, dried, soaked overnight and drained
- 1 bay leaf
- 2 tablespoons Cajun seasoning
- 1 celery stalk, chopped
- Salt and black pepper to the taste
- ½ green bell pepper, chopped
- 1 teaspoon parsley, dried
- 5 cups water
- ¼ teaspoon cumin, ground
- 1 garlic clove, chopped
- 1 small yellow onion, chopped

Directions:

1. In your instant pot, mix beans with sausage, bay leaf, Cajun seasoning, celery, salt, pepper, bell pepper, parsley, cumin, garlic, onion and water, stir, cover and cook at High for 30 minutes.
2. Release the pressure, uncover the pot, divide mix into bowls and serve.

Enjoy!

Nutrition:

- Calories 248
- Fat 5
- Fiber 12.3
- Carbs 40
- Protein 15.4

Pork Sausages And Mashed Potatoes

It is a very simple combination!

Preparation time: 15 minutes
Cooking time: 15 minutes
Servings: 6
Ingredients:

For the potatoes:

- 4 potatoes, peeled and cut into cubes
- Sat and black pepper to the taste
- 1 teaspoon mustard powder
- 1 tablespoon butter
- 4 ounces milk, warm
- 6 ounces water
- 1 tablespoon cheddar cheese, grated

For the sausages:

- 6 pork sausages
- 2 tablespoons extra virgin olive oil
- ½ cup onion jam
- 3 ounces red wine
- 3 ounces water
- Salt and black pepper to the taste
- 1 tablespoon cornstarch mixed with 1 tablespoon water

Directions:

1. Put potatoes in your instant pot, add 6 ounces water, salt and pepper, stir, cover and cook on High for 5 minutes.
2. Release the pressure quickly, drain potatoes and put them in a bowl.
3. Add warm milk, butter, mustard and more salt and pepper, and mash well.
4. Add cheese, stir again and leave aside for now.
5. Set your instant pot on Sauté mode, add oil and heat it up.
6. Add sausages and brown them on all sides.
7. Add onion jam, wine and 3 ounces water.
8. Add salt and pepper to the taste, cover the pot and cook at High for 8 minutes.
9. Release the pressure quickly and divide sausages among plates.
10. Add cornstarch mix to the pot and stir well.
11. Drizzle the sauce over sausages and serve them with mashed potatoes.

Enjoy!

Nutrition:

- Calories 435
- Fat 23
- Fiber 5
- Carbs 44.2
- Protein 15

Delicious Meatloaf

Did you know you can make a delicious meatloaf in your instant pot?

Preparation time: 10 minutes
Cooking time: 40 minutes
Servings: 6
Ingredients:

- 1/3 cup milk
- ½ cup panko breadcrumbs
- 1 yellow onion, grated
- Salt and black pepper to the taste
- 2 eggs, whisked
- 2 pounds ground meat
- 2 cups water
- ¼ cup ketchup

Directions:

1. In a bowl, mix breadcrumbs with milk, stir and leave aside for 5 minutes.
2. Add onion, salt, pepper and eggs and stir.
3. Add ground meat and stir very well again.
4. Place this on a greased tin foil and shape a loaf.
5. Add ketchup on top.
6. Put the water in your instant pot, arrange meatloaf in the steamer basket of the pot, cover and cook at High for 35 minutes.
7. Release the pressure for 10 minutes, uncover, take meatloaf out, leave it to cool down for 5 minutes, slices and serve it.

Enjoy!

Nutrition:

- Calories 300
- Fat 18
- Fiber 1
- Carbs 10
- Protein 24

Special Meatloaf

It's a special meatloaf recipe you just have to try!

Preparation time: 10 minutes
Cooking time: 25 minutes
Servings: 8
Ingredients:

- 2 pounds ground beef
- 3 bread slices
- ½ cup milk
- ¾ cup parmesan, grated
- Salt and black pepper to the taste
- 2 tablespoons parsley, dried
- 2 cups water
- 8 bacon slices
- 3 eggs, whisked
- ½ cup BBQ sauce

Directions:

1. In a bowl, mix bread slices with milk and leave aside for 5 minutes.
2. Add meat, cheese, salt, pepper, eggs and parsley and stir well.
3. Shape a loaf, place on a tin foil, arrange bacon slices on top, tuck them underneath and spread half of the BBQ sauce all over.
4. Put 2 cups water in the instant pot, place meatloaf in the steamer basket of the pot, cover and cook on High for 20 minutes.
5. Release the pressure, uncover the pot, transfer meat loaf to a pan and spread the rest of the BBQ sauce over it.
6. Introduce in preheated broiler for 5 minutes, transfer to a platter and slice.

Enjoy!

Nutrition:

- Calories 227
- Fat 14.5
- Fiber 1
- Carbs 8.8
- Protein 15

Meatball Delight

It's going to become your favorite kind of meal!

Preparation time: 10 minutes
Cooking time: 10 minutes
Servings: 8
Ingredients:

- 1 and ½ pounds ground pork meat
- 2 tablespoons parsley, chopped
- 1 egg
- 2 bread slices, soaked in water
- 2 garlic cloves, minced
- Salt and black pepper to the taste
- ¾ cup beef stock
- ½ teaspoon nutmeg
- ¼ cup flour
- 1 teaspoon Worcestershire sauce
- ½ teaspoon paprika
- 2 tablespoons extra virgin olive oil
- 2 carrots, chopped
- ¾ cup fresh peas
- 2 potatoes, cubed
- 1 bay leaf
- ¼ cup white wine

Directions:

1. In a bowl, mix ground meat with soaked bread, egg, salt, pepper, parsley, paprika, garlic and nutmeg and stir well.
2. Add 1 tablespoons stock and Worcestershire sauce and stir again
3. Shape meatballs and dust them with flour
4. Set your instant pot on Sauté mode, add oil and heat it up.
5. Add meatballs and brown them on all sides.
6. Add carrots, peas, potatoes, bay leaf, stock and wine, cover the pot and cook at High for 6 minutes.
7. Release the pressure, uncover the pot, discard bay leaf, divide meatballs mix into bowls and serve.

Enjoy!
Nutrition:

- Calories 400
- Fat 13
- Fiber 7
- Carbs 24
- Protein 17

Meatballs And Tomato Sauce

These meatballs will taste divine! Serve them with some spaghetti!

Preparation time: 10 minutes
Cooking time: 10 minutes
Servings: 6
Ingredients:

- 1 onion, chopped
- 1/3 cup parmesan, grated
- ½ cup bread crumbs
- ½ teaspoon oregano, dried
- Salt and black pepper to the taste
- ½ cup milk
- 1 pound ground meat
- 1 tablespoon extra virgin olive oil
- 1 egg, whisked
- 1 carrot, chopped
- ½ celery stalk, chopped
- 2 and ¾ cups tomato puree
- 2 cups water

Directions:

1. In a bowl, mix bread crumbs with cheese, half of the onion, oregano, salt and pepper and stir.
2. Add milk and meat and stir well.
3. Add the egg and stir well again.
4. Set your instant pot on Sauté mode, add oil and heat it up.
5. Add onion, stir and cook for 3 minutes.
6. Add celery and carrot, tomato puree, water and salt and stir again.
7. Shape meatballs and add them to the pot, toss them to coat, cover and cook at High for 5 minutes.
8. Release the pressure naturally for 10 minutes and serve with your favorite spaghetti.

Enjoy!
Nutrition:

- Calories 150
- Fat 3
- Fiber 1
- Carbs 4
- Protein 8

Tasty Fish With Orange Sauce

This is a very light and tasty recipe you can make for a romantic dinner!

Preparation time: 10 minutes
Cooking time: 7 minutes
Servings: 4
Ingredients:

- 4 white fish fillets
- 4 spring onions, chopped
- A drizzle of extra virgin olive oil
- A small piece of ginger, chopped
- Salt and black pepper to the taste
- Juice and zest from 1 orange
- 1 cup fish stock

Directions:

1. Pat dry fish fillets, season with salt, pepper and rub them with the olive oil.
2. Put stock, ginger, orange juice, orange zest and onions in your instant pot.
3. Put fish fillets in the steamer basket, cover the pot and cook at High for 7 minutes.
4. Release the pressure, divide fish among plates and drizzle the orange sauce on top.

Enjoy!

Nutrition:

- Calories 170
- Fat 2
- Fiber 0.4
- Carbs 10
- Protein 23

Delicious Steamed Fish

This is a very healthy dish you can make in your instant pot!

Preparation time: 10 minutes
Cooking time: 10 minutes
Servings: 4
Ingredients:

- 4 white fish fillets
- 1 cup olives, pitted and chopped
- 1 pound cherry tomatoes, cut into halves
- A pinch of thyme, dried
- 1 garlic clove, minced
- A drizzle of olive oil
- Salt and black pepper to the taste
- 1 cup water

Directions:

1. Put the water in your instant pot.
2. Put fish fillets in the steamer basket of the pot.
3. Add tomatoes and olives on top.
4. Also add garlic, thyme, oil, salt and pepper.
5. Cover the pot and cook on Low for 10 minutes.
6. Release the pressure, uncover the pot, divide fish, olives and tomatoes mix among plates and serve.

Enjoy!

Nutrition:

- Calories 157
- Fat 3.2
- Fiber 0
- Carbs 0
- Protein 29

Fish Curry

This is an Indian style dish you must try soon!

Preparation time: 10 minutes
Cooking time: 15 minutes
Servings: 6
Ingredients:

- 6 fish fillets, cut into medium pieces
- 1 tomato, chopped
- 14 ounces coconut milk
- 2 onions, sliced
- 2 capsicums, cut into strips
- 2 garlic cloves, minced
- 6 curry leaves
- 1 tablespoons coriander, ground
- 1 tablespoon ginger, finely grated
- ½ teaspoon turmeric, ground
- 2 teaspoons cumin, ground
- Salt and black pepper to the taste
- ½ teaspoon fenugreek, ground
- 1 teaspoon hot pepper flakes
- 2 tablespoons lemon juice

Directions:

1. Set your instant pot on Sauté mode, add oil and curry leaves and fry for 1 minute.
2. Add ginger, onion and garlic, stir and cook for 2 minutes.
3. Add coriander, turmeric, cumin, fenugreek and hot pepper, stir and cook 2 minutes.
4. Add coconut milk, tomatoes, fish and capsicum, stir, cover and cook on Low for 5 minutes.
5. Release the pressure naturally, add salt and pepper to the taste, stir and divide into bowls.
6. Serve with lemon juice on top.

Enjoy!

Nutrition:

- Calories 230
- Fat 10
- Fiber 3
- Carbs 12
- Protein 23

Mediterranean Fish

This has such an elegant taste!

Preparation time: 10 minutes
Cooking time: 10 minutes
Servings: 4
Ingredients:

- 4 cod fillets
- 17 ounces tomatoes, cut into halves
- 1 garlic clove, crushed
- 1 cup olives, pitted and chopped
- 2 tablespoons capers, drained and chopped
- Salt and black pepper to the taste
- 1 tablespoon parsley, chopped
- 1 tablespoon extra virgin olive oil

Directions:

1. Put tomatoes on the bottom of a heat proof bowl.
2. Add parsley, salt and pepper and toss to coat.
3. Place fish fillets on top, add olive oil, salt, pepper, garlic, olives and capers.
4. Place the bowl in the steamer basket of the pot, cover and cook at High for 5 minutes.
5. Release the pressure naturally, divide among plates and serve.

Enjoy!

Nutrition:

- Calories 170
- Fat 9
- Fiber 1
- Carbs 4
- Protein 23

Cod And Peas

The combination of the cod and the greens is the best!

Preparation time: 15 minutes
Cooking time: 5
Servings: 4
Ingredients:

- 16 ounces cod fillets
- 1 tablespoon parsley, chopped
- 10 ounces peas
- 9 ounces wine
- ½ teaspoon oregano, dried
- ½ teaspoon paprika
- 2 garlic cloves, chopped
- Salt and pepper to the taste

Directions:

1. In your food processor mix garlic with parsley, oregano and paprika and blend well.
2. Add wine, blend again and leave aside for now.
3. Place fish fillets in the steamer basket of your instant pot, add salt and pepper, cover and cook at High for 2 minutes.
4. Release the pressure and divide fish among plates.
5. Add peas to the steamer basket, cover the pot again and cook at High for 2 minutes.
6. Release the pressure again and arrange peas next to fish fillets.
7. Serve with herbs dressing on top.

Enjoy!

Nutrition:

- Calories 200
- Fat 2
- Fiber 2
- Carbs 10
- Protein 20

Poached Salmon

It's tasty and light!

Preparation time: 10 minutes
Cooking time: 5 minutes
Servings: 4
Ingredients:

- 16 ounces salmon fillet, skin on
- Zest from 1 lemon
- 4 scallions, chopped
- 3 black peppercorns
- ½ teaspoon fennel seeds
- 1 bay leaf
- 1 teaspoon white wine vinegar
- 2 cups chicken stock
- ½ cup dry white wine
- ¼ cup dill, chopped
- Salt and black pepper to the taste

Directions:

1. Put salmon in the steamer basket of your instant pot and season with salt and pepper.
2. Add stock, scallions, lemon zest, peppercorns, fennel, vinegar, bay leaf, wine, stock and dill to your pot.
3. Cover and cook at High for 5 minutes.
4. Release the pressure, uncover pot and divide salmon among plates.
5. Set the pot on Simmer mode and cook the liquid for a few minutes more.
6. Drizzle over salmon and serve.

Enjoy!

Nutrition:

- Calories 140
- Fat 4
- Fiber 0
- Carbs 2
- Protein 23

Crispy Salmon Fillet

Get your dinner ready in only a few minutes!

Preparation time: 5 minutes
Cooking time: 10 minutes
Servings: 2
Ingredients:

- 2 salmon fillets, frozen
- 1 cup water
- Salt and black pepper to the taste
- 2 tablespoons extra virgin olive oil

Directions:

1. Put the water in your instant pot.
2. Place salmon in the steamer basket, cover and cook on Low for 3 minutes.
3. Release pressure quick, transfer salmon to paper towels and pat dry them.
4. Heat up a pan with the oil over medium high heat, add salmon fillets skin side down, season with salt and pepper to the taste and cook for 2 minutes.
5. Divide among plates and serve with your favorite salad on the side.

Enjoy!

Nutrition:

- Calories 230
- Fat 12
- Fiber 1
- Carbs 0
- Protein 29

Delicious Salmon And Rice

Serve this with a side salad and enjoy!

Preparation time: 5 minutes
Cooking time: 5 minutes
Servings: 2
Ingredients:

- 2 wild salmon fillets, frozen
- Salt and black pepper to the taste
- ½ cup jasmine rice
- 1 cup chicken stock
- ¼ cup vegetable soup mix, dried
- 1 tablespoon butter
- A pinch of saffron

Directions:

1. In your instant pot, mix stock with rice, soup mix, butter and saffron and stir.
2. Season salmon with salt and pepper, place in the steamer basket of your pot, cover and cook on High for 5 minutes.
3. Release the pressure, divide salmon among plates, add rice mix on the side and serve.

Enjoy!

Nutrition:

- Calories 300
- Fat 8
- Fiber 0.5
- Carbs 30
- Protein 25

Salmon And Tasty Veggies

This is one of the tastiest salmon dishes ever!

Preparation time: 10 minutes
Cooking time: 10 minutes
Servings: 2
Ingredients:

- 2 salmon fillets, skin on
- 1 bay leaf
- 1 cup water
- 1 cinnamon stick
- 3 cloves
- 1 tablespoon canola oil
- 1 cup baby carrots
- 2 cups broccoli florets
- Salt and black pepper to the taste
- Lime wedges for serving

Directions:

1. Put the water in your instant pot.
2. Add bay leaf, cinnamon stick and cloves.
3. Place salmon fillets in the steamer basket of your pot after you've brushed them with canola oil.
4. Season with salt and pepper, add broccoli and carrots, cover the pot and cook at High for 6 minutes.
5. Release the pressure for 4 minutes, uncover the pot, divide salmon and veggies among plates.
6. Drizzle the sauce from the pot after you've discarded cinnamon, cloves and bay leaf and serve with lime wedges on the side.

Enjoy!

Nutrition:

- Calories 170
- Fat 4.5
- Fiber 3.7
- Carbs 13
- Protein 17

Spicy Salmon

You will love this spicy dish!

Preparation time: 10 minutes
Cooking time: 5 minutes
Servings: 4
Ingredients:

- 4 salmon fillets
- 2 tablespoons assorted chili pepper
- Juice of 1 lemon
- 1 lemon, sliced
- 1 cup water
- Salt and black pepper to the taste

Directions:

1. Place salmon fillets in the steamer basket of your pot, add salt, pepper, lemon juice, lemon slices and chili pepper.
2. Add 1 cup water to the pot, cover and cook at High for 5 minutes.
3. Release the pressure, divide salmon and lemon slices among plates and serve.

Enjoy!

Nutrition:

- Calories 120
- Fat 2
- Fiber 0.5
- Carbs 13
- Protein 5

Special Salmon Dish

This is a special and sophisticated dish!

Preparation time: 10 minutes
Cooking time: 15 minutes
Servings: 4
Ingredients:

- 4 salmon fillets
- 1 lemon, sliced
- 1 white onion, chopped
- 3 tomatoes, sliced
- 4 thyme springs
- 4 parsley springs
- 3 tablespoons extra virgin olive oil
- Salt and black pepper to the taste
- 2 cups water

Directions:

1. Drizzle the oil on a parchment paper.
2. Add a layer of tomatoes, salt and pepper.
3. Drizzle some oil again, add fish and season them with salt and pepper.
4. Drizzle some more oil, add thyme and parsley springs, onions, lemon slices, salt and pepper.
5. Fold and wrap packet, place in the steamer basket of your instant pot.
6. Add 2 cups water to the pot, cover and cook on Low for 15 minutes.
7. Release the pressure, uncover the pot, open packet, divide fish mix among plates and serve.

Enjoy!

Nutrition:

- Calories 180
- Fat 5
- Fiber 1
- Carbs 0
- Protein 31

Salmon Burger

This is more healthy than any other burgers you've ever had!

Preparation time: 10 minutes
Cooking time: 10 minutes
Servings: 4
Ingredients:

- 1 teaspoon extra virgin olive oil
- ½ cup panko
- 1 pound salmon meat, minced
- 2 tablespoons lemon zest
- Salt and black pepper to the taste
- Mustard for serving
- Tomatoes slices for serving
- Arugula leaves for serving

Directions:

- Put salmon in your food processor and blend it.
- Transfer to a bowl, add panko, salt, pepper and lemon zest and stir well.
- Shape 4 patties and place them on a working surface.
- Set your instant pot on Sauté mode, add oil and heat it up.
- Add patties, cook for 3 minutes on each side and divide them on buns.
- Serve with tomatoes, arugula and mustard.

Enjoy!

Nutrition:

- Calories 170
- Fat 9
- Fiber 0
- Carbs 1
- Protein 22

Excellent Fish Dish

This is excellent!

Preparation time: 10 minutes
Cooking time: 25 minutes
Servings: 6
Ingredients:

- 17 ounces white fish, cut into medium chunks
- 1 yellow onion, chopped
- 13 ounces potatoes, peeled and cut into chunks
- 13 ounces milk
- Salt and black pepper to the taste
- 14 ounces chicken stock
- 14 ounces water
- 14 ounces half and half

Directions:

1. In your instant pot mix fish with onion, potatoes, water, milk and stock.
2. Cover and cook at High for 10 minutes.
3. Release the pressure, uncover and set the pot on Simmer mode.
4. Add salt, pepper, half and half, stir and cook for 10 minutes.
5. Divide among bowls and serve.

Enjoy!

Nutrition:

- Calories 194
- Fat 4.4
- Fiber 2
- Carbs 21
- Protein 17

Salmon And Raspberry Sauce

It's so delicious and very easy make!

Preparation time: 2 hours
Cooking time: 5 minutes
Servings: 6
Ingredients:

- 6 salmon steaks
- 2 tablespoons extra virgin olive oil
- 4 leeks, sliced
- 2 garlic cloves, minced
- 2 tablespoons parsley, chopped
- 1 cup clam juice
- 2 tablespoons lemon juice
- Salt and white pepper to the taste
- 1 teaspoon sherry
- 1/3 cup dill, finely chopped
- Raspberries for serving

For the raspberry vinegar:

- 2 pints red raspberries
- 1-pint cider vinegar

Directions:

1. Mix red raspberries with vinegar and stir well.
2. Add salmon steaks and leave aside in the fridge for 2 hours.
3. Set your instant pot on Sauté mode, add oil and heat it up.
4. Add parsley, leeks and garlic, stir and cook for 2 minutes.
5. Add clam and lemon juice, sherry, salt, pepper and dill and stir.
6. Add salmon steaks, cover and cook at High for 3 minutes.
7. Release pressure, uncover pot, divide salmon among plates and serve with leeks and fresh raspberries.

Enjoy!

Nutrition:

- Calories 670
- Fat 46
- Fiber 1
- Carbs 18
- Protein 81

Fish Pudding

Have you ever tried this kind of pudding before? It's really good!

Preparation time: 10 minutes

Cooking time: 20 minutes

Servings: 4

Ingredients:

- 1 pound cod fillets, cut into medium pieces
- 2 tablespoons parsley, chopped
- 4 ounces bread crumbs
- 2 teaspoons lemon juice
- 2 eggs, whisked
- 2 ounces butter
- ½ pint milk
- ½ pint shrimp sauce
- Salt and black pepper to the taste
- ½ pint water

Directions:

1. In a bowl, mix fish with crumbs, lemon juice, parsley, salt and pepper and stir.
2. Heat up a pan with the butter over medium high heat.
3. Put milk in a pot and bring to a boil over medium high heat.
4. Pour butter and milk over the egg and stir well.
5. Add this to fish and leave aside for 3 minutes.
6. Pour everything into a greased pudding dish and place in the steamer basket of your pot.
7. Add ½ pint water to the pot, cover and cook at High for 15 minutes.
8. Release the pressure, uncover, divide among plates and serve with shrimp sauce.

Enjoy!

Nutrition:

- Calories 200
- Fat 3
- Fiber 1
- Carbs 8
- Protein 9

Jambalaya

This is so popular! You need to learn how to make it!

Preparation time: 10 minutes
Cooking time: 4 minutes
Servings: 8
Ingredients:

- 1 pound chicken breast, chopped
- 1 pound shrimp, peeled and deveined
- 2 tablespoons extra virgin olive oil
- 1 pound sausage, already cooked and chopped
- 2 cups onions, chopped
- 1 and ½ cups rice
- 2 tablespoons garlic, chopped
- 2 cups green, yellow and red bell peppers, chopped
- 3 and ½ cups chicken stock
- 1 tablespoon Creole seasoning
- 1 tablespoon Worcestershire sauce
- 1 cup tomatoes, crushed

Directions:

1. Set your instant pot on Sauté mode, add chicken and Creole seasoning, stir, brown on all sides and transfer to a bowl.
2. Add oil and heat it up.
3. Add peppers, onions and garlic, stir and cook for 2 minutes.
4. Add rice, stir and cook for 2 minutes.
5. Add tomato puree, stock, Worcestershire sauce and return chicken, stir, cover and cook for 10 minutes.
6. Release the pressure, add sausage and shrimp, stir, cover and cook at High for 2 minutes.
7. Release the pressure, uncover, divide among plates and serve.

Enjoy!

Nutrition:

- Calories 250
- Fat 13
- Fiber 1
- Carbs 22
- Protein 27

Tuna And Noodle Dish

It's a delight!

Preparation time: 10 minutes
Cooking time: 15 minutes
Servings: 4
Ingredients:

- 8 ounces egg noodles
- ½ cup red onion, chopped
- 1 tablespoon extra virgin olive oil
- 1 and ¼ cups water
- 14 ounces canned tomatoes, chopped and mixed with oregano, basil and garlic
- Salt and black pepper to the taste
- 14 ounces canned tuna, drained
- 8 ounces artichoke hearts, drained and chopped
- 1 tablespoon parsley, chopped
- Crumbled feta cheese

Directions:

1. Set your instant pot on Sauté mode, add oil and heat it up.
2. Add onion, stir and cook for 2 minutes.
3. Add tomatoes, noodles, salt, pepper and water, set the pot on Simmer and cook for 10 minutes.
4. Add tuna and artichokes, stir, cover and cook at High for 5 minutes.
5. Release pressure, divide tuna and noodles among plates, sprinkle cheese and parsley on top and serve.

Enjoy!
Nutrition:

- Calories 300
- Fat 4
- Fiber 9
- Carbs 23
- Protein 29

Cheesy Tuna

You just need your instant pot to make this great dish!

Preparation time: 5 minutes
Cooking time: 5 minutes
Servings: 4
Ingredients:

- 14 ounces canned tuna, drained
- 16 ounces egg noodles
- 28 ounces cream of mushroom
- 1 cup peas, frozen
- 3 cups water
- 4 ounces cheddar cheese, grated
- ¼ cup breadcrumbs

Directions:

1. Add pasta and water to your instant pot.
2. Also add tuna, peas and cream, stir, cover, cook at High for 4 minutes and release pressure.
3. Add cheese and stir.
4. Transfer everything to a baking dish, spread breadcrumbs all over and introduce in preheated broiler for 3 minutes.
5. Divide among plates and serve.

Enjoy!

Nutrition:

- Calories 270
- Fat 12
- Fiber 0.5
- Carbs 20
- Protein 15

Roasted Mackerel

You definitely must try this recipe!

Preparation time: 10 minutes
Cooking time: 6 minutes
Servings: 4

Ingredients:

- 18 ounces mackerel, cut into pieces
- 3 garlic cloves, minced
- 8 shallots, chopped
- 1 teaspoon dried shrimp powder
- 1 teaspoon turmeric powder
- 1 tablespoon chili paste
- 2 lemongrass sticks, cut into halves
- 1 small piece of ginger, chopped
- 6 stalks laska leaves
- 3 and ½ ounces water
- 5 tablespoons vegetable oil
- 1 and 1/3 tablespoons tamarind paste mixed with 3 and ½ ounces water
- Salt to the taste
- 1 tablespoon sugar

Directions:

1. In your blender, mix garlic with shallots, chili paste, turmeric powder and shrimp powder and blend well.
2. Set your instant pot on Sauté mode, add oil and heat it up.
3. Add fish pieces; spices paste, ginger, lemongrass and laska leaves and cook for 1 minute.
4. Add tamarind mix, water, salt and sugar, stir, cover and cook at High for 5 minutes.
5. Release the pressure, uncover the pot, divide among plates and serve.

Enjoy!

Nutrition:

- Calories 189
- Fat 11
- Fiber 0
- Carbs 1
- Protein 20

Miso Mackerel

This is a bit different from all the other mackerel recipes! Try it!

Preparation time: 10 minutes
Cooking time: 50 minutes
Servings: 4
Ingredients:

- 2 pounds mackerel, cut into big pieces
- 1 cup water
- 1 garlic clove, crushed
- 1 shallot, sliced
- 1 inch ginger piece, chopped
- 1/3 cup sake
- 1/3 cup mirin
- ¼ cup miso
- 1 sweet onion, thinly sliced
- 2 celery stalks, sliced
- 1 tablespoon rice vinegar
- 1 teaspoon Japanese hot mustard
- Salt to the taste
- 1 teaspoon sugar

Directions:

1. Set your instant pot on Sauté mode, add mirin, sake, ginger, garlic and shallot, stir and boil for 2 minutes.
2. Add miso and water and stir.
3. Add mackerel, cover the pot and cook at High for 45 minutes.
4. Meanwhile, put onion and celery in a bowl and cover with ice water.
5. In another bowl, mix vinegar with salt, sugar and mustard and stir well.
6. Release the pressure from the pot naturally for 10 minutes and divide mackerel among plates.
7. Drain onion and celery well and mix with mustard dressing.
8. Divide along mackerel and serve.

Enjoy!

Nutrition:

- Calories 290
- Fat 13
- Fiber 0
- Carbs 15
- Protein 24

Tasty Mackerel With Lemon

The taste is fabulous!

Preparation time: 10 minutes
Cooking time: 10 minutes
Servings: 4
Ingredients:

- 4 mackerels
- 3 ounces breadcrumbs
- Juice and rind of 1 lemon
- 1 tablespoon chives, finely chopped
- Salt and black pepper to the taste
- 1 egg, whisked
- 1 tablespoon butter
- 1 tablespoon vegetable oil
- 2 tablespoons margarine
- 10 ounces water
- 3 lemon wedges

Directions:

1. In a bowl, mix breadcrumbs with lemon juice, lemon rind, salt, pepper, egg and chives and stir very well.
2. Coat mackerel with this mix.
3. Set your instant pot on Sauté mode, add oil and butter and heat up.
4. Add fish, brown on all sides and transfer to a plate.
5. Clean the pot and add the water.
6. Grease a heat proof dish with the margarine and introduce in the pot.
7. Add fish, cover the pot and cook at High for 6 minutes.
8. Release the pressure. Divide mackerel among plates and serve with lemon wedges.

Enjoy!

Nutrition:

- Calories 140
- Fat 7.8
- Fiber 0
- Carbs 1
- Protein 13

Steamed Mussels

These mussels are perfect!

Preparation time: 10 minutes
Cooking time: 5 minutes
Servings: 4
Ingredients:

- 2 pounds mussels, cleaned and scrubbed
- 1 radicchio, cut into thin strips
- 1 white onion, chopped
- 1 pound baby spinach
- ½ cup dry white wine
- 1 garlic clove, crushed
- ½ cup water
- A drizzle of extra virgin olive oil

Directions:

1. Arrange baby spinach and radicchio on appetizer plates.
2. Set instant pot on Sauté mode, add oil and heat it up.
3. Add garlic and onion, stir and cook for 4 minutes.
4. Add wine, stir and cook for 1 minute.
5. Place mussels in the steamer basket of the pot, cover and cook on Low for 1 minute.
6. Release the pressure and divide mussels on top of spinach and radicchio.
7. Add cooking liquid all over and serve.

Enjoy!

Nutrition:

- Calories 50
- Fat 1
- Fiber 1
- Carbs 0.3
- Protein 1.1

Delicious Mussels

This is a Neapolitan style dish you have to try!

Preparation time: 10 minutes
Cooking time: 5 minutes
Servings: 3
Ingredients:

- 28 ounces canned tomatoes, crushed
- ½ cup white onion, chopped
- 2 jalapeno peppers, chopped
- ¼ cup dry white wine
- ¼ cup extra virgin olive oil
- ¼ cup balsamic vinegar
- 2 pounds mussels, cleaned and scrubbed
- 2 tablespoons red pepper flakes
- 2 garlic cloves, minced
- Salt to the taste
- ½ cup basil, chopped
- Lemon wedges for serving

Directions:

1. Set your instant pot on Sauté mode, add tomatoes, onion, jalapenos, wine, oil, vinegar, garlic and pepper flakes, stir and bring to a boil.
2. Add mussels, stir, cover and cook on Low for 4 minutes.
3. Release pressure, uncover, discard unopened mussels, add salt and basil, stir, divide among bowls and serve with lemon wedges.

Enjoy!

Nutrition:

- Calories 50
- Fat 0.2
- Fiber 0.2
- Carbs 1
- Protein 1.5

Tasty Mussels And Spicy Sauce

This is a tasty, flavored and fulfilling dish!

Preparation time: 10 minutes
Cooking time: 4 minutes
Servings: 4
Ingredients:

- 2 pounds mussels, scrubbed and debearded
- 2 tablespoons extra virgin olive oil
- 1 yellow onion, chopped
- ½ teaspoon red pepper flakes
- 14 ounces tomatoes, chopped
- 2 teaspoons garlic, minced
- ½ cup chicken stock
- 2 teaspoons oregano, dried

Directions:

1. Set your instant pot on Sauté mode, add oil and heat it up.
2. Add onions, stir and cook for 3 minutes.
3. Add pepper flakes and garlic, stir and cook for 1 minute.
4. Add stock, oregano and tomatoes and stir well.
5. Add mussels, stir, cover and cook on Low for 2 minutes.
6. Release the pressure quickly, discard unopened mussels, divide among bowls and serve.

Enjoy!
Nutrition:

- Calories 60
- Fat 0.2
- Fiber 0.2
- Carbs 1
- Protein 1.3

Mussels With Sausage

It's a great combination!

Preparation time: 5 minutes
Cooking time: 5 minutes
Servings: 4
Ingredients:

- 2 pounds mussels, scrubbed and debearded
- 12 ounces amber beer
- 1 tablespoon extra virgin olive oil
- 1 yellow onion, chopped
- 8 ounces spicy sausage
- 1 tablespoon paprika

Directions:

1. Set your instant pot on Sauté mode, add oil and heat it up.
2. Add onion, stir and cook for 2 minutes.
3. Add sausages and cook for 4 minutes.
4. Add paprika, beer and mussels, stir, cover and cook on Low for 2 minutes.
5. Release the pressure, uncover, discard unopened mussels, transfer to bowls and serve.

Enjoy!
Nutrition:

- Calories 100
- Fat 4
- Fiber 1
- Carbs 3
- Protein 14

Tasty Cioppino

This is so tasty and rich!

Preparation time: 10 minutes
Cooking time: 15 minutes
Servings: 4
Ingredients:

- 12 shell clams
- 12 mussels
- 1 and ½ pounds big shrimp, peeled and deveined
- 1 and ½ pounds fish fillets, cut into medium pieces
- 1 cup butter
- 2 yellow onions, chopped
- 3 garlic cloves, minced
- ½ cup parsley, chopped
- 20 ounces canned tomatoes, chopped
- 8 ounces clam juice
- 1 and ½ cups white wine
- 2 bay leaves
- ½ teaspoon marjoram, dried
- 1 tablespoon basil, dried
- Salt and black pepper to the taste

Directions:

1. Set your instant pot on Sauté mode, add butter and melt it.
2. Add onion and garlic, stir and cook for 2 minutes.
3. Add clam juice, tomatoes, wine, parsley, basil, bay leaves, marjoram, salt and pepper, stir, cover and cook at High for 10 minutes.
4. Release the pressure and switch pot to Sauté mode again.
5. Add clams and mussels, stir and cook for 8 minutes.
6. Discard unopened mussels and clams, add fish and shrimp, stir and cook for 4 minutes.
7. Divide among bowls and serve.

Enjoy!

Nutrition:

- Calories 300
- Fat 12
- Fiber 12
- Carbs 10
- Protein 20

Tasty Clams

You need to try this recipe today!

Preparation time: 10 minutes
Cooking time: 15 minutes
Servings: 4
Ingredients:

- 15 small clams
- 30 mussels, scrubbed and debearded
- 2 chorizo links, sliced
- 1 pound baby red potatoes
- 1 yellow onion, chopped
- 10 ounces beer
- 2 tablespoons parsley, chopped
- 1 teaspoon extra virgin olive oil
- Lemon wedges for serving

Directions:

1. Set your instant pot on Sauté mode, add oil and heat it up.
2. Add chorizo and onions, stir and cook for 4 minutes.
3. Add clams, mussels, potatoes and beer, stir, cover and cook at High for 10 minutes.
4. Release the pressure, uncover, add parsley, stir, divide among bowls and serve with lemon wedges on the side.

Enjoy!

Nutrition:

- Calories 203
- Fat 3
- Fiber 8
- Carbs 10
- Protein 20

Amazing Clams

These are so delicious! If you want something special for dinner, then this is the best idea!

Preparation time: 10 minutes
Cooking time: 5 minutes
Servings: 4
Ingredients:

- 24 clams, shucked
- 3 garlic cloves, minced
- 4 tablespoons butter
- ¼ cup parsley, chopped
- ¼ cup parmesan cheese, grated
- 1 teaspoon oregano, dried
- 1 cup breadcrumbs
- 2 cups water
- Lemon wedges

Directions:

1. In a bowl, mix breadcrumbs with parmesan, oregano, parsley, butter and garlic and stir.
2. Place 1 tablespoon of this mix in exposed clams.
3. Place the clams in the steamer basket of the pot, add 2 cups water to the pot, cover and cook at High for 4 minutes.
4. Release the pressure, uncover, divide among plates and serve with lemon wedges.

Enjoy!
Nutrition:

- Calories 80
- Fat 5
- Fiber 0
- Carbs 6
- Protein 3

Simple Crab Dish

It is so simple to make a tasty crab dish in your instant pot!

Preparation time: 5 minutes
Cooking time: 3 minutes
Servings: 4
Ingredients:

- 4 pounds king crab legs, broken in half
- 3 lemon wedges
- ¼ cup butter
- 1 cup water

Directions:

1. Put crab legs in the steamer basket of the pot.
2. Add water to the pot, cover and cook at High for 3 minutes.
3. Release the pressure, uncover, transfer crab legs to a bowl and butter and serve with lemon wedges on the side.

Enjoy!
Nutrition:

- Calories 50
- Fat 0.2
- Fiber 0.2
- Carbs 0
- Protein 7

Special Shrimp Delight

It will make you wonder why you didn't make it before!

Preparation time: 10 minutes
Cooking time: 5 minutes
Servings: 4
Ingredients:

- 1 and ½ pounds shrimp, peeled and deveined
- 2 tablespoons extra virgin olive oil
- 1 cup yellow onion, chopped
- 2 tablespoons parsley, chopped
- 4 garlic cloves, minced
- 2 teaspoons hot paprika
- ½ cup fish stock
- ¼ cup dry white wine
- 1 cup tomato sauce
- A pinch of saffron
- A pinch of sugar
- 1 teaspoon hot pepper, crushed
- ¼ teaspoon thyme dried
- 1 bay leaf
- Salt and black pepper to the taste

Directions:

1. Set your instant pot on Sauté mode, add oil and heat up.
2. Add shrimp, cook for 1 minute and transfer to a platter.
3. Add onion, stir and cook for 2 minutes.
4. Add parsley, garlic, paprika and wine, stir and cook for 2 minutes.
5. Add stock, tomato sauce, red pepper, sugar, saffron, thyme, bay leaf, salt and pepper.
6. Cover and cook at High for 4 minutes.
7. Release the pressure, uncover, add shrimp, cover again and cook at High for 2 minutes.
8. Release pressure, again, uncover, divide shrimp mix among plates and serve.

Enjoy!

Nutrition:

- Calories 566
- Fat 20
- Fiber 8
- Carbs 30
- Protein 40

Shrimp Paella

It only takes about 5 minutes to cook this wonderful paella!

Preparation time: 10 minutes
Cooking time: 5 minutes
Servings: 4
Ingredients:

- 20 shrimp, deveined
- 1 cup jasmine rice
- ¼ cup butter
- Salt and black pepper to the taste
- ¼ cup parsley, chopped
- A pinch of red pepper, crushed
- A pinch of saffron
- Juice of 1 lemon
- 1 and ½ cups water
- 4 garlic cloves, minced
- Melted butter for serving
- Hard cheese, grated for serving
- Parsley, chopped for serving

Directions:

1. Put shrimp in your instant pot.
2. Add rice, butter, salt, pepper, parsley, red pepper, saffron, lemon juice, water and garlic.
3. Stir, cover and cook at High for 5 minutes.
4. Release pressure, uncover pot, takes shrimps and peel them
5. Return to pot, stir well and divide into bowls.
6. Add melted butter, cheese and parsley on top and serve.

Enjoy!

Nutrition:

- Calories 320
- Fat 4
- Fiber 1.4
- Carbs 12
- Protein 22

Quick Shrimp Boil

This is a fresh dish you can serve on a hot summer day!

Preparation time: 10 minutes
Cooking time: 5 minutes
Servings: 4
Ingredients:

- 1 and ½ pounds shrimp, head removed
- 12 ounces Andouille sausage, already cooked and chopped
- 4 ears of corn, each cut into 3 pieces
- 1 tablespoon old bay seasoning
- 16 ounces beer
- Salt and black pepper to the taste
- 1 teaspoon red pepper flakes, crushed
- 2 sweet onions, cut into wedges
- 1 pound potatoes, cut into medium chunks
- 8 garlic cloves, crushed
- French baguettes for serving

Directions:

1. In your instant pot, mix beer with old bay seasoning, red pepper flakes, salt, black pepper, onions, garlic, potatoes, corn, sausage pieces and shrimp.
2. Cover the pot and cook at High for 5 minutes.
3. Release the pressure, uncover the pot, divide shrimp boil into bowls and serve with French baguettes on the side.

Enjoy!

Nutrition:

- Calories 360
- Fat 10
- Fiber 9
- Carbs 41
- Protein 30

Shrimp Curry

This Indian style dish will surprise you and everyone around the table!

Preparation time: 10 minutes
Cooking time: 30 minutes
Servings: 4
Ingredients:

- 1 pound big shrimp, peeled and deveined
- 1/3 cup butter
- 2 bay leaves
- 1 cinnamon stick
- 10 cloves
- 3 cardamom pods
- 2 red onions, chopped
- 14 red chilies, dried
- 3 green chilies, chopped
- ½ cup cashews
- 1 tablespoon garlic paste
- 1 tablespoon ginger paste
- 4 tomatoes, chopped
- Salt to the taste
- 1 teaspoon sugar
- 1 teaspoon fenugreek leaves, dried
- ½ cup cream

Directions:

1. Set your instant pot on Sauté mode, add butter and melt it.
2. Add bay leaves, cardamom, cinnamon stick and onion, stir and cook for 3 minutes.
3. Add red chilies, green chilies, cashews, tomatoes, garlic paste and ginger paste and stir.
4. Add salt, stir, cover and cook at High for 15 minutes.
5. Release the pressure, transfer everything to your blender and pulse well.
6. Strain into a pan and heat it up over medium high heat.
7. Add shrimp, stir, cover and cook for 12 minutes.
8. Add fenugreek, cream and sugar, stir, cook for 2 minutes, take off heat and divide among plates.

Enjoy!

Nutrition:

- Calories 299
- Fat 9
- Fiber 3
- Carbs 26
- Protein 27

Different Shrimp Curry

This is another tasty shrimp curry recipe! Try it soon!

Preparation time: 10 minutes
Cooking time: 6 minutes
Servings: 4
Ingredients:

- 1 pound shrimp, peeled and deveined
- 1 cup bouillon
- 4 lemon slices
- Salt and black pepper to the taste
- ½ teaspoon curry powder
- ¼ cup mushrooms, sliced
- ¼ cup yellow onion, chopped
- 2 tablespoons shortening
- ½ cup raisins
- 3 tablespoons flour
- 1 cup milk

Directions:

1. Set your instant pot on Sauté mode, add shortenings and heat up.
2. Add onion and mushroom, stir and cook for 2 minutes.
3. Add salt, pepper, curry powder, lemon, bouillon, raisins and shrimp.
4. Stir, cover and cook at High for 2 minutes.
5. Meanwhile, in a bowl mix flour with milk and whisk well.
6. Release the pressure from the pot, uncover, add flour and milk mix, stir well and cook until curry thickens on Simmer mode.
7. Divide among bowls and serve.

Enjoy!

Nutrition:

- Calories 300
- Fat 7
- Fiber 2.5
- Carbs 34
- Protein 29

Shrimp And Dill Sauce

This shrimp dish is so satisfying and delicious!

Preparation time: 10 minutes

Cooking time: 10 minutes

Servings: 4

Ingredients:

- 1 pound shrimp, peeled and deveined
- 2 tablespoons shortening
- 1 tablespoon yellow onion, chopped
- 1 cup white wine
- 2 tablespoons cornstarch
- ¾ cup milk
- 1 teaspoon dill weed

Directions:

1. Set your instant pot on Sauté mode, add shortening and heat it up.
2. Add onion, stir and cook for 2 minutes.
3. Add shrimp and wine, stir, cover and cook at High for 2 minutes.
4. Release the pressure, uncover pot and set it on Simmer mode.
5. In a bowl, mix cornstarch with milk and stir.
6. Add this to shrimp and stir until it thickens.
7. Add dill weed, stir, simmer for 5 minutes, divide among bowls and serve.

Enjoy!

Nutrition:

- Calories 300
- Fat 10
- Fiber 0
- Carbs 7
- Protein 10

Shrimp And Potatoes Mix

Try this simple and very delicious shrimp stew soon!

Preparation time: 10 minutes
Cooking time: 15 minutes
Servings: 4
Ingredients:

- 2 pounds shrimp, peeled and deveined
- 1 pound tomatoes, peeled and chopped
- 8 potatoes, cut into quarters
- Salt to the taste
- 4 tablespoons extra virgin olive oil
- 4 onions, chopped
- 1 teaspoon coriander, ground
- 1 teaspoon curry powder
- Juice of 1 lemon
- 1 tablespoon watercress

Directions:

1. Put potatoes in the steamer basket of the pot, add some water to the pot, cover and cook at High for 10 minutes.
2. Release the pressure, transfer potatoes to a bowl and clean up your pot.
3. Set the pot on Sauté mode, add oil and heat it up.
4. Add onions, stir and cook for 5 minutes.
5. Add salt, coriander and curry, stir and cook for 5 minutes.
6. Add tomatoes, shrimp, lemon juice and return potatoes as well.
7. Stir, cover and cook at High for 3 minutes.
8. Release the pressure again, divide among bowls and serve with watercress on top.

Enjoy!

Nutrition:

- Calories 140
- Fat 2
- Fiber 0
- Carbs 5
- Protein 19

Shrimp Creole

This is an amazing option for dinner! You will become a huge fan in no time!

Preparation time: 10 minutes
Cooking time: 5 minutes
Servings: 4
Ingredients:

- 1 cup already cooked shrimp
- 1 and ½ cups already cooked, rice
- ½ teaspoon sugar
- 2 teaspoons vinegar
- 1 cup tomato juice
- Salt to the taste
- 1 teaspoons chili powder
- 1 yellow onion, chopped
- 1 cup celery, chopped
- 2 tablespoons shortening

Directions:

1. Set the pot on Sauté mode, add shortening and heat it up.
2. Add onion and celery, stir and cook for 2 minutes.
3. Add salt, chili powder, tomato juice, vinegar, sugar, shrimp and rice.
4. Stir, cover and cook at High for 3 minutes.
5. Release the pressure, uncover pot, divide among plates and serve.

Enjoy!

Nutrition:

- Calories 294
- Fat 9
- Fiber 1.5
- Carbs 27
- Protein 24

Shrimp Teriyaki

It's a unique dish with a perfect taste!

Preparation time: 10 minutes
Cooking time: 4 minutes
Servings: 4
Ingredients:

- 1 pounds shrimp, peeled and deveined
- 2 tablespoons soy sauce
- ½ pound pea pods
- 3 tablespoons vinegar
- ¾ cup pineapple juice
- 1 cup chicken stock
- 3 tablespoons sugar

Directions:

1. Put shrimp and pea pods in your instant pot.
2. In a bowl, mix soy sauce with vinegar, pineapple juice, stock and sugar and stir well.
3. Pour this into the pot, stir, cover and cook at High for 3 minutes.
4. Release the pressure, uncover, divide among plates and serve.

Enjoy!
Nutrition:

- Calories 200
- Fat 4.2
- Fiber 0.7
- Carbs 13
- Protein 38

Surprising Shrimp Dish

It's a very delicious way to cook shrimp!

Preparation time: 20 minutes
Cooking time: 10 minutes
Servings: 4
Ingredients:

- 18 ounces shrimp, peeled and deveined
- Salt to the taste
- ½ tablespoon mustard seeds
- 3 ounces mustard oil
- 1 teaspoon turmeric powder
- 2 green chilies, cut into halves lengthwise
- 2 onions, finely chopped
- 4 ounces curd, beaten
- 1 inch ginger, chopped
- Already cooker rice for serving

Directions:

1. Put mustard seeds in a bowl, add water to cover, leave aside for 10 minutes, drain and grind very well.
2. Put shrimp in a bowl, add mustard oil, turmeric, mustard paste, salt, onions, chilies, curd and ginger, toss to coat and leave aside for 10 minutes.
3. Transfer everything to your instant pot, cover and cook on Low for 10 minutes.
4. Release the pressure, divide among plates and serve with boiled rice.

Enjoy!
Nutrition:

- Calories 200
- Fat 2
- Fiber 1
- Carbs 7
- Protein 11

Shrimp Scampi

It's time you tried something new!

Preparation time: 10 minutes
Cooking time: 4 minutes
Servings: 4
Ingredients:

- 1 pound shrimp, cooked, peeled and deveined
- 2 tablespoons extra virgin olive oil
- 1 garlic clove, minced
- 10 ounces canned tomatoes, chopped
- 1/3 cup tomato paste
- ¼ teaspoon oregano, dried
- 1 tablespoon parsley, finely chopped
- 1/3 cup water
- 1 cup parmesan, grated
- Already cooked spaghetti for serving

Directions:

1. Set your instant pot on Sauté mode, add oil and heat up.
2. Add garlic, stir and brown for 2 minutes.
3. Add shrimp, tomato paste, tomatoes, water, oregano and parsley, stir, cover and cook at High for 3 minutes.
4. Release pressure, divide among plates and serve with your favorite spaghetti.
5. Sprinkle parmesan at the end.

Enjoy!

Nutrition:

- Calories 288
- Fat 20
- Fiber 0
- Carbs 0.01
- Protein 23

Fish And Shrimp

If you love seafood and fish then you will love this dish!

Preparation time: 10 minutes
Cooking time: 10 minutes
Servings: 4
Ingredients:

- 2 pounds flounder
- ½ cup water
- ½ pound shrimp, cooked, peeled and deveined
- 2 tablespoons butter
- Salt and black pepper to the taste
- 4 lemon wedges

Directions:

1. Season fish with salt and pepper and place in the steamer basket of the pot.
2. Add water to the pot, cover and cook at High for 10 minutes.
3. Release the pressure uncover the pot, transfer fish to plates and leave aside.
4. Discard water, clean pot and set on Sauté mode.
5. Add butter and melt it.
6. Add shrimp, salt and pepper, stir and divide among plates on top of fish and serve with lemon wedges on the side.

Enjoy!

Nutrition:

- Calories 200
- Fat 0.2
- Fiber 0.2
- Carbs 1
- Protein 12

Shrimp With Risotto And Herbs

This is a complete meal for you and your family!

Preparation time: 10 minutes
Cooking time: 20 minutes
Servings: 4
Ingredients:

- 4 tablespoons butter
- 2 garlic cloves, minced
- 1 yellow onion, chopped
- 1 and ½ cups Arborio rice
- 2 tablespoons dry white wine
- 4 and ½ cups chicken stock
- Salt and black pepper to the taste
- 1 pound shrimp, peeled and deveined
- ¾ cup parmesan, grated
- ¼ cup tarragon and parsley, chopped

Directions:

1. Set your instant pot on Sauté mode, add 2 tablespoons butter and melt.
2. Add garlic and onion, stir and cook for 4 minutes.
3. Add rice, stir and cook for 1 minute.
4. Add wine, stir and cook 30 seconds more.
5. Add 3 cups stock, salt, and pepper, stir, cover and cook at High for 9 minutes.
6. Release the pressure, uncover the pot, add shrimp, the rest of the stock, set the pot on Sauté mode again and cook for 5 minutes stirring from time to time.
7. Add cheese, the rest of the butter, tarragon and parsley, stir, divide among plates and serve.

Enjoy!

Nutrition:

- Calories 400
- Fat 8
- Fiber 4
- Carbs 15
- Protein 29

Octopus And Potatoes

This is an exotic and delicious salad!

Preparation time: 10 minutes
Cooking time: 35 minutes
Servings: 6
Ingredients:

- 2 pounds octopus, cleaned, head removed, emptied, tentacles separated
- 2 pounds potatoes.
- Water
- 3 garlic cloves, crushed
- ½ teaspoon peppercorns
- 1 bay leaf
- 2 tablespoons parsley, finely chopped
- 5 tablespoons vinegar
- Salt and black pepper salad
- 2 tablespoons extra virgin olive oil

Directions:

1. Put potatoes in your instant pot, add water to cover them, salt and pepper, cover the pot and cook at High for 15 minutes.
2. Release the pressure, transfer potatoes to a bowl, peeled and chopped.
3. Put octopus in your instant pot, add more water, bay leaf, 1 garlic clove, peppercorns and more salt.
4. Stir, cover and cook at High for 20 minutes.
5. Release the pressure, drain octopus, chop it and add to potatoes.
6. In a bowl, mix olive oil with vinegar, 2 garlic cloves, salt and pepper and stir very well.
7. Add this to octopus salad, also add parsley, toss to coat and serve.

Enjoy!
Nutrition:

- Calories 300
- Fat 12
- Fiber 2
- Carbs 14
- Protein 20

Seafood Gumbo

This gumbo is amazing!

Preparation time: 10 minutes
Cooking time: 25 minutes
Servings: 10
Ingredients:

- ¾ cup vegetable oil
- 1 and ¼ cups flour
- 1 cup white onions, chopped
- ½ cup celery, chopped
- 1 cup green bell pepper, chopped
- 4 garlic cloves, chopped
- 2 tablespoons peanut oil
- 6 plum tomatoes, chopped
- A pinch of cayenne pepper
- 3 bay leaves
- ½ teaspoon onion powder
- ½ teaspoon garlic powder
- 1 teaspoon thyme, dried
- 1 teaspoon celery seeds
- 1 teaspoon sweet paprika
- 1 pound sausage, sliced
- 2 quarts chicken stock
- 24 shrimp, peeled and deveined
- 24 crawfish tails
- 24 oysters
- ½ pound crab meat
- Salt and black pepper to the taste

Directions:

1. Heat up a pan with the vegetable oil over medium heat, add flour and stir for 3-4 minutes.
2. Set your instant pot on Sauté mode, add peanut oil and heat it up.
3. Add celery, peppers, onions and garlic, stir and cook for 10 minutes.
4. Add sausage, tomatoes, stock, bay leaves, cayenne, onion and garlic powder, thyme, paprika and celery seeds, stir and cook for 3 minutes.
5. Add flour mix you've made earlier, stir until it combines.
6. Add shrimp, crawfish, crab, oysters, salt and pepper, stir, cover and cook at High for 15 minutes.
7. Release the pressure, uncover, divide gumbo among bowls and serve.

Enjoy!
Nutrition:

- Calories 800
- Fat 58
- Fiber 3
- Carbs 35
- Protein 36

Octopus Stew

This is a Portuguese stew we found just for you!

Preparation time: 1 day
Cooking time: 8 minutes
Servings: 4
Ingredients:

- 1 octopus, already prepared
- 1 cup red wine
- 1 cup white wine
- 1 cup water
- ½ cup vegetable oil
- ½ cup extra virgin olive oil
- 2 teaspoons pepper sauce
- 1 tablespoon hot sauce
- 1 tablespoon paprika
- 1 tablespoon tomato sauce
- Salt and black pepper to the taste
- ½ bunch parsley, chopped
- 2 garlic cloves, minced
- 1 yellow onion, chopped
- 4 potatoes, cut into quarters.

Directions:

1. Put octopus in a bowl and add white wine, red wine, water, vegetable oil, pepper sauce, hot sauce, paprika, tomato paste, salt, pepper and parsley.
2. Toss to coat, cover and keep in a cold place for 1 day.
3. Set your instant pot on Sauté mode, add olive oil and heat it up.
4. Add onions and potatoes, stir and cook for 3 minutes.
5. Add octopus and its marinade, stir, cover and cook at High for 8 minutes.
6. Release the pressure, uncover the pot, divide stew among bowls and serve.

Enjoy!

Nutrition:

- Calories 210
- Fat 9
- Fiber 0
- Carbs 4
- Protein 32

Greek Octopus

This is a light dish you may serve next time you have a party!

Preparation time: 10 minutes
Cooking time: 16 minutes
Servings: 6
Ingredients:

- 1 octopus, cleaned and prepared
- 2 rosemary springs
- 2 teaspoons oregano, dried
- ½ yellow onion, roughly chopped
- 4 thyme springs
- ½ lemon
- 1 teaspoon black peppercorns
- 3 tablespoons extra virgin olive oil

For the marinade:

- ¼ cup extra virgin olive oil
- Juice of ½ lemon
- 4 garlic cloves, minced
- 2 thyme springs
- 1 rosemary spring
- Salt and black pepper to the taste

Directions:

1. Put the octopus in your instant pot.
2. Add oregano, 2 rosemary springs, 4 thyme springs, onion, lemon, 3 tablespoons olive oil, peppercorns and salt.
3. Stir, cover and cook on Low for 10 minutes.
4. Release the pressure, uncover the pot, transfer octopus on a cutting board, cut tentacles and place them in a bowl.
5. Add ¼ cup olive oil, lemon juice, garlic, 1 rosemary springs, 2 thyme springs, salt and pepper, toss to coat and leave aside for 1 hour.
6. Heat up your grill over medium heat, add octopus, grill for 3 minutes on each side and divide among plates.
7. Drizzle the marinade over octopus and serve.

Enjoy!

Nutrition:

- Calories 161
- Fat 1
- Fiber 0
- Carbs 1
- Protein 9

Stuffed Squid

This is something you must try!

Preparation time: 10 minutes
Cooking time: 20 minutes
Servings: 4
Ingredients:

- 4 squid
- 1 cup sticky rice
- 14 ounces dashi stock
- 2 tablespoons sake
- 4 tablespoons soy sauce
- 1 tablespoon mirin
- 2 tablespoons sugar

Directions:

1. Chop tentacles from 1 squid and mix with the rice.
2. Fill each squid with rice and seal ends with toothpicks.
3. Place squid in your instant pot, add stock, soy sauce, sake, sugar and mirin.
4. Cover and cook at High for 15 minutes.
5. Release the pressure, uncover the pot, divide stuffed squid among plates and serve.

Enjoy!

Nutrition:

- Calories 148
- Fat 2.4
- Fiber 1.1
- Carbs 7
- Protein 11

Squid Masala

It's something different and really tasty!

Preparation time: 10 minutes
Cooking time: 15 minutes
Servings: 4
Ingredients:

- 17 ounces squids
- 1 and ½ tablespoons red chili powder
- Salt and black pepper to the taste
- ¼ teaspoon turmeric powder
- 2 cups water
- 5 pieces coconut
- 4 garlic cloves, minced
- ½ teaspoons cumin seeds
- 3 tablespoons extra virgin olive oil
- ¼ teaspoon mustard seeds
- 1 inch ginger pieces, chopped

Directions:

1. Put squids in your instant pot.
2. Add chili powder, turmeric, salt, pepper and water, stir, cover and cook on High for 15 minutes.
3. Meanwhile, in your blender, mix coconut with ginger, garlic and cumin and blend well.
4. Heat up a pan with the oil over medium high heat, add mustard seeds and toast for 2-3 minutes.
5. Release the pressure from the pot and transfer squid and water to the pan.
6. Stir and mix with coconut blend.
7. Cook until everything thickens, divide among plates and serve.

Enjoy!

Nutrition:

- Calories 255
- Fat 0
- Fiber 1
- Carbs 7
- Protein 9

Braised Squid

It's an Italian-style dish! It's very tasty and rich!

Preparation time: 10 minutes
Cooking time: 20 minutes
Servings: 4
Ingredients:

- 1 pound squid, cleaned and cut
- 1 pound fresh peas
- ½ pounds canned tomatoes, crushed
- 1 yellow onion, chopped
- A splash of white wine
- A drizzle of olive oil
- Salt and black pepper to the taste

Directions:

1. Set your instant pot on Sauté mode, add some oil and heat it up.
2. Add onion, stir and cook for 3 minutes.
3. Add squid, stir and cook for 3 more minutes.
4. Add wine, tomatoes and peas, stir, cover and cook for 20 minutes.
5. Release the pressure, uncover the pot, add salt and pepper to the taste, stir, divide among plates and serve.

Enjoy!

Nutrition:

- Calories 145
- Fat 1
- Fiber 0
- Carbs 7
- Protein 12

Squid Roast

This is the best squid roast ever!

Preparation time: 10 minutes
Cooking time: 25 minutes
Servings: 4
Ingredients:

- 1 pound squid, cleaned and cut into small pieces
- 10 garlic cloves, minced
- 2-inch ginger piece, grated
- 2 green chilies, chopped
- 2 yellow onions, chopped
- 1 curry leaf
- ½ tablespoon lemon juice
- ¼ cup coconut, sliced
- 1 tablespoon coriander powder
- ¾ tablespoon chili powder
- 1 teaspoon garam masala
- Salt and black pepper to the taste
- A pinch of turmeric
- 1 teaspoon mustard seeds
- ¾ cup water
- 3 tablespoons vegetable oil

Directions:

1. Set your instant pot on Sauté mode, add oil and heat it up.
2. Add mustard seeds and fry for 1 minute.
3. Add coconut and cook 2 minutes.
4. Add ginger, onions, garlic and chilies, stir and cook 30 seconds.
5. Add salt, pepper, curry leaf, coriander powder, chili powder, garam masala, turmeric, water, lemon juice, and squid.
6. Stir, cover and cook on Low for 25 minutes.
7. Release pressure, uncover, divide among plates and serve.

Enjoy!

Nutrition:

- Calories 209
- Fat 10
- Fiber 0.5
- Carbs 9.3
- Protein 20

Artichokes With Lemon Sauce

You will learn to appreciate this amazing veggie from now on!

Preparation time: 10 minutes
Cooking time: 20 minutes
Servings: 4
Ingredients:

- 4 artichokes
- 1 tablespoon tarragon, chopped
- 2 cups chicken stock
- 2 lemons
- 1 celery stalk, chopped
- ½ cup extra virgin olive oil
- Salt to the taste

Directions:

1. Discard stems and petal tips from artichokes.
2. Zest lemons, cut into 4 slices and place them in your instant pot.
3. Place an artichoke on each lemon slices, add stock, cover pot and cook at High for 20 minutes.
4. Release the pressure fast, uncover the pot and transfer artichokes to a platter.
5. Meanwhile, In your food processor, mix tarragon with lemon zest, with the pulp from the second lemon, celery, salt and olive oil and pulse very well.
6. Drizzle this over artichokes and serve.

Enjoy!

Nutrition:

- Calories 200
- Fat 12
- Fiber 9
- Carbs 20
- Protein 6

Tasty Artichoke Hearts

This is a very simple and easy instant pot veggie recipe!

Preparation time: 10 minutes

Cooking time: 40 minutes

Servings: 4

Ingredients:

- 4 big artichokes, washed, stems and petal tips cut off
- Salt and black pepper to the taste
- 2 tablespoons lemon juice
- ¼ cup extra virgin olive oil
- 2 teaspoons balsamic vinegar
- 1 teaspoon oregano
- 2 cups water
- 2 garlic cloves, minced

Directions:

1. Put artichokes in the steamer basket of your instant pot.
2. Add 2 cups water to the pot, cover and steam them for 8 minutes.
3. Meanwhile, in a bowl, mix lemon juice with vinegar, oil, salt, pepper, garlic and oregano and stir very well.
4. Release the pressure from the pot, transfer artichokes to a plate, cut them into halves, take out the hearts and arrange them on a platter.
5. Drizzle the vinaigrette over artichokes and leave them aside for 30 minutes.
6. Heat up your kitchen grill over medium heat, add artichokes and cook for 3 minutes on each side.
7. Serve them warm.

Enjoy!

Nutrition:

- Calories 120
- Fat 2
- Fiber 1
- Carbs 1
- Protein 4

Artichokes And Spinach Dip

This is a creamy dip you can make in your instant pot! Serve it at a party!

Preparation time: 10 minutes

Cooking time: 5 minutes

Servings: 6

Ingredients:

- 14 ounces canned artichoke hearts
- 8 ounces cream cheese
- 16 ounces parmesan cheese, grated
- 10 ounces spinach
- ½ cup chicken stock
- 8 ounces mozzarella, shredded
- ½ cup sour cream
- 3 garlic cloves, minced
- ½ cup mayonnaise
- 1 teaspoon onion powder

Directions:

1. In your instant pot, mix artichokes with stock, garlic, spinach, cream cheese, sour cream, onion powder and mayo, stir, cover and cook at High for 5 minutes.
2. Release the pressure fast, uncover the pot, add, mozzarella and parmesan, stir well and transfer to a bowl.
3. Serve with corn chips on the side.

Enjoy!

Nutrition:

- Calories 288
- Fat 20
- Fiber 0
- Carbs 8
- Protein 15

Artichokes With Tasty Dip

This is a special recipe for a special occasion!

Preparation time: 10 minutes
Cooking time: 22 minutes
Servings: 2
Ingredients:

- 2 artichokes, washed, stems and petal tips cut off
- 1 bay leaf
- 1 cup water
- 2 garlic cloves, chopped
- 1 lemon cut into halves

For the sauce:

- ¼ cup coconut oil
- ¼ cup extra virgin olive oil
- 3 anchovy fillets
- 3 garlic cloves

Directions:

1. Put artichokes in the steamer basket of the instant pot, add water in the pot, lemon halves, 2 garlic cloves and bay leaf, cover and cook at High for 20 minutes.
2. Release the pressure naturally for 10 minutes, uncover the pot and divide artichokes among plates.
3. In your food processor, mix coconut oil with anchovy, 3 garlic cloves and olive oil and blend very well.
4. Pour this into a bowl and serve your artichokes with this dip.

Enjoy!

Nutrition:

- Calories 300
- Fat 14
- Fiber 9
- Carbs 45
- Protein 15

Wrapped Asparagus Canes

This will impress even the most pretentious guests!

Preparation time: 5 minutes
Cooking time: 4 minutes
Servings: 4
Ingredients:

- 1 pound asparagus, trimmed
- 8 ounces prosciutto slices
- 2 cups water
- A pinch of salt

Directions:

1. Wrap asparagus spears in prosciutto slices and place them on the bottom of the steamer basket in your instant pot.
2. Add 2 cups water to the pot, add a pinch of salt, cover and cook at High for 4 minutes.
3. Release the pressure naturally, uncover, transfer asparagus canes on a platter and serve at room temperature.

Enjoy!

Nutrition:

- Calories 60
- Fat 3
- Fiber 1
- Carbs 3
- Protein 4

Asparagus And Shrimp

This is a tasty dish and a great combination!

Preparation time: 4 minutes
Cooking time: 3 minutes
Servings: 4
Ingredients:

- 1 cup water
- 1 pound shrimp, peeled and deveined
- 1 teaspoon extra virgin olive oil
- 1 bunch asparagus, trimmed
- ½ tablespoon Cajun seasoning

Directions:

1. Put the water in your instant pot.
2. Put asparagus in the steamer basket of the pot and add shrimp on top.
3. Drizzle olive oil, sprinkle Cajun seasoning, stir, cover and cook on Low for 2 minutes.
4. Release the pressure naturally, transfer asparagus and shrimp to plates and serve.

Enjoy!

Nutrition:

- Calories 150
- Fat 1.4
- Fiber 4
- Carbs 15
- Protein 23

Delicious Beet Salad

This is so delicious and super easy to make!

Preparation time: 10 minutes
Cooking time: 30 minutes
Servings: 4
Ingredients:

- 4 beets
- 1 cup water
- 2 tablespoons balsamic vinegar
- A bunch of parsley, chopped
- Salt and black pepper to the taste
- 1 tablespoon extra virgin olive oil
- 1 garlic clove, chopped
- 2 tablespoons capers

Directions:

1. Put the beets in the steamer basket of your instant pot, add 1 cup water to the pot, cover and cook for 20 minutes at High.
2. Meanwhile, in a bowl, mix parsley with garlic, salt, pepper, olive oil and capers and stir very well.
3. Release the pressure from the pot, uncover, transfer beets to a cutting board, leave them to cool down, peel them, slice them and arrange them on a platter.
4. Add vinegar over them and drizzle the parsley dressing at the end.

Enjoy!

Nutrition:

- Calories 44
- Fat 2.4
- Fiber 1
- Carbs 0
- Protein 1

Delicious Beets And Blue Cheese

This dish is so yummy and amazing!

Preparation time: 10 minutes
Cooking time: 20 minutes
Servings: 6
Ingredients:

- 6 beets
- Salt and black pepper to the taste
- ¼ cup blue cheese, crumbled
- 1 cup water

Directions:

1. Put the beets in the steamer basket of your instant pot, add 1 cup water to the pot, cover and cook at High for 20 minutes.
2. Release the pressure naturally, uncover the pot, transfer beets to a cutting board, leave aside to cool down, peel and cut them into quarters.
3. Put beets in a bowl, add blue cheese, salt and pepper to the taste, stir and serve.

Enjoy!

Nutrition:

- Calories 160
- Fat 1
- Fiber 5
- Carbs 10
- Protein 7

Beet And Orange Salad

You've got to try this wonderful salad as soon as possible!

Preparation time: 10 minutes
Cooking time: 10 minutes
Servings: 4
Ingredients:

- 1 and ½ pounds beets
- 2 teaspoons orange zest, grated
- 3 strips orange peel
- 2 tablespoons cider vinegar
- ½ cup orange juice
- 2 tablespoons brown sugar
- 2 scallions, chopped
- 2 teaspoons mustard
- 2 cups arugula and mustard greens

Directions:

1. Scrub beets well cut them in halves and put them in a bowl.
2. In your instant pot, mix orange peel strips with vinegar and orange juice and stir.
3. Add beets, cover the pot, cook at High for 7 minutes and release the pressure naturally.
4. Uncover, pot, take beets and transfer them to a bowl.
5. Discard peel strips from the pot, add mustard and sugar and stir well.
6. Add scallions and grated orange zest to beets and toss them.
7. Add liquid from the pot over beets, toss to coat and serve on plates on top of mixed salad greens.

Enjoy!

Nutrition:

- Calories 140
- Fat 6
- Fiber 3.1
- Carbs 11
- Protein 4

Beet And Tomato Salad

This is a light and very healthy salad you can enjoy tonight for dinner!

Preparation time: 30 minutes
Cooking time: 30 minutes
Servings: 8
Ingredients:

- 1 and ½ cups water
- 8 small beets, trimmed
- 1 red onion, sliced
- 4 ounces goat cheese
- 1 cup apple cider vinegar
- 1 cup water
- 2 teaspoons pickling juice
- Salt and black pepper to the taste
- 2 tablespoons sugar
- 1 pint mixed cherry tomatoes, cut into halves
- 2 ounces pecans
- 2 tablespoons extra virgin olive oil

Directions:

1. Put beets in the steamer basket of your instant pot, add 1 and ½ cups water, cover and cook at High for 20 minutes.
2. Release the pressure, uncover the pot, transfer beets to a cutting board, leave them to cool down, peel and chop them and put them in a bowl.
3. Clean your instant pot, add 1 cup water, vinegar, sugar, pickling juice and salt to the taste, stir, cover and cook at High for 2 minutes.
4. Release the pressure, strain liquid into a bowl, add onions, stir and leave aside for 10 minutes.
5. Add tomatoes over beets and onions and stir.
6. In a bowl, mix 4 tablespoons of liquid from the onions with 2 tablespoons olive oil, salt and pepper and stir.
7. Add this to beets salad and stir.
8. Also, add goat cheese and pecans, toss to coat and serve.

Enjoy!

Nutrition:

- Calories 163
- Fat 8
- Fiber 4
- Carbs 12
- Protein 4.5

Stuffed Bell Peppers

It's a fun dish you need to try!

Preparation time: 15 minutes
Cooking time: 15 minutes
Servings: 4
Ingredients:

- 1 pound turkey meat, ground
- 1 cup water
- 2 green onions, chopped
- 5 ounces canned green chilies, chopped
- 1 jalapeno pepper, chopped
- 2 teaspoons chili powder
- ½ cup whole wheat panko
- 1 teaspoon garlic powder
- 1 teaspoon cumin, ground
- Salt to the taste
- 4 bell peppers, tops, and seeds discarded
- 4 pepper jack cheese slices
- 1 avocado, chopped
- Crushed tortilla chips
- Pico de gallo

For the chipotle sauce:

- Zest from 1 lime
- Juice from 1 lime
- ½ cup sour cream
- 2 tablespoons chipotle in adobo sauce
- 1/8 teaspoon garlic powder

Directions:

1. In a bowl, mix sour cream with chipotle in adobo sauce, lime zest and lime juice and garlic powder, stir well and keep in the fridge until you serve it.
2. In a bowl, mix turkey meat with green onions, green chilies, bread crumbs, jalapeno, cumin, salt, chili powder and garlic powder, stir very well and stuff your peppers with this mix.
3. Add 1 cup water to your instant pot, add peppers in the steamer basket, cover and cook at High for 15 minutes.
4. Release the pressure naturally for 10 minutes, transfer bell peppers to a pan, add cheese on top, introduce in preheated broiler and broil until cheese is browned.
5. Divide bell peppers on plates, top with the chipotle sauce you've made earlier and serve.

Enjoy!

Nutrition:

- Calories 177
- Fat 5
- Fiber 3.3
- Carbs 22
- Protein 13

Special Stuffed Bell Peppers

This is a different and unique recipe!

Preparation time: 10 minutes
Cooking time: 15 minutes
Servings: 4
Ingredients:

- 4 bell peppers, tops and seeds removed
- Salt and black pepper to the taste
- 16 ounces beef meat, ground
- 1 cup white rice, already cooked
- 1 egg
- ½ cup milk
- 2 onions, chopped
- 8 ounces water
- 10 ounces canned tomato soup

Directions:

1. Put some water in a pot, bring to a boil over medium heat, add bell peppers, blanch them for 3 minutes, drain and transfer them to a working surface.
2. In a bowl, mix beef with rice, salt, pepper, egg, milk and onions and stir very well.
3. Stuff bell peppers with this mix and place them in your instant pot.
4. Add tomato soup mixed with water, cover pot and cook at High for 12 minutes.
5. Release the pressure fast, divide bell peppers among plates, drizzle tomato sauce on top and serve.

Enjoy!

Nutrition:

- Calories 200
- Fat 12
- Fiber 1.5
- Carbs 13
- Proteins 12

Broccoli And Garlic

This is so simple to make at home in your instant pot!

Preparation time: 10 minutes
Cooking time: 12 minutes
Servings: 4
Ingredients:

- 1 broccoli head, cut into 4 pieces
- ½ cup water
- 1 tablespoon peanut oil
- 6 garlic cloves, minced
- 1 tablespoon Chinese rice wine
- Salt to the taste

Directions:

1. Put broccoli in the steamer basket of you instant pot, add ½ cup water to the pot, cover and cook on Low for 12 minutes.
2. Release the pressure, transfer broccoli to a bowl filled with cold water, drain and place it in a bowl.
3. Heat up a pan with the oil over medium high heat, add garlic, stir and cook for 3 minutes.
4. Add broccoli and rice wine, stir and cook for 1 minute more.
5. Add salt, stir and cook 30 seconds.
6. Transfer to plates and serve.

Enjoy!

Nutrition:

- Calories 100
- Fat 1
- Fiber 0
- Carbs 3
- Protein 6

Brussels Sprouts With Pomegranate

This is so delicious and light!

Preparation time: 5 minutes
Cooking time: 10 minutes
Servings: 4
Ingredients:

- 1 pound Brussels sprouts
- Salt and black pepper to the taste
- 1 pomegranate, seeds separated
- ¼ cup pine nuts, toasted
- A drizzle of extra virgin olive oil
- 1 cup water

Directions:

1. Put Brussels sprouts in the pressure cooker of your instant pot, add 1 cup water to the pot, cover and cook at High for 4 minutes.
2. Release the pressure, uncover your pot and transfer sprouts to a bowl.
3. Add salt, pepper, pine nuts, pomegranate seeds and pine nuts and stir.
4. Add olive oil, toss to coat and serve.

Enjoy!

Nutrition:

- Calories 100
- Fat 1
- Fiber 4
- Carbs 11
- Protein 4

Brussels Sprouts And Bacon

This is the perfect dinner idea for tonight!

Preparation time: 4 minutes
Cooking time: 6 minutes
Servings: 4
Ingredients:

- 1 pound Brussels sprouts, trimmed and cut into halves
- Salt and black pepper to the taste
- ½ cup bacon, chopped
- 1 tablespoon mustard
- 1 cup chicken stock
- 1 tablespoon butter
- 2 tablespoons dill, finely chopped

Directions:

1. Set your instant pot on Sauté mode, add bacon and cook it until it's crispy.
2. Add sprouts, stir and cook for 2 minutes.
3. Add stock, mustard, salt and pepper, stir, cover and cook at High for 4 minutes.
4. Release pressure, uncover the pot, add butter and dill, set the pot on Sauté mode again, stir and divide among serving plates.

Enjoy!

Nutrition:

- Calories 175
- Fat 11
- Fiber 5.6
- Carbs 14
- Protein 6.6

Brussels Sprouts With Parmesan

It's an interesting combination worth trying!

Preparation time: 10 minutes
Cooking time: 6 minutes
Servings: 4
Ingredients:

- 1 pound Brussels sprouts, washed
- Juice of 1 lemon
- Salt and black pepper to the taste
- 2 tablespoons butter
- 1 cup water
- 3 tablespoons parmesan, grated

Directions:

1. Put sprouts in your instant pot, add salt, pepper and water, stir, cover and cook at High for 3 minutes.
2. Release the pressure, transfer sprouts to a bowl, discard water and clean your pot.
3. Set your pot on Sauté mode, add butter and melt it.
4. Add lemon juice and stir well.
5. Add sprouts, stir and transfer to plates.
6. Add more salt and pepper if needed and parmesan cheese on top.

Enjoy!

Nutrition:

- Calories 160
- Fat 2
- Fiber 1
- Carbs 7
- Protein 12

Brussels Sprouts And Potatoes

This is one of the best Brussels sprouts dishes!

Preparation time: 10 minutes
Cooking time: 5 minutes
Servings: 4
Ingredients:

- 1 and ½ pounds Brussels sprouts, washed and trimmed
- 1 cup new potatoes, chopped
- 1 and ½ tablespoons bread crumbs
- ½ cup beef stock
- Salt and black pepper to the taste
- 1 and ½ tablespoons butter

Directions:

1. Put sprouts and potatoes in your instant pot.
2. Add stock, salt and pepper, cover and cook at High for 5 minutes.
3. Release the pressure, uncover pot, set on Sauté mode, add butter and bread crumbs, toss to coat well, divide among plates and serve.

Enjoy!

Nutrition:

- Calories 100
- Fat 2.5
- Fiber 4.6
- Carbs 18
- Protein 4

Savoy Cabbage And Cream

You've got try this recipe at least once!

Preparation time: 10 minutes
Cooking time: 9 minutes
Servings: 4
Ingredients:

- 1 cup bacon, chopped
- 1 medium Savoy cabbage head, chopped
- 1 yellow onion, chopped
- 2 cups bone stock
- ¼ teaspoon nutmeg
- Salt and black pepper to the taste
- 1 bay leaf
- 1 cup coconut milk
- 2 tablespoons parsley flakes

Directions:

1. Set your instant pot on Sauté mode, add bacon and onion, stir and cook until bacon is crispy.
2. Add stock, cabbage, bay leaf, salt, pepper and nutmeg, stir, cover and cook on High for 5 minutes.
3. Release the pressure, uncover the pot and set it on Sauté mode again.
4. Add milk, more salt and pepper if needed and parsley, stir and cook for 4 minutes.
5. Divide among plates and serve.

Enjoy!

Nutrition:

- Calories 160
- Fat 10
- Fiber 2.2
- Carbs 13
- Protein 5

Special Cabbage Dish

It's so flavored! We love this dish so much!

Preparation time: 10 minutes
Cooking time: 8 minutes
Servings: 8
Ingredients:

- 1 green cabbage head, chopped
- ¼ cup butter
- 2 cups chicken stock
- 3 bacon slices, chopped
- Salt and black pepper to the taste

Directions:

1. Set your instant pot on Sauté mode, add bacon, stir and cook for 4 minutes.
2. Add butter and stir until it melts.
3. Add cabbage, stock, salt and pepper, stir, cover and cook at High for 3 minutes.
4. Release the pressure, uncover, transfer cabbage to plates and serve.

Enjoy!

Nutrition:

- Calories 100
- Fat 4
- Fiber 3
- Carbs 7
- Protein 2

Tasty Cabbage And Sausages

This is a very easy and delicious dish!

Preparation time: 10 minutes
Cooking time: 5 minutes
Servings: 4
Ingredients:

- 3 tablespoons butter
- 1 green cabbage head, chopped
- Salt and black pepper to the taste
- 1 pound sausage links, sliced
- 15 ounces canned tomatoes, chopped
- ½ cup yellow onion, chopped
- 2 teaspoons turmeric

Directions:

1. Set your instant pot on Sauté mode, add sausage slices, stir and cook until they brown.
2. Drain excess grease, add butter, cabbage, tomatoes salt, pepper, onion and turmeric, stir, cover and cook at High for 2 minutes.
3. Release the pressure fast, uncover, divide cabbage and sausages among plates and serve.

Enjoy!

Nutrition:

- Calories 140
- Fat 6
- Fiber 4
- Carbs 11
- Protein 10

Sweet And Spicy Cabbage

This is unbelievable!

Preparation time: 10 minutes
Cooking time: 8 minutes
Servings: 4
Ingredients:

- 1 cabbage, cut into 8 wedges
- 1 tablespoon sesame seed oil
- 1 carrots, grated
- ¼ cup apple cider vinegar
- 1 and ¼ cups apple+2 teaspoons water
- 1 teaspoon raw sugar
- ½ teaspoon cayenne pepper
- ½ teaspoon red pepper flakes
- 2 teaspoons cornstarch

Directions:

1. Set your instant pot on Sauté mode, add oil and heat it up.
2. Add cabbage, stir and cook for 3 minutes.
3. Add carrots, 1 and ¼ cups water, sugar, vinegar, cayenne and pepper flakes, stir, cover and cook at High for 5 minutes.
4. Release the pressure, uncover the pot and divide cabbage and carrots mix among plates.
5. Add cornstarch mixed with 2 teaspoons water to the pot, set the pot on Simmer mode, stir very well and bring to a boil.
6. Drizzle over cabbage and serve.

Enjoy!
Nutrition:

- Calories 90
- Fat 4.5
- Fiber 2.1
- Carbs 11
- Protein 1

Sweet Carrots

These are so delicious! Your kids will love them!

Preparation time: 10 minutes
Cooking time: 15 minutes
Servings: 4
Ingredients:

- 2 cups baby carrots
- A pinch of salt
- 1 tablespoon brown sugar
- ½ tablespoon butter
- ½ cup water

Directions:

1. In your instant pot, mix butter with water, salt and sugar and stir well.
2. Set the pot on Sauté mode and cook everything for 30 seconds.
3. Add carrots, stir, cover and cook at High for 15 minutes.
4. Release the pressure, uncover the pot, set it on Sauté mode again and cook everything for 1 more minute.
5. Serve hot.

Enjoy!

Nutrition:

- Calories 60
- Fat 0.1
- Fiber 1
- Carbs 4
- Protein 1

Maple Glazed Carrots

This is a dish you can make tonight! You don't need to much time to make and it will be delicious!

Preparation time: 10 minutes
Cooking time: 4 minutes
Servings: 4
Ingredients:

- 2 pounds carrots, peeled and sliced on the diagonal
- 1 tablespoon maple syrup
- Black pepper to the taste
- 1 tablespoon butter
- 1 cup water
- ¼ cup raisins

Directions:

1. Put carrots in your instant pot.
2. Add water and raisins, cover and cook at High for 4 minutes.
3. Release the pressure, uncover, add butter and maple syrup, stir, divide carrots among plates and sprinkle black pepper before serving them.

Enjoy!

Nutrition:

- Calories 60
- Fat 1.1
- Fiber 2.6
- Carbs 12
- Protein 1

Special Carrots Dish

This is another great idea for a quick lunch or dinner!

Preparation time: 10 minutes
Cooking time: 2 minutes
Servings: 4
Ingredients:

- 16 ounces baby carrots
- Salt and black pepper to the taste
- 2 tablespoons butter
- 4 ounces molasses
- 2 ounces water
- 2 tablespoon dill, chopped

Directions:

1. Put carrot, water, salt, pepper and molasses in your instant pot, stir, cover and cook at High for 3 minutes.
2. Release the pressure, uncover the pot, add butter and dill, stir, divide among plates and serve.

Enjoy!

Nutrition:

- Calories 60
- Fat 1
- Fiber 2
- Carbs 4
- Protein 3

Tasty Cauliflower And Pasta

If you are in the mood for something tasty and healthy, then try this dish!

Preparation time: 10 minutes
Cooking time: 10 minutes
Servings: 4
Ingredients:

- 2 tablespoons butter
- 8 cups cauliflower florets
- 2 garlic cloves, minced
- 1 cup chicken stock
- Salt to the taste
- 2 cups spinach, chopped
- 1 pound fettuccine paste
- 2 green onions, chopped
- 1 tablespoon gorgonzola cheese, grated
- 3 sun-dried tomatoes, chopped
- A splash of balsamic vinegar

Directions:

1. Set your instant pot on Sauté mode, add butter and melt it.
2. Add garlic, stir and cook for 2 minutes.
3. Add stock, salt and cauliflower, stir, cover and cook at High for 6 minutes.
4. Release the pressure for 10 minutes, transfer cauliflower to your blender and pulse well.
5. Add spinach and green onions and stir gently.
6. Heat up a pot with some water and a pinch of salt over medium high heat, bring to a boil, add pasta, cook according to instructions, drain and divide among plates.
7. Add cauliflower sauce, gorgonzola, sun-dried tomatoes and a splash of vinegar on top, toss to coat and serve.

Enjoy!
Nutrition:

- Calories 160
- Fat 5
- Fiber 3
- Carbs 23
- Protein 13

Collard Greens And Bacon

Believe it or not, this is an amazing recipe!

Preparation time: 10 minutes
Cooking time: 26 minutes
Servings: 6
Ingredients:

- 1 pound collard greens, trimmed
- ¼ pound bacon, chopped
- Salt and black pepper to the taste
- ½ cup water

Directions:

1. Set your instant pot on Sauté mode, add bacon, stir and cook for 5 minutes.
2. Add collard greens, salt, pepper and water, stir, cover and cook at High for 20 minutes.
3. Release the pressure, uncover, divide mix among plates and serve.

Enjoy!

Nutrition:

- Calories 130
- Fat 8
- Fiber 2
- Carbs 4
- Protein 6

Collard Greens Delight

This is a real delight that you will enjoy for sure!

Preparation time: 10 minutes
Cooking time: 20 minutes
Servings: 4
Ingredients:

- 1 bunch collard greens, trimmed
- 2 tablespoons extra virgin olive oil
- ½ cup chicken stock
- 2 tablespoons tomato puree
- 1 yellow onion, chopped
- 3 garlic cloves, minced
- Salt and black pepper to the taste
- 1 tablespoon balsamic vinegar
- 1 teaspoon sugar

Directions:

1. In your instant pot, mix stock with oil, garlic, vinegar, onion and tomato puree and stir.
2. Add collard greens after you've rolled them in cigar-shaped bundles.
3. Add salt, pepper and sugar, cover and cook at High for 20 minutes.
4. Release the pressure fast, uncover pot, divide collard greens among plates and serve.

Enjoy!

Nutrition:

- Calories 130
- Fat 7
- Fiber 4.5
- Carbs 12
- Protein 4
- Sugar 4

Classic Collard Greens Dish

This dish is a southern classic!

Preparation time: 10 minutes
Cooking time: 25 minutes
Servings: 8
Ingredients:

- 1 sweet onion, chopped
- 2 tablespoons extra virgin olive oil
- 3 garlic cloves, crushed
- 2 and ½ pounds collard greens, chopped
- Salt and black pepper to the taste
- 2 cups chicken stock
- 2 tablespoons apple cider vinegar
- 1 tablespoon brown sugar
- ½ teaspoon crushed red pepper
- 2 smoked turkey wings

Directions:

1. Set your instant pot on Sauté mode, add oil and heat it up.
2. Add onions, stir and cook for 2 minutes.
3. Add garlic, stir and cook for 1 minute.
4. Add stock, greens, vinegar, salt, pepper, crushed red pepper and sugar and stir gently.
5. Add smoked turkey, cover and cook at High for 20 minutes.
6. Release the pressure fast, uncover, divide greens and turkey among plates and serve.

Enjoy!

Nutrition:

- Calories 100
- Fat 1.4
- Fiber 1.7
- Carbs 4
- Protein 6

Braised Endives

This is a French style dish!

Preparation time: 10 minutes
Cooking time: 7 minutes
Servings: 4
Ingredients:

- 4 endives, trimmed and cut into halves
- Salt and black pepper to the taste
- 1 tablespoon lemon juice
- 1 tablespoon butter

Directions:

1. Set your instant pot on Sauté mode.
2. Add butter and melt it.
3. Arrange endives in the pot, add salt and pepper and the lemon juice, cover and cook at High for 7 minutes.
4. Release the pressure naturally, arrange endives on a platter, add cooking juice all over them and serve.

Enjoy!
Nutrition:

- Calories 80
- Fat 3.1
- Fiber 0.5
- Carbs 12
- Protein 1.2

Special Endives Dish

Simply enjoy the taste!

Preparation time: 10 minutes
Cooking time: 20 minutes
Servings: 4
Ingredients:

- 4 endives, trimmed
- Salt and black pepper to the taste
- 1 tablespoon white flour
- 4 slices ham
- 2 tablespoons butter
- ½ teaspoon nutmeg
- 14 ounces milk

Directions:

1. Put the endives in the steamer basket of your instant pot, add some water to the pot, cover and cook at High for 10 minutes.
2. Meanwhile, heat up a pan with the butter over medium heat, stir and melt it.
3. Add flour, stir well and cook for 3 minutes.
4. Add milk, salt, pepper and nutmeg, stir well, reduce heat to low and cook for 10 minutes.
5. Release the pressure from the pot, uncover it, transfer them to a cutting board and roll each in a slice of ham.
6. Arrange endives in a pan, add milk mix over them, introduce in preheated broiler and broil for 10 minutes.
7. Slice, arrange on plates and serve.

Enjoy!

Nutrition:

- Calories 120
- Fat 1
- Fiber 2
- Carbs 6
- Protein 23

Sautéed Endives

You've got to try this dish soon!

Preparation time: 10 minutes
Cooking time: 15 minutes
Servings: 4
Ingredients:

- 8 endives, trimmed
- Salt and black pepper to the taste
- 4 tablespoon butter
- Juice of ½ lemon
- ½ cup water
- 1 teaspoon sugar
- 2 tablespoons parsley, chopped

Directions:

1. Put the endives in your instant pot, add 1 tablespoon butter, lemon juice, ½ cup water, sugar, salt and pepper, stir gently, cover and cook at High for 10 minutes.
2. Release the pressure fast, uncover the pot and transfer endives to a plate.
3. Heat up a pan with 3 tablespoons butter over medium high heat, add endives, more salt and pepper if needed and parsley, stir and cook for 5 minutes.
4. Transfer endives to plates and serve.

Enjoy!

Nutrition:

- Calories 90
- Fat 1
- Fiber 4
- Carbs 4
- Protein 2

Endives Risotto

This Belgian style risotto is a delight!

Preparation time: 10 minutes
Cooking time: 20 minutes
Servings: 2
Ingredients:

- ¾ cup rice
- 2 Belgian endives, trimmed and cut into halves lengthwise and roughly chopped
- ½ yellow onion, chopped
- 2 tablespoons extra virgin olive oil
- ½ cup white wine
- 2 cups veggie stock
- 2 ounces parmesan, grated
- 3 tablespoons heavy cream
- Salt and black pepper to the taste

Directions:

1. Set your instant pot on Sauté mode, add oil and heat it up.
2. Add onion, stir and sauté for 4 minutes.
3. Add endives, stir and cook for 4 minutes more.
4. Add rice, wine, salt, pepper, stock, stir, cover and cook at High for 10 minutes.
5. Release the pressure fast, uncover pot and set it on Sauté mode again.
6. Add cheese and heavy cream, stir, cook for 1 minute, transfer to plates and serve.

Enjoy!

Nutrition:

- Calories 260
- Fat 5
- Fiber 5
- Carbs 13
- Protein 16

Eggplant Ratatouille

This is a veggie dish you will adore!

Preparation time: 15 minutes
Cooking time: 8 minutes
Servings: 6
Ingredients:

- 1 big eggplant, peeled and thinly sliced
- 2 garlic cloves, minced
- 3 tablespoons extra virgin olive oil
- Salt and black pepper to the taste
- 1 cup onion, chopped
- 1 green bell pepper, chopped
- 1 red bell pepper, chopped
- ½ cup water
- 1 teaspoon thyme
- 14 ounces canned tomatoes, chopped
- A pinch of sugar
- 1 cup basil, chopped

Directions:

1. Set your instant pot on Sauté mode, add oil and heat it up.
2. Add green and red bell pepper, onion and garlic, stir and cook for 3 minutes.
3. Add eggplant, water, salt, pepper, thyme, sugar and tomatoes, cover the pot and cook at High for 4 minutes.
4. Release the pressure fast, uncover the pot, add basil, stir gently, divide among plates and serve.

Enjoy!

Nutrition:

- Calories 109
- Fat 5
- Fiber 3
- Carbs 14
- Protein 2

Special Eggplant Dish

Go and get your ingredients and start making this amazing mix!

Preparation time: 10 minutes
Cooking time: 8 minutes
Servings: 2
Ingredients:

- 4 cups eggplant, cubed
- 1 tablespoon extra virgin olive oil
- 3 garlic cloves, minced
- 1 tablespoon garlic powder
- Salt and black pepper to the taste
- 1 cup marinara sauce
- ½ cup water

Directions:

1. Set your instant pot on Sauté mode, add the oil and heat it up.
2. Add garlic, stir and cook for 2 minutes.
3. Add eggplant, salt, pepper, garlic powder, marinara sauce and water, stir gently, cover and cook at High for 8 minutes.
4. Release the pressure fast, uncover the pot and serve your eggplant mix right away with your favorite spaghetti.

Enjoy!
Nutrition:

- Calories 130
- Fat 3
- Fiber 2
- Carbs 3
- Protein 3

Babaganoush

This spread is just wonderful!

Preparation time: 10 minutes
Cooking time: 4 minutes
Servings: 6
Ingredients:

- 2 pounds eggplant, peeled and cut into medium chunks
- Salt and black pepper to the taste
- ¼ cup extra virgin olive oil
- ½ cup water
- 4 garlic cloves
- ¼ cup lemon juice
- 1 bunch thyme, chopped
- 1 tablespoon tahini
- A drizzle of olive oil
- 3 olives, pitted and sliced

Directions:

1. Put the eggplant pieces in your instant pot, add ¼ cup oil, set the pot on Sauté mode and heat everything up.
2. Add garlic, water, salt and pepper, stir, cover and cook at High for 3 minutes.
3. Release the pressure, uncover the pot, transfer eggplant pieces and garlic to your blender, add lemon juice and tahini and pulse well.
4. Add thyme and blend again.
5. Transfer eggplant spread to a bowl, top with olive slices and a drizzle of oil and serve.

Nutrition:

- Calories 70
- Fat 2
- Fiber 2
- Carbs 7
- Protein 1

Eggplant Surprise

It's going to be a real surprise for you and your loved ones!

Preparation time: 10 minutes
Cooking time: 7 minutes
Servings: 4
Ingredients:

- 1 eggplant, roughly chopped
- 3 zucchinis, roughly chopped
- 3 tomatoes, sliced
- 2 tablespoons lemon juice
- Salt and black pepper to the taste
- 1 teaspoon thyme, dried
- 1 teaspoon oregano, dried
- 3 tablespoons extra virgin olive oil

Directions:

1. Put eggplant pieces in your instant pot.
2. Add zucchinis and tomatoes.
3. In a bowl, mix lemon juice with salt, pepper, thyme, oregano and oil and stir well.
4. Pour this over veggies, toss to coat, cover the pot and cook at High for 7 minutes.
5. Release the pressure, uncover the pot, divide among plates and serve.

Enjoy!

Nutrition:

- Calories 140
- Fat 3.4
- Fiber 7
- Carbs 20
- Protein 5

Tasty Braised Fennel

You will love fennel from now on!

Preparation time: 10 minutes
Cooking time: 12 minutes
Servings: 4
Ingredients:

- 2 fennel bulbs, trimmed and cut into quarters
- 3 tablespoons extra virgin olive oil
- Salt and black pepper to the taste
- 1 garlic clove, chopped
- 1 dried red pepper
- ¾ cup veggie stock
- Juice of ½ lemon
- ¼ cup white wine
- ¼ cup parmesan, grated

Directions:

1. Set your instant pot on Sauté mode, add oil and heat it up.
2. Add garlic and red pepper, stir, cook for 2 minutes and discard garlic.
3. Add fennel, stir and brown it for 8 minutes.
4. Add salt, pepper, stock, wine, cover and cook at High for 4 minutes.
5. Release the pressure, uncover the pot, add lemon juice, more salt and pepper if needed and cheese.
6. Toss to coat, divide among plates and serve.

Enjoy!

Nutrition:

- Calories 70
- Fat 1
- Fiber 2
- Carbs 2
- Protein 1

Fennel Risotto

This is simple to make and it will taste great!

Preparation time: 10 minutes
Cooking time: 10 minutes
Servings: 2
Ingredients:

- 1 and ½ cups Arborio rice
- 1 yellow onion, chopped
- 3 cups chicken stock
- 1 fennel bulb, trimmed and chopped
- 2 tablespoons butter
- 1 tablespoon extra virgin olive oil
- ¼ cup white wine
- Salt and black pepper to the taste
- ½ teaspoon thyme, dried
- 3 tablespoons tomato paste
- 1/3 cup parmesan cheese, grated

Directions:

1. Set your instant pot on Sauté mode, add butter and melt it.
2. Add fennel and onion, stir, sauté for 4 minutes and transfer to a bowl.
3. Add oil to your pot and heat it up.
4. Add rice, stir and cook for 3 minutes.
5. Add tomato paste, stock, fennel, onions, wine, salt, pepper and thyme, stir, cover and cook at High for 8 minutes.
6. Release the pressure, uncover, add cheese, stir, divide among plates and serve.

Enjoy!
Nutrition:

- Calories 200
- Fat 10
- Fiber 2
- Carbs 20
- Protein 12

Kale With Garlic And Lemon

Kale is a very delicious green veggie! Try this next recipe and enjoy!

Preparation time: 10 minutes
Cooking time: 5 minutes
Servings: 4
Ingredients:

- 3 garlic cloves, chopped
- 1 tablespoon extra virgin olive oil
- 1 pound kale, trimmed
- Salt and black pepper to the taste
- ½ cup water
- Juice of ½ lemon

Directions:

1. Set the instant pot on Sauté mode, add oil and heat it up.
2. Add garlic, stir and cook for 2 minutes.
3. Add kale and water, cover and cook at High for 5 minutes.
4. Release the pressure, uncover the pot, add salt, pepper and lemon juice, stir, divide among plates and serve.

Enjoy!
Nutrition:

- Calories 60
- Fat 3
- Fiber 1
- Carbs 2.4
- Protein 0.7

Braised Kale

Everyone will love this dish!

Preparation time: 10 minutes
Cooking time: 10 minutes
Servings: 2
Ingredients:

- 10 ounces kale, chopped
- 1 yellow onion, thinly sliced
- 1 tablespoon kale
- 3 carrots, sliced
- ½ cup chicken stock
- 5 garlic cloves, chopped
- Salt and black pepper to the taste
- A splash of balsamic vinegar
- ¼ teaspoon red pepper flakes

Directions:

1. Set your instant pot on Sauté mode, add ghee and melt it.
2. Add carrots and onion, stir and sauté for 2 minutes.
3. Add garlic, stir and cook for 1 minute more.
4. Add kale, stock, salt and pepper, stir, cover and cook at High for 7 minutes.
5. Release the pressure, uncover the pot, add vinegar and pepper flakes, toss to coat, divide among plates and serve.

Enjoy!

Nutrition:

- Calories 60
- Fat 2
- Fiber 2
- Carbs 4
- Protein 1

Kale And Bacon

It's so tasty and incredibly easy to make!

Preparation time: 10 minutes
Cooking time: 10 minute
Servings: 4
Ingredients:

- 6 bacon slices, chopped
- 1 tablespoon vegetable oil
- 1 onion, thinly sliced
- 6 garlic cloves, chopped
- 1 and ½ cups chicken stock
- 1 tablespoon brown sugar
- 2 tablespoons apple cider vinegar
- 10 ounces kale leaves, chopped
- 1 teaspoon red chili, crushed
- 1 teaspoon liquid smoke
- Salt and black pepper to the taste

Directions:

1. Set your instant pot on Sauté mode, add oil and heat it up.
2. Add bacon, stir and cook for 1-2 minutes.
3. Add onion, stir and cook for 3 minutes.
4. Add garlic, stir and cook for 1 minute.
5. Add vinegar, stock, sugar, liquid smoke, red chilies, salt, pepper, kale, stir, cover and cook at High for 5 minutes.
6. Release the pressure fast, uncover, divide among plates and serve.

Enjoy!
Nutrition:

- Calories 140
- Fat 7
- Fiber 1
- Carbs 7
- Protein 2

Okra Pilaf

It's so delicious!

Preparation time: 10 minutes
Cooking time: 25 minutes
Servings: 4
Ingredients:

- 2 cups okra, sliced
- 4 bacon slices, chopped
- 2 teaspoons paprika
- 1 cup brown rice
- 1 cup tomatoes, chopped
- 2 and ¼ cups water
- Salt and black pepper to the taste

Directions:

1. Set your instant pot on Sauté mode, add bacon and brown it for 2 minutes.
2. Add okra, stir and cook 5 minutes.
3. Add paprika and rice, stir and cook for 2 minutes.
4. Add salt, pepper, water and tomatoes, stir, cover and cook for 16 minutes.
5. Release the pressure, uncover pot, divide pilaf among plates and serve.

Enjoy!
Nutrition:

- Calories 300
- Fat 11
- Fiber 4.2
- Carbs 41
- Protein 7.8

Okra And Corn

You can serve this with some fried chicken!

Preparation time: 10 minutes
Cooking time: 17 minutes
Servings: 6
Ingredients:

- 1 pound okra, trimmed
- 6 scallions, chopped
- 3 green bell peppers, chopped
- Salt and black pepper to the taste
- 2 tablespoons vegetable oil
- 1 teaspoon sugar
- 28 ounces canned tomatoes, chopped
- 1 cup corn kernels

Directions:

1. Set your instant pot on Sauté mode, add oil and heat it up.
2. Add scallions and bell peppers, stir and cook for 5 minutes.
3. Add okra, salt, pepper, sugar and tomatoes, stir, cover and cook at High for 10 minutes.
4. Release the pressure fast, uncover, add corn, cover pot again and cook at High for 2 minutes.
5. Release pressure again, transfer okra mix on plates and serve.

Enjoy!
Nutrition:

- Calories 140
- Fat 5
- Fiber 6
- Carbs 22
- Protein 4
- Sugar 9

Steamed Leeks

It's not just delicious! It's so simple to make it!

Preparation time: 10 minutes
Cooking time: 10 minutes
Servings: 4
Ingredients:

- 4 leeks, washed, roots and ends cut off
- Salt and black pepper to the taste
- 1/3 cup water
- 1 tablespoon butter

Directions:

1. Put leeks in your instant pot, add water and butter, salt and pepper to the taste, stir, cover and cook at High for 5 minutes.
2. Release the pressure fast, uncover the pot, set it on Sauté mode and cook leeks for 5 more minutes.
3. Divide among plates and serve.

Enjoy!
Nutrition:

- Calories 70
- Fat 4
- Fiber 1.4
- Carbs 10
- Protein 1.2

Crispy Potatoes

Use your instant pot to make the best crispy potatoes ever!

Preparation time: 10 minutes
Cooking time: 7 minutes
Servings: 4
Ingredients:

- ½ cup water
- 1 pound gold potatoes, cubed
- Salt and black pepper to the taste
- 2 tablespoons ghee
- Juice of ½ lemon
- ¼ cup parsley leaves, chopped

Directions:

1. Put the water in your instant pot, add potatoes in the steamer basket, cover and cook at High for 5 minutes.
2. Release the pressure naturally, uncover the pot and set it on Sauté mode.
3. Add ghee, lemon juice, parsley, salt and pepper, stir and cook for 2 minutes.
4. Transfer to plates and serve.

Enjoy!
Nutrition:

- Calories 132
- Fat 1
- Fiber 0
- Carbs 23
- Protein 3

Roasted Potatoes

This recipe might sound surreal, but we can assure you can make it using your instant pot!

Preparation time: 10 minutes
Cooking time: 17 minutes
Servings: 4
Ingredients:

- 2 pounds baby potatoes
- 5 tablespoons vegetable oil
- Salt and black pepper to the taste
- 1 rosemary spring
- 5 garlic cloves
- ½ cup stock

Directions:

1. Set your instant pot on Sauté mode, add oil and heat it up.
2. Add potatoes, rosemary and garlic, stir and brown them for 10 minutes.
3. Prick each potato with a knife, add stock, salt and pepper to the pot, cover and cook at High for 7 minutes.
4. Release the pressure, uncover the pot, divide potatoes among plates and serve.

Enjoy!
Nutrition:

- Calories 50
- Fat 1.4
- Fiber 1
- Carbs 7.4
- Protein 1

Zucchinis And Tomatoes

Do you feel like eating something light tonight? Then try this great recipe!

Preparation time: 10 minutes
Cooking time: 12 minutes
Servings: 4
Ingredients:

- 6 zucchinis, roughly chopped
- 2 yellow onions, chopped
- 1 tablespoon vegetable oil
- 1 cup tomato puree
- 1 pound cherry tomatoes, cut into halves
- A drizzle of olive oil
- Salt and black pepper to the taste
- 2 garlic cloves, minced
- 1 bunch basil, chopped

Directions:

1. Set your instant pot on Sauté mode, add vegetable oil and heat it up.
2. Add onion, stir and cook for 5 minutes.
3. Add tomatoes, tomato puree, zucchinis, salt and pepper, stir, cover and cook at High for 5 minutes.
4. Release the pressure, uncover the pot, add garlic and basil, stir and divide among plates.
5. Drizzle some olive oil at the end and serve.

Enjoy!
Nutrition:

- Calories 155
- Fat 2
- Fiber 4
- Carbs 12
- Protein 22

Turnips And Carrots

This dish is wonderful and very delicious!

Preparation time: 5 minutes
Cooking time: 9 minutes
Servings: 4
Ingredients:

- 2 turnips, peeled and sliced
- 3 carrots, sliced
- 1 small onion, chopped
- 1 teaspoon cumin, ground
- 1 tablespoon extra virgin olive oil
- 1 cup water
- Salt and black pepper to the taste
- 1 teaspoon lemon juice

Directions:

1. Set your instant pot on Sauté mode, add oil and heat it up.
2. Add onion, stir and sauté for 2 minutes.
3. Add turnips, carrots, cumin and lemon juice, stir and cook for 1 minute.
4. Add salt, pepper, and water, stir, cover and cook at High for 6 minutes.
5. Release the pressure, uncover the pot, divide turnips and carrots among plates and serve.

Enjoy!

Nutrition:

- Calories 70
- Fat 0
- Fiber 1
- Carbs 0.4
- Protein 2

Spicy Turnips

This is an authentic Indian style dish!

Preparation time: 10 minutes
Cooking time: 22 minutes
Servings: 4
Ingredients:

- 20 ounces turnips, peeled and chopped
- 1 teaspoon garlic, minced
- 1 teaspoon ginger, grated
- 2 yellow onions, chopped
- 2 tomatoes, chopped
- 1 teaspoon sugar
- 1 teaspoon cumin powder
- 1 teaspoon coriander powder
- 2 green chilies, chopped
- ½ teaspoon turmeric powder
- 1 cup water
- 2 tablespoons butter
- Salt to the taste
- A handful coriander leaves, chopped

Directions:

1. Set your instant pot on Sauté mode, add butter and melt it.
2. Add green chilies, garlic and ginger, stir and cook for 1 minute.
3. Add onions, stir and cook 3 minutes.
4. Add salt, tomatoes, turmeric, cumin and coriander powder, stir and cook 3 minutes.
5. Add turnips and water, stir, cover and cook on Low for 15 minutes.
6. Release the pressure, uncover the pot, add sugar and coriander, stir, divide among plates and serve.

Enjoy!

Nutrition:

- Calories 80
- Fat 2.4
- Fiber 4
- Carbs 12
- Protein 3

Stuffed Tomatoes

You will feel full and satisfied with this great dish!

Preparation time: 10 minutes
Cooking time: 10 minutes
Servings: 4
Ingredients:

- 4 tomatoes, tops cut off and pulp scooped
- Salt and black pepper to the taste
- 1 yellow onion, chopped
- 1 tablespoon butter
- 2 tablespoons celery, chopped
- ½ cup mushrooms, chopped
- 1 slice of bread, crumbled
- 1 cup cottage cheese
- ¼ teaspoon caraway seeds
- 1 tablespoon parsley, chopped
- ½ cup water

Directions:

1. Chop tomato pulp and put it in a bowl.
2. Heat up a pan with the butter over medium high heat, add onion and celery, stir and cook for 3 minutes.
3. Add tomato pulp and mushrooms, stir and cook for 1 minute more.
4. Add salt, pepper, crumbled bread, cheese, caraway seeds and parsley, stir and cook for 4 minutes more.
5. Fill each tomato with this mix and arrange them in the steamer basket of your instant pot.
6. Add the water to the pot, cover and cook at High for 2 minutes.
7. Release the pressure fast, uncover the pot, transfer stuffed potatoes to plates and serve.

Enjoy!

Nutrition:

- Calories 140
- Fat 3
- Fiber 1.4
- Carbs 10
- Protein 4

Tasty Chicken Soup

It's a Mexican style soup your family will love!

Preparation time: 10 minutes
Cooking time: 17 minutes
Servings: 4
Ingredients:

- 4 chicken breasts, skinless and boneless
- 2 tablespoons extra virgin olive oil
- 1 onion, chopped
- 3 garlic cloves, minced
- 16 ounces jarred chunky salsa
- 29 ounces canned tomatoes, peeled and chopped
- 29 ounces canned chicken stock
- Salt and black pepper to the taste
- 2 tablespoons parsley, dried
- 1 teaspoon garlic powder
- 1 tablespoon onion powder
- 1 tablespoon chili powder
- 15 ounces frozen corn
- 32 ounces canned black beans, drained

Directions:

1. Set your instant pot on Sauté mode, add oil and heat it up.
2. Add onion, stir and cook 5 minutes.
3. Add garlic, stir and cook for 1 minute more.
4. Add chicken breasts, salsa, tomatoes, stock, salt, pepper, parsley, garlic powder, onion and chili powder, stir, cover and cook at High for 8 minutes.
5. Release the pressure for 10 minutes, uncover the pot, transfer chicken breasts to a cutting board, shred with 2 forks and return to pot.
6. Add beans and corn, set the pot on Simmer mode and cook for 2-3 minutes more.
7. Divide into soup bowls and serve.

Enjoy!

Nutrition:

- Calories 210
- Fat 4.4
- Fiber 4.3
- Carbs 18
- Protein 26

Tasty Corn Soup

It's very exciting to learn something new each day! Today, you get to learn how to make the best corn soup!

Preparation time: 10 minutes
Cooking time: 15 minutes
Servings: 4
Ingredients:

- 2 leeks, chopped
- 2 tablespoons butter
- 2 garlic cloves, minced
- 6 ears of corn, kernels cut off, cobs reserved
- 2 bay leaves
- 4 tarragon sprigs, chopped
- 1-quart chicken stock
- Salt and black pepper to the taste
- A drizzle of extra virgin olive oil
- 1 tablespoon chives, chopped

Directions:

1. Set your instant pot on Sauté mode, add butter and melt it.
2. Add garlic and leeks, stir and cook for 4 minutes.
3. Add corn, corn cobs, bay leaves, tarragon and stock to cover everything, cover pot and cook at High for 15 minutes.
4. Release the pressure, uncover the pot, discard bay leaves and corn cobs and transfer everything to your blender.
5. Pulse well o obtain a smooth soup, add the rest of the stock and blend again.
6. Add salt and pepper to the taste, stir well, divide into soup bowls and serve cold with chives and olive oil on top.

Enjoy!

Nutrition:

- Calories 300
- Fat 8.3
- Fiber 8
- Carbs 50
- Protein 13

Butternut Squash Soup

It's so creamy and smooth! It's so good!

Preparation time: 10 minutes
Cooking time: 16 minutes
Servings: 6
Ingredients:

- 1 and ½ pounds butternut squash, baked, peeled and cubed
- ½ cup green onions, chopped
- 3 tablespoons butter
- ½ cup carrots, chopped
- ½ cup celery, chopped
- 29 ounces canned chicken stock
- 1 garlic clove, minced
- ½ teaspoon Italian seasoning
- 15 ounces canned tomatoes and their juice, chopped
- Salt and black pepper to the taste
- 1/8 teaspoon red pepper flakes, dried
- 1 cup orzo, already cooked
- 1/8 teaspoon nutmeg, grated
- 1 and ½ cup half and half
- 1 cup chicken meat, already cooked and shredded
- Some green onions, chopped for serving

Directions:

1. Set your instant pot on Sauté mode, add butter and melt it.
2. Add celery, carrots and onions, stir and cook for 3 minutes.
3. Add garlic, stir and cook for 1 minute more.
4. Add squash, tomatoes, stock, Italian seasoning, salt, pepper, pepper flakes and nutmeg.
5. Stir, cover and cook at High for 10 minutes.
6. Release the pressure fast, uncover and puree everything with your immersion blender.
7. Set the pot on Simmer mode, add half and half, orzo and chicken, stir and cook for 3 minutes.
8. Divide soup into bowls, sprinkle green onions on top and serve.

Enjoy!
Nutrition:

- Calories 130
- Fat 2.3
- Fiber 0.4
- Carbs 18
- Protein 6

Potato And Cheese Soup

This is one of the best combinations you could ever make!

Preparation time: 10 minutes
Cooking time: 10 minutes
Servings: 6
Ingredients:

- 6 cups potatoes, cubed
- 2 tablespoons butter
- ½ cup yellow onion, chopped
- 28 ounces canned chicken stock
- Salt and black pepper to the taste
- 2 tablespoons parsley, dried
- 1/8 red pepper flakes
- 2 tablespoons cornstarch
- 2 tablespoons water
- 3 ounces cream cheese, cubed
- 2 cups half and half
- 1 cup cheddar cheese, shredded
- 1 cup corn
- 6 bacon slices, cooked and crumbled

Directions:

1. Set your instant pot on Sauté mode, add butter and melt it.
2. Add onion, stir and cook 5 minutes
3. Add half of the stock, salt, pepper, pepper flakes and parsley and stir.
4. Put potatoes in the steamer basket, cover the pot and cook at High for 4 minutes.
5. Release the pressure fast, uncover pot and transfer potatoes to a bowl.
6. In another bowl, mix cornstarch with water and stir well.
7. Set the pot to Simmer mode, add cornstarch, cream cheese and shredded cheese and stir well.
8. Also add the rest of the stock, corn, bacon, potatoes, half and half.
9. Stir, bring to a simmer, ladle into bowls and serve.

Enjoy!

Nutrition:

- Calories 188
- Fat 7.14
- Fiber 1.5
- Carbs 22
- Protein 9

Split Pea Soup

Make sure you try this creamy soup as soon as possible!

Preparation time: 10 minutes
Cooking time: 20 minutes
Servings: 6
Ingredients:

- 2 tablespoons butter
- 1 pound chicken sausage, ground
- 1 yellow onion, chopped
- ½ cup carrots, chopped
- ½ cup celery, chopped
- 2 garlic cloves, minced
- 29 ounces chicken stock
- Salt and black pepper to the taste
- 2 cups water
- 16 ounces split peas, rinsed
- ½ cup half and half
- ¼ teaspoon red pepper flakes, dried

Directions:

1. Set the pot on Sauté mode, add sausage, brown it on all sides and transfer to a plate.
2. Add butter to your instant pot and melt it.
3. Add celery, onions, and carrots, stir and cook 4 minutes.
4. Add garlic, stir and cook for 1 minute.
5. Add water, stock, peas and pepper flakes, stir, cover and cook at High for 10 minutes.
6. Release the pressure, puree the mix using an immersion blender and set the pot on Simmer mode.
7. Add sausage, salt, pepper and half and half, stir, bring to a simmer and ladle into soup bowls.

Enjoy!

Nutrition:

- Calories 30
- Fat 11
- Fiber 12
- Carbs 14
- Protein 20

Beef And Rice Soup

If your loved ones need a hearty and rich soup, then this is the one you have to make for them!

Preparation time: 10 minutes
Cooking time: 15 minutes
Servings: 6
Ingredients:

- 1 pound beef meat, ground
- 3 garlic cloves, minced
- 1 yellow onion, chopped
- 1 tablespoon vegetable oil
- 1 celery rib, chopped
- 28 ounces canned beef stock
- 14 ounces canned tomatoes, crushed
- ½ cup white rice
- 12 ounces spicy V8 juice
- 15 ounces canned garbanzo beans, rinsed
- 1 potato, cubed
- Salt and black pepper to the taste
- ½ cup frozen peas
- 2 carrots, thinly sliced

Directions:

1. Set your instant pot on Sauté mode, add beef, stir, cook until it browns and transfer to a plate.
2. Add the oil to your pot and heat it up.
3. Add celery and onion, stir and cook for 5 minutes.
4. Add garlic, stir and cook for 1 minute more.
5. Add V8 juice, stock, tomatoes, rice, beans, carrots, potatoes, beef, salt and pepper, stir, cover and cook at High for 5 minutes.
6. Release the pressure, uncover the pot and set it on Simmer mode.
7. Add more salt and pepper if needed and peas, stir, bring to a simmer, transfer to bowls and serve hot.

Enjoy!
Nutrition:

- Calories 230
- Fat 7
- Fiber 4
- Carbs 10
- Protein 3

Chicken Noodle Soup

This is a comfort food everyone loves for sure!

Preparation time: 10 minutes
Cooking time: 12 minutes
Servings: 6
Ingredients:

- 1 yellow onion, chopped
- 1 tablespoon butter
- 1 celery rib, chopped
- 4 carrots, sliced
- Salt and black pepper to the taste
- 6 cups chicken stock
- 2 cups chicken, already cooked and shredded
- Egg noodles, already cooked

Directions:

1. Set your instant pot on Sauté mode, add butter and heat it up.
2. Add onion, stir and cook 2 minutes.
3. Add celery and carrots, stir and cook 5 minutes.
4. Add chicken, stock, stir, cover pot and cook at High for 5 minutes.
5. Release the pressure, uncover the pot, add salt and pepper to the taste and stir.
6. Divide noodles into soup bowls, add soup over them and serve.

Enjoy!
Nutrition:

- Calories 100
- Fat 1
- Fiber 1
- Carbs 4
- Protein 7

Chicken And Wild Rice Soup

If you are looking for a special soup, then this one is perfect for you!

Preparation time: 10 minutes
Cooking time: 15 minutes
Servings: 6
Ingredients:

- 1 cup yellow onion, chopped
- 2 tablespoons butter
- 1 cup celery, chopped
- 1 cup carrots, chopped
- 28 ounces chicken stock
- 2 chicken breasts, skinless and boneless and chopped
- 6 ounces wild rice
- A pinch of red pepper flakes
- Salt and black pepper to the taste
- 1 tablespoon parsley, dried
- 2 tablespoons cornstarch mixed with 2 tablespoons water
- 1 cup milk
- 1 cup half and half
- 4 ounces cream cheese, cubed

Directions:

1. Set your instant pot on Sauté mode, add butter and melt it.
2. Add carrot, onion and celery, stir and cook for 5 minutes.
3. Add rice, chicken, stock, parsley, salt and pepper, stir, cover and cook at High for 5 minutes.
4. Release the pressure, uncover, add cornstarch mixed with water, stir and set the pot on Simmer mode.
5. Add cheese, milk and half and half, stir, heat up, transfer to bowls and serve.

Enjoy!

Nutrition:

- Calories 200
- Fat 7
- Fiber 1
- Carbs 19
- Protein 5

Creamy Tomato Soup

This next recipe will hypnotize your taste buds!

Preparation time: 10 minutes
Cooking time: 6 minutes
Servings: 8
Ingredients:

- 1 yellow onion, chopped
- 3 tablespoons butter
- 1 carrot, chopped
- 2 celery stalks, chopped
- 2 garlic cloves, minced
- 29 ounces canned chicken stock
- Salt and black pepper to the taste
- ¼ cup basil, chopped
- 3 pounds tomatoes, peeled, cored and cut into quarters
- 1 tablespoon tomato paste
- 1 cup half and half
- ½ cup parmesan cheese, shredded

Directions:

1. Set your instant pot on Sauté mode, add butter and melt it.
2. Add onion, carrots and celery, stir and cook for 3 minutes.
3. Add garlic, stir and cook for 1 minute more.
4. Add tomatoes, tomato paste, stock, basil, salt and pepper, stir, cover and cook at High for 5 minutes.
5. Release the pressure, uncover pot and puree soup using and immersion blender.
6. Add half and half and cheese, stir, set the pot on Simmer mode and heat everything up.
7. Divide into soup bowls and serve.

Enjoy!

Nutrition:

- Calories 280
- Fat 8
- Fiber 4
- Carbs 32
- Protein 24

Zuppa Toscana

It's very flavored and creamy!

Preparation time: 10 minutes
Cooking time: 17 minutes
Servings: 8
Ingredients:

- 1 pound chicken sausage, ground
- 6 bacon slices, chopped
- 3 garlic cloves, minced
- 1 cup yellow onion, chopped
- 1 tablespoon butter
- 40 ounces chicken stock
- Salt and black pepper to the taste
- A pinch of red pepper flakes
- 3 potatoes, cubed
- 3 tablespoons cornstarch
- 12 ounces evaporated milk
- 1 cup parmesan, shredded
- 2 cup spinach, chopped

Directions:

1. Set your instant pot on Sauté mode, add bacon, stir, cook until it's crispy and transfer to a plate.
2. Add sausage to the pot, stir, cook until it browns on all sides and also transfer to a plate.
3. Add butter to the pot and melt it.
4. Add onion, stir and cook for 5 minutes.
5. Add garlic, stir and cook for 1 minute.
6. Add 1/3 of the stock, salt, pepper and pepper flakes and stir.
7. Place potatoes in the steamer basket of the pot, cover and cook at High for 4 minutes.
8. Release the pressure fast, uncover and transfer potatoes to a bowl.
9. Add the rest of the stock to the pot, cornstarch mixed with some evaporated milk and the milk, stir and set the pot on Simmer mode.
10. Add parmesan, sausage, bacon, potatoes, spinach, more salt and pepper if needed, stir, divide into bowls and serve.

Enjoy!

Nutrition:

- Calories 170
- Fat 4
- Fiber 2
- Carbs 24
- Protein 10

Minestrone Soup

We are sure everyone has heard about this great soup! Then let's make it today!

Preparation time: 10 minutes
Cooking time: 15 minutes
Servings: 8
Ingredients:

- 1 tablespoon extra virgin olive oil
- 1 celery stalk, chopped
- 2 carrots, chopped
- 1 onion, chopped
- 1 cup corn kernels
- 1 zucchini, chopped
- 3 pounds tomatoes, peeled and chopped
- 4 garlic cloves, minced
- 29 ounces canned chicken stock
- 1 cup uncooked pasta
- Salt and black pepper to the taste
- 1 teaspoon Italian seasoning
- 2 cups baby spinach
- 15 ounces canned kidney beans
- 1 cup asiago cheese, grated
- 2 tablespoons basil, chopped

Directions:

1. Set your instant pot on Sauté mode, ad oil and heat it up.
2. Add onion, stir and cook for 5 minutes.
3. Add carrots, garlic, celery, corn and zucchini, stir and cook 5 minutes.
4. Add tomatoes, stock, Italian seasoning, pasta, salt and pepper, stir, cover and cook at High for 4 minutes.
5. Release the pressure fast, uncover, add beans, basil and spinach.
6. Add more salt and pepper if needed, divide into bowls, add cheese on top and serve.

Enjoy!

Nutrition:

- Calories 110
- Fat 2
- Fiber 4
- Carbs 18
- Protein 5

Different Tomato Soup

You get to discover one of the most delicious soups ever!

Preparation time: 10 minutes
Cooking time: 45 minutes
Servings: 6
Ingredients:

For the roasted tomatoes:

- 14 garlic cloves, crushed
- 3 pounds cherry tomatoes, cut into halves
- Salt and black pepper to the taste
- 2 tablespoons extra virgin olive oil
- ½ teaspoon red pepper flakes

For the soup:

- 1 yellow onion, chopped
- 2 tablespoons olive oil
- 1 red bell pepper, chopped
- 3 tablespoons tomato paste
- 2 celery ribs, chopped
- 2 cups chicken stock
- 1 teaspoon garlic powder
- 1 teaspoon onion powder
- ½ tablespoon basil, dried
- ½ teaspoon red pepper flakes
- Salt and black pepper to the taste
- 1 cup heavy cream

For serving:

- Basil leaves, chopped
- ½ cup parmesan, grated

Directions:

1. Place tomatoes and garlic in a baking tray, drizzle 2 tablespoons oil, season with salt, pepper and ½ teaspoons red pepper flakes, toss to coat, introduce in the oven at 425 degrees F and roast for 25 minutes.
2. Take tomatoes out of the oven and leave them aside for now.
3. Set your instant pot on Sauté mode, add 2 tablespoons oil and heat it up.
4. Add onion, bell pepper and celery and stir.
5. Also add salt, pepper, garlic powder, onion powder, dried basil and ½ teaspoon pepper flakes, stir and cook for 3 minutes.
6. Add tomato paste, roasted tomatoes and garlic and stir.
7. Add stock, cover pot and cook at High for 10 minutes.
8. Release the pressure naturally, uncover the pot and set it on Sauté mode.
9. Add heavy cream and blend everything using an immersion blender.
10. Divide in bowls, add basil leaves and cheese on top and serve.

Enjoy!

Nutrition:

- Calories 150
- Fat 1
- Fiber 3
- Carbs 3
- Protein 4

Delicious Carrot Soup

It's a creamy soup you can make very fast in your instant pot!

Preparation time: 10 minutes
Cooking time: 16 minutes
Servings: 4

Ingredients:

- 1 tablespoon vegetable oil
- 1 onion, chopped
- 1 tablespoon butter
- 1 garlic clove, minced
- 1 pound carrots, chopped
- 1 small ginger piece, grated
- Salt and black pepper to the taste
- ¼ teaspoon brown sugar
- 2 cups chicken stock
- 1 tablespoon Sriracha
- 14 ounces canned coconut milk
- Cilantro leaves, chopped for serving

Directions:

1. Set your instant pot on Sauté mode, add butter and oil and heat them up.
2. Add onion, stir and cook for 3 minutes.
3. Add ginger and garlic, stir and cook for 1 minute.
4. Add sugar, carrots, salt and pepper, stir and cook 2 minutes more.
5. Add sriracha sauce, coconut milk, stock, stir, cover and cook at High for 6 minutes.
6. Release the pressure for 10 minutes, uncover, blend soup with an immersion blender, add more salt and pepper if needed and divide into soup bowls.
7. Add cilantro on top and serve.

Enjoy!

Nutrition:

- Calories 60
- Fat 1
- Fiber 3.1
- Carbs 12
- Protein 2

Ham And White Bean Soup

It's hearty and rustic! Try it!

Preparation time: 10 minutes
Cooking time: 15 minutes
Servings: 8
Ingredients:

- 1 pound white beans, soaked for 1 hour and drained
- 1 carrot, chopped
- 1 tablespoon extra virgin olive oil
- 1 yellow onion, chopped
- 3 garlic cloves, minced
- 1 tomato, peeled and chopped
- 1 pound ham, chopped
- Salt and black pepper to the taste
- 4 cups water
- 4 cups veggie stock
- 1 teaspoon mint, dried
- 1 teaspoon paprika
- 1 teaspoon thyme, dried

Directions:

1. Set your instant pot on Sauté mode, add oil and heat it up.
2. Add carrot, onion, garlic, tomato, stir and cook for 5 minutes.
3. Add beans, ham, salt, pepper, water, stock, mint, paprika and thyme, stir, cover and cook at High for 15 minutes.
4. Release the pressure for 10 minutes, uncover, divide into soup bowls and serve.

Enjoy!

Nutrition:

- Calories 177
- Fat 2
- Fiber 1
- Carbs 26
- Protein 14

Lentils Soup

It's a delicious and easy soup!

Preparation time: 10 minutes
Cooking time: 30 minutes
Servings: 4
Ingredients:

- 2 celery stalks, chopped
- 1 tablespoon olive oil
- 1 small onion, chopped
- 2 carrots, chopped
- ½ pound chicken sausage, ground
- 3 and ½ cups beef stock
- 2 teaspoons garlic, minced
- 1 cup lentils
- 15 ounces canned tomatoes, chopped
- Salt and black pepper to the taste
- 2 cups spinach

Directions:

1. Set your instant pot on Sauté mode, add oil and heat it up.
2. Add celery, onion, carrots, stir and cook for 4 minutes.
3. Add chicken sausage, stir and cook 5 minutes.
4. Add stock, garlic, lentils, tomatoes, salt, pepper and spinach, stir, cover and cook at High for 25 minutes.
5. Release the pressure fast, uncover, divide into soup bowls and serve.

Enjoy!

Nutrition:

- Calories 175
- Fat 1
- Fiber 1
- Carbs 2
- Protein 2

Cabbage Soup

Just trust us and try this special soup soon!

Preparation time: 10 minutes
Cooking time: 10 minutes
Servings: 4
Ingredients:

- 1 cabbage head, chopped
- 12 ounces baby carrots
- 3 celery stalks, chopped
- ½ onion, chopped
- 1 packet veggie soup mix
- 2 tablespoons olive oil
- 12 ounces soy burger
- 3 teaspoons garlic, minced
- ¼ cup cilantro, chopped
- 4 cups chicken stock
- Salt and black pepper to the taste

Directions:

1. In your instant pot, mix cabbage with celery, carrots, onion, veggie soup mix, soy burger, stock, olive oil and garlic, stir, cover and cook on High for 5 minutes.
2. Release pressure, uncover the pot, add salt, pepper and cilantro, stir again well, divide into soup bowls and serve.

Enjoy!

Nutrition:

- Calories 100
- Fat 1
- Fiber 2
- Carbs 10
- Protein 10

Tasty Cream Of Asparagus

It is so delicious and creamy! We love this soup!

Preparation time: 10 minutes
Cooking time: 25 minutes
Servings: 4
Ingredients:

- 2 pounds green asparagus, trimmed, tips cut off and cut into medium pieces
- 3 tablespoons butter
- 1 yellow onion, chopped
- 6 cups chicken stock
- ¼ teaspoon lemon juice
- ½ cup crème fraiche
- Salt and white pepper to the taste

Directions:

1. Set your instant pot on Sauté mode, add butter and melt it.
2. Add asparagus, salt and pepper, stir and cook for 5 minutes.
3. Add 5 cups stock, cover pot and cook on Low for 15 minutes.
4. Release the pressure, uncover the pot and transfer soup to your blender.
5. Pulse very well and return to pot.
6. Set the pot on Simmer mode, add crème fraiche, the rest of the stock, salt and pepper and lemon juice, bring to a boil, divide into soup bowls and serve.

Enjoy!
Nutrition:

- Calories 80
- Fat 8
- Fiber 1
- Carbs 16
- Protein 6.3

Artichoke Soup

You will love artichokes once you learn how to make this next dish!

Preparation time: 10 minutes
Cooking time: 20 minutes
Servings: 4
Ingredients:

- 5 artichoke hearts, washed and trimmed
- 1 leek, sliced
- 5 tablespoons butter
- 6 garlic cloves, minced
- ½ cup shallots, chopped
- 8 ounces gold potatoes, chopped
- 12 cups chicken stock
- 1 bay leaf
- 4 parsley springs
- 2 thyme springs
- ¼ teaspoon black peppercorns, crushed
- Salt to the taste
- ¼ cup cream

Directions:

1. Set your instant pot on Sauté mode, add butter and melt it.
2. Add artichoke hearts, shallots, leek and garlic, stir and brown for 3-4 minutes.
3. Add potatoes, stock, bay leaf, thyme, parsley, peppercorns and salt, stir, cover and cook at High for 15 minutes.
4. Release the pressure, uncover the pot, discard herbs, blend well using an immersion blender, add salt to the taste and cream, stir well, divide into bowls and serve.

Enjoy!

Nutrition:

- Calories 95
- Fat 2
- Fiber 4
- Carbs 15
- Protein 4

Beet Soup

It's an amazing soup with such an intense taste and color!

Preparation time: 10 minutes
Cooking time: 10 minutes
Servings: 4
Ingredients:

- 1 tablespoon sesame oil
- 1 cup red lentils
- 1 red onion, chopped
- 2 carrots, chopped
- 3 beets, chopped
- 3 bay leaves
- 6 cups veggie stock
- ½ teaspoon thyme leaves, chopped
- 3 tablespoons dark miso
- 1 and ½ tablespoons parsley, chopped
- Salt and black pepper to the taste

Directions:

1. Set your instant pot on Sauté mode, add oil and heat it up.
2. Add onion, stir and cook for 5 minutes.
3. Add lentils, carrots, beets, thyme, bay leaves, stock, salt and pepper, stir, cover and cook at High for 5 minutes.
4. Release the pressure, uncover the pot, discard bay leaves, puree soup using an immersion blender, add miso mixed with some water, more salt and pepper if needed and parsley, stir, divide into soup bowls and serve.

Enjoy!
Nutrition:

- Calories 100
- Fat 4
- Fiber 2
- Carbs 8
- Protein 3

Cream Of Broccoli

Make sure you prepare this soup as soon as possible!

Preparation time: 10 minutes
Cooking time: 10 minutes
Servings: 4
Ingredients:

- 1 yellow onion, chopped
- 3 carrots, chopped
- 1 potato, chopped
- 1 broccoli head, florets separated and chopped
- 1 tablespoons olive oil
- 2 cups chicken stock
- 5 garlic cloves, minced
- Salt and black pepper to the taste
- 2 tablespoons cream
- Cheddar cheese, grated for serving
- 1 tablespoon chives, chopped

Directions:

1. Set your instant pot on Sauté mode, add oil and heat it up.
2. Add onion and garlic, stir and cook for 2 minutes.
3. Add broccoli, carrots, potato, stock, salt and pepper, stir, cover and cook at High for 5 minutes.
4. Release the pressure, uncover the pot, set it on Simmer mode, add cream, cheese and chives, stir, heat up for 2 minutes, divide into bowls and serve.

Enjoy!

Nutrition:

- Calories 180
- Fat 11
- Fiber 3
- Carbs 14
- Protein 6

Celery Soup

This is so simple and yet so tasty!

Preparation time: 10 minutes
Cooking time: 17 minutes
Servings: 2
Ingredients:

- 1 yellow onion, chopped
- 7 celery stalks, chopped
- 3 potatoes, chopped
- 1 teaspoon extra virgin olive oil
- Salt and black pepper to the taste
- 4 cups veggie stock
- 1 tablespoon curry powder
- 1 teaspoon celery seeds
- A handful parsley, chopped for serving

Directions:

1. Set your instant pot on Sauté mode, add oil and heat it up.
2. Add onion, celery seeds and curry powder, stir and cook for 1 minute.
3. Add celery and potatoes, stir and cook for 5 minutes.
4. Add stock, salt, pepper stir, cover and cook at High for 10 minutes.
5. Release the pressure, uncover the pot, blend well using an immersion blender, add parsley, stir, divide into soup bowls and serve.

Enjoy!

Nutrition:

- Calories 90
- Fat 4
- Fiber 4
- Carbs 8.5
- Protein 2

Chestnut Soup

If you are planning a sophisticated dinner, then you should consider making this soup!

Preparation time: 10 minutes

Cooking time: 25 minutes

Servings: 4

Ingredients:

- 1 pound canned chestnuts, drained and rinsed
- 1 celery stalk, chopped
- 4 tablespoons butter
- 1 yellow onion, chopped
- 1 sage spring, chopped
- Salt and white pepper to the taste
- 1 bay leaf
- 1 potato, chopped
- 4 cups chicken stock
- 2 tablespoons rum
- A pinch of nutmeg
- Whole cream for serving
- Sage leaves, chopped for serving

Directions:

1. Set your instant pot on Sauté mode, add butter and melt it.
2. Add onion, sage, celery, salt and pepper, stir and cook for 5 minutes.
3. Add chestnuts, potato, bay leaf and stock, stir, cover and cook on Low for 20 minutes.
4. Release the pressure, uncover the pot, add nutmeg and rum, discard bay leaf and blend soup using an immersion blender.
5. Divide soup into bowls, add cream and sage leaves on top and serve.

Enjoy!

Nutrition:

- Calories 230
- Fat 13
- Fiber 2
- Carbs 22
- Protein 2.1

Easy Fennel Soup

It's so refreshing and amazing!

Preparation time: 10 minutes
Cooking time: 15 minutes
Servings: 3
Ingredients:

- 1 fennel bulb, chopped
- 1 bay leaf
- 1 leek, chopped
- 2 cups water
- 1 tablespoon extra virgin olive oil
- ½ cube vegetable bouillon
- Salt and black pepper to the taste
- 2 teaspoons parmesan cheese, grated

Directions:

1. In your instant pot, mix fennel with leek, bay leaf, vegetable bouillon and water.
2. Stir, cover and cook at High for 15 minutes.
3. Release the pressure, uncover the pot, add cheese, oil, salt and pepper, stir, divide into bowls and serve.

Enjoy!

Nutrition:

- Calories 100
- Fat 2.2
- Fiber 4
- Carbs 15
- Protein 5

Cauliflower Soup

You must try this cauliflower soup right away!

Preparation time: 10 minutes
Cooking time: 10 minutes
Servings: 6
Ingredients:

- 1 small onion, chopped
- 1 cauliflower head, florets separated and chopped
- 2 tablespoons butter
- 3 cups chicken stock
- Salt and black pepper to the taste
- 1 teaspoon garlic powder
- 4 ounces cream cheese, cubed
- 1 cup cheddar cheese, grated
- ½ cup half and half

Directions:

1. Set your instant pot on Sauté mode, add butter and melt it.
2. Add onion, stir and cook for 3 minutes.
3. Add cauliflower, stock, salt, pepper and garlic powder, stir, cover and cook at High for 5 minutes.
4. Release the pressure, uncover the pot, blend everything using an immersion blender, add more salt and pepper if needed, cream cheese, grated cheese and half and half.
5. Stir, set the pot on Simmer mode, heat up for 2 minutes, divide into soup bowls and serve.

Enjoy!

Nutrition:

- Calories 78
- Fat 1.2
- Fiber 1
- Carbs 10
- Protein 3

Turkey And Sweet Potato Soup

Learn how to make one of the most delicious soups ever!

Preparation time: 10 minutes
Cooking time: 12 minutes
Servings: 4
Ingredients:

- 1 pound Italian turkey sausage, chopped
- 1 yellow onion, chopped
- 2 celery stalks, chopped
- 2 carrots, chopped
- 1 big sweet potato, cubed
- 5 cups turkey stock
- 2 garlic cloves, minced
- 1 teaspoon red pepper flakes
- 1 teaspoon basil, dried
- 1 teaspoon oregano, dried
- Salt and black pepper to the taste
- 1 teaspoon thyme, dried
- 5 ounces spinach, chopped
- 2 bay leaves

Directions:

1. Set your instant pot on Sauté mode, add sausage, brown it and transfer to a plate.
2. Add onion, celery and carrots, stir and cook for 2 minutes.
3. Add potato, stir and cook 2 minutes.
4. Add stock, garlic, red pepper, salt, pepper, basil, oregano, thyme, spinach and bay leaves,
5. Stir, cover and cook at High for 4 minutes.
6. Release the pressure, uncover the pot, discard bay leaves, divide soup into bowls and serve.

Enjoy!

Nutrition:

- Calories 190
- Fat 12
- Fiber 1
- Carbs 2
- Protein 5

Chicken Meatball Soup

A cold winter day just became better with this soup!

Preparation time: 10 minutes

Cooking time: 20 minutes

Servings: 6

Ingredients:

- 1 and ½ pounds chicken breast, ground
- Salt and black pepper to the taste
- 2 tablespoons arrowroot powder
- 1 teaspoon garlic powder
- ½ teaspoon crushed red pepper
- 1 teaspoon onion powder
- ½ tablespoon basil, dried
- ½ tablespoon oregano, dried
- 2 tablespoons nutritional yeast

For the soup:

- 6 cups chicken stock
- 4 celery stalks, chopped
- 3 carrots, chopped
- 2 yellow onions, chopped
- 1 bunch kale, chopped
- 2 teaspoons thyme, dried
- 2 garlic cloves, minced
- ½ teaspoon red pepper, crushed
- 2 eggs, whisked
- 2 tablespoons extra virgin olive oil

Directions:

1. Set your instant pot on Sauté mode, add oil and heat it up.
2. Add onions, celery and carrots, stir and cook for 3 minutes.
3. Add garlic, salt, pepper, kale, stock, 2 teaspoons thyme and ½ teaspoon red pepper, stir and continue cooking.
4. Meanwhile, in a bowl mix chicken meat with arrow powder, salt, pepper, ½ teaspoon red pepper, garlic powder, onion powder, oregano, basil and yeast and stir well.
5. Shape meatballs using your hands and drop them gently into the soup.
6. Cover pot and cook at High for 15 minutes.
7. Release the pressure, uncover the pot and set it on Sauté mode again.
8. Add eggs slowly, stir and cook for 2 minutes.
9. Divide into soup bowls and serve hot.

Enjoy!

Nutrition:

- Calories 190
- Fat 2.8
- Fiber 2.3
- Carbs 10
- Protein 29

Veggie Soup

You will enjoy a delicious soup in no time!

Preparation time: 10 minutes
Cooking time: 15 minutes
Servings: 4
Ingredients:

- 1 brown onion, chopped
- 1 tablespoon coconut oil
- Salt and black pepper to the taste
- ½ red chili, chopped
- 2 carrots, chopped
- 2 celery sticks, chopped
- 6 big mushrooms, sliced
- 4 garlic cloves, minced
- A handful dried porcini mushrooms
- 3.5 ounces kale leaves, roughly chopped
- 1 cup tomatoes, chopped
- 1 zucchini, chopped
- 4 cups veggie stock
- 1 bay leaf
- 1 teaspoon lemon zest
- A handful parsley, chopped

Directions:

1. Set your instant pot on Sauté mode, add oil and heat it up.
2. Add onion, celery, carrots, salt and pepper, stir and cook for 1 minute.
3. Add chili, dried mushrooms, mushrooms, garlic, stir and cook for 2 minutes.
4. Add kale leaves, zucchini, tomatoes, bay leaf and stock, stir, cover and cook at High for 10 minutes.
5. Release the pressure naturally, uncover the pot, divide soup into bowls, add lemon zest and parsley on top and serve.

Enjoy!

Nutrition:

- Calories 80
- Fat 1
- Fiber 2
- Carbs 14
- Protein 2

Chicken Chili Soup

You can even serve this for dinner!

Preparation time: 10 minutes
Cooking time: 30 minutes
Servings: 4
Ingredients:

- 1 white onion, chopped
- 2 tablespoons olive oil
- 1 jalapeno pepper, chopped
- 4 garlic cloves, minced
- 2 teaspoons oregano, dried
- 1 teaspoon cumin
- ½ teaspoon red pepper flakes, crushed
- 3 cups chicken stock
- 1 pound chicken breast, skinless and boneless
- 30 ounces canned cannellini beans, drained
- Salt and black pepper to the taste
- Cilantro, chopped for serving
- Tortilla chips, for serving
- Lime wedges for serving

Directions:

1. Set your instant pot on Sauté mode, add oil and heat it up.
2. Add jalapeno and onion, stir and cook for 3 minutes.
3. Add garlic, stir and cook for 1 minute.
4. Add oregano, cumin, pepper flakes, stock, chicken, beans, salt and pepper, stir, cover and cook on Low for 30 minutes.
5. Release the pressure, uncover the pot, shred meat with 2 forks, add more salt and pepper, stir and divide into soup bowls.
6. Serve with cilantro on top and with tortilla chips and lime wedges on the side.

Enjoy!

Nutrition:

- Calories 200
- Fat 8
- Fiber 6
- Carbs 17
- Protein 19

Broccoli And Bacon Soup

It's a great combination of ingredients you should try!

Preparation time: 10 minutes
Cooking time: 10 minutes
Servings: 6
Ingredients:

- 4 bacon slices, chopped
- 1 teaspoon olive oil
- 2 small broccoli heads, chopped
- 1 leek, chopped
- 1 celery rib, chopped
- 2 cups spinach, chopped
- 4 tablespoons basmati rice
- 1 tablespoon parmesan, grated
- 1-quart veggie stock
- Salt and black pepper to the taste

Directions:

1. Set your instant pot on Sauté mode, add oil and bacon, cook until it's crispy, transfer to a plate and leave aside.
2. Add broccoli, leek, celery, spinach, rice, salt, pepper and veggie stock, stir, cover and cook at High for 6 minutes.
3. Release the pressure, uncover, add more salt and pepper if needed, add bacon, divide into soup bowls and serve with parmesan on top.

Enjoy!

Nutrition:

- Calories 151
- Fat 2.2
- Fiber 7
- Carbs 26
- Protein 10

Chorizo, Chicken and Kale Soup

You need to try this great and tasty soup!

Preparation time: 10 minutes
Cooking time: 10 minutes
Servings: 8
Ingredients:

- 9 ounces chorizo, casings removed
- 2 tablespoons olive oil
- 4 chicken thighs, chopped
- Salt and black pepper to the taste
- 4 garlic cloves, minced
- 2 yellow onions, chopped
- 4 cups chicken stock
- 15 ounces canned tomatoes, chopped
- 3 potatoes, chopped
- 2 bay leaves
- 5 ounces baby kale
- 14 ounces garbanzo beans, drained

Directions:

1. Set your instant pot on Sauté mode, add oil and heat it up.
2. Add chorizo, chicken and onion, stir and cook 5 minutes.
3. Add garlic, stir and cook for 1 minute.
4. Add stock, tomatoes and bay leaves and stir again.
5. Also add, kale and potatoes, salt and pepper, stir, cover and cook at High for 4 minutes.
6. Release the pressure, uncover the pot, add beans, more salt and pepper if needed, stir, divide into bowls and serve.

Enjoy!

Nutrition:

- Calories 200
- Fat 9
- Fiber 2
- Carbs 19
- Protein 11

Endive Soup

It's simply a fabulous soup!

Preparation time: 10 minutes
Cooking time: 25 minutes
Servings: 4
Ingredients:

- 1 tablespoon canola oil
- 2 teaspoons sesame oil
- 2 scallions, chopped
- 3 garlic cloves chopped
- 1 tablespoon ginger, grated
- 1 teaspoon chili sauce
- ½ cup uncooked rice
- 6 cups veggie stock
- 1 and ½ tablespoons soy sauce
- 3 endives, trimmed and roughly chopped
- Salt and white pepper to the taste

Directions:

1. Set your instant pot on Sauté mode, add canola and sesame oil and heat it up.
2. Add scallions and garlic, stir and cook for 4 minutes.
3. Add chili sauce and ginger, stir and cook for 1 minute.
4. Add stock and soy sauce, stir and cook for 2 minutes.
5. Add rice, stir, cover and cook at High for 15 minutes.
6. Release the pressure, uncover the pot, add salt, pepper and endives, stir, cover again and cook at High for 5 minutes.
7. Release the pressure again, uncover the pot, stir soup, divide into bowls and serve.

Enjoy!

Nutrition:

- Calories 207
- Fat 9
- Fiber 12
- Carbs 12
- Protein 11.5

Chicken Enchilada Soup

Do you feel like eating something different today? Then try this soup!

Preparation time: 10 minutes
Cooking time: 30 minutes
Servings: 4
Ingredients:

- 2 chicken breasts, boneless and skinless and chopped
- 1 and ¼ cup jarred red enchilada sauce
- 3 cups chicken stock
- 14 ounces canned tomatoes, chopped
- 28 ounces canned black beans, drained
- 15 ounces canned corn, drained
- Salt and black pepper to the taste
- 4 ounces canned green chilies, chopped
- 2 garlic cloves, minced
- 1 cup white onion, chopped
- ½ cup quinoa
- 1 teaspoon cumin, ground
- 1 teaspoon oregano

For serving:

- Chopped cilantro
- Chopped avocado
- Chopped red onion
- Shredded cheddar cheese

Directions:

1. In your instant pot, mix chicken with enchilada sauce, stock, tomatoes, black beans, corn, green chilies, salt, pepper, garlic, onion, quinoa, cumin and oregano, stir, cover and cook on Medium heat for 25 minutes.
2. Release the pressure, uncover the pot, divide soup into bowls and serve with chopped cilantro, avocado and red onion on top and with shredded cheese sprinkled all over.

Enjoy!

Nutrition:

- Calories 400
- Fat 23
- Fiber 3
- Carbs 23
- Protein 27

Beef And Barley Soup

It's a perfect soup!

Preparation time: 10 minutes
Cooking time: 25 minutes
Servings: 4
Ingredients:

- 1 and ½ pounds beef stew meat, chopped
- 2 tablespoons vegetable oil
- Salt and black pepper to the taste
- 10 baby bell mushrooms, cut into quarters
- 3 cups mixed onion, carrots and celery
- 8 garlic cloves, minced
- 6 cups beef stock
- 2 bay leaves
- 1 cup water
- ½ teaspoon thyme, dried
- 1 potato, chopped
- 2/3 cup barley

Directions:

1. Set your instant pot on Sauté mode, add oil and heat it up.
2. Add meat, salt and pepper, stir, cook for 3 minutes and transfer to a plate.
3. Add mushrooms, stir, brown them for 2 minutes and transfer to a plate.
4. Add mixed veggies to the pot, stir and cook for 4 minutes.
5. Return meat, mushrooms to the pot and stir everything.
6. Also add bay leaves, thyme, water, stock, salt and pepper, stir, cover and cook at High for 16 minutes.
7. Release the pressure, uncover the pot, add potatoes and barley, stir, cover and cook on Low for 1 hour.
8. Release the pressure again, stir soup, divide it into bowls and serve.

Enjoy!

Nutrition:

- Calories 120
- Fat 3
- Fiber 2
- Carbs 11
- Protein 5

Beef Stew

Your kids will adore this stew!

Preparation time: 10 minutes
Cooking time: 30 minutes
Servings: 8
Ingredients:

- 1 tablespoon vegetable oil
- 2 pounds beef stew, cubed
- 1 yellow onion, chopped
- 5 carrots, chopped
- 8 potatoes, cubed
- Salt and black pepper to the taste
- 2 teaspoons cornstarch
- 2 beef bouillon cubes
- 2 cups water

Directions:

1. Set your instant pot on Sauté mode, add oil and heat it up.
2. Add beef and onion, stir and cook until it browns on all sides.
3. Add carrots, water and bouillon, stir, cover and cook on Medium for 20 minutes.
4. Put water in a pot, add some salt, bring to a boil over medium high heat, add potatoes, cook for 10 minutes and drain them.
5. Release the pressure, uncover the pot and set it on Simmer mode.
6. Add cornstarch mixed with some water, salt, pepper and potatoes, stir, bring to a boil, take off heat and divide stew among plates.

Enjoy!
Nutrition:

- Calories 300
- Fat 12
- Fiber 5
- Carbs 1
- Protein 25

Tasty Pork Stew

This is a fall recipe, made with the best ingredients!

Preparation time: 10 minutes
Cooking time: 30 minutes
Servings: 4
Ingredients:

- 1 and ½ pounds pork shoulder, cubed
- 1 yellow onion, chopped
- 3 tablespoons extra virgin olive oil
- 1 red bell pepper, chopped
- 2 garlic cloves, chopped
- 1 rutabaga, cubed
- Salt and black pepper to the taste
- 8 baby potatoes
- 4 carrots, cut into big chunks
- ½ cup chicken stock
- 14 ounces canned tomatoes, chopped

Directions:

1. Set your instant pot on Sauté mode, add 2 tablespoons oil and heat it up.
2. Add pork, salt and pepper, brown on all sides and transfer to a bowl.
3. Add onions, garlic, bell pepper and the rest of the oil to the pot, stir and cook for 3 minutes.
4. Return pork to pot, add carrots, potatoes, rutabaga, salt, pepper, tomatoes and stock, stir, cover and cook on Medium for 20 minutes.
5. Release the pressure, uncover the pot, stir stew one more time, divide into bowls and serve.

Enjoy!

Nutrition:

- Calories 272
- Fat 6
- Fiber 3
- Carbs 27
- Protein 24

Delicious Chicken Stew

This is just perfect for a holiday meal!

Preparation time: 10 minutes
Cooking time: 1 hour and 15 minutes
Servings: 6
Ingredients:

- 6 chicken thighs
- 1 teaspoon vegetable oil
- Salt and black pepper to the taste
- 1 yellow onion, chopped
- ¼ pound baby carrots, sliced
- 1 celery stalk, chopped
- ½ teaspoon thyme, dried
- 2 tablespoons tomato paste
- ½ cup white wine
- 2 cups chicken stock
- 15 ounces canned tomatoes, chopped
- ¾ pound baby carrots
- 1 and ½ pounds new potatoes

Directions:

1. Set your instant pot on Sauté mode, add oil and heat it up.
2. Add chicken, salt and pepper, brown for 4 minutes on each side and transfer to a plate.
3. Add celery, onion, tomato paste, carrots, thyme, salt and pepper, stir and cook for 5 minutes.
4. Add wine, stir, bring to a boil and simmer for 3 minutes.
5. Add stock, return chicken, add tomatoes and put potatoes in the steamer basket of your pot.
6. Cover pot and cook at High for 30 minutes.
7. Release the pressure, uncover the pot, take potatoes out of the pot and put them in a bowl.
8. Transfer chicken pieces to a cutting board, leave aside to cool down for a few minutes, discard bones, shred meat and return it to the stew.
9. Add more salt and pepper if needed, stir, divide into bowls and serve hot.

Enjoy!

Nutrition:

- Calories 271
- Fat 2
- Fiber 4
- Carbs 18
- Protein 15

Simple Fish Chowder

Follow the directions and obtain the best fish chowder ever!

Preparation time: 10 minutes
Cooking time: 10 minutes
Servings: 4
Ingredients:

- 1 yellow onion, chopped
- 2 celery ribs, chopped
- ¾ cup bacon, chopped
- 1 carrot, chopped
- 2 garlic cloves, chopped
- 3 cups potatoes, cubed
- 4 cups chicken stock
- 1 pound haddock fillets
- 2 tablespoons butter
- 1 cup frozen corn
- Salt and white pepper to the taste
- 1 tablespoon potato starch
- 2 cups heavy cream

Directions:

1. Set your instant pot on Sauté mode, add butter and melt it.
2. Add bacon, stir and cook until it's crispy.
3. Add garlic, celery and onion, stir and cook fro 3 minutes.
4. Add salt, pepper, fish, potatoes, corn and stock, stir, cover and cook at High for 5 minutes.
5. Release the pressure naturally, uncover the pot, add heavy cream mixed with potato starch, stir well, set the pot on Simmer mode and cook everything for 3 minutes.
6. Divide into bowls and serve.

Enjoy!

Nutrition:

- Calories 195
- Fat 4.4
- Fiber 2
- Carbs 21
- Protein 17

Fast Bean Stew

It easy! It's fast! It's tasty!

Preparation time: 10 minutes
Cooking time: 25 minutes
Servings: 4
Ingredients:

- 1 yellow onion, chopped
- 2 carrots, chopped
- 1 garlic head, halved
- 1 pound chickpeas, drained
- 22 ounces canned tomatoes, chopped
- 22 ounces water
- 1 teaspoon oregano, dried
- 3 bay leaves
- 2 tablespoons olive oil
- Salt and black pepper to the taste
- ½ teaspoon red pepper flakes
- A drizzle of olive oil for serving
- 2 tablespoons parmesan cheese, grated

Directions:

1. Put onion, carrots, garlic, chickpeas, tomatoes, water, oregano, bay leaves, 2 tablespoons olive oil, salt, and pepper in your instant pot.
2. Cover, cook at High for 25 minutes and release pressure.
3. Ladle into bowls, add parmesan, pepper flakes and a drizzle of oil on top and serve.

Enjoy!
Nutrition:

- Calories 164
- Fat 2
- Fiber 9
- Carbs 28
- Protein 8.2

Sweet Potato Stew

It's a Moroccan style stew just for you!

Preparation time: 10 minutes
Cooking time: 20 minutes
Servings: 4
Ingredients:

- 1 big onion, chopped
- 1 sweet potato, cubed
- 3 garlic cloves, chopped
- 1 celery stalk, chopped
- 2 carrots, chopped
- 1 cup green lentils
- ½ cup red lentils
- 2 cups veggie stock
- ¼ cup raisins
- 14 ounces canned tomatoes, chopped
- Salt and black pepper to the taste

For the spice blend:

- 1 teaspoon cumin
- 1 teaspoon turmeric
- ½ teaspoon cinnamon
- 1 teaspoon paprika
- 2 teaspoons coriander
- ¼ teaspoon ginger, grated
- A pinch of cloves
- A pinch of chili flakes

Directions:

1. Set your instant pot on Sauté mode, add onions and brown them for 2 minutes adding some of the stock from time to time.
2. Add garlic, stir and cook for 1 minute.
3. Add carrots, raisins, celery, and sweet potatoes, stir and cook for 1 minute.
4. Add red and green lentils, stock, tomatoes, salt, pepper, turmeric, cinnamon, paprika, cumin, coriander, ginger, cloves and chili flakes, stir, cover and cook at High for 15 minutes.
5. Release the pressure, uncover the pot, stir stew one more time, add more salt and pepper if needed, ladle into bowls and serve.

Enjoy!

Nutrition:

- Calories 150
- Fat 9
- Fiber 3
- Protein 4
- Carbs 25

Spinach Stew

It gives you so many nutrients and vitamins!

Preparation time: 10 minutes
Cooking time: 30 minutes
Servings: 4
Ingredients:

- 1 small yellow onion, chopped
- 2 teaspoons olive oil
- 1 celery stalk, chopped
- 2 carrots, chopped
- 4 garlic cloves, minced
- 1 teaspoon turmeric
- 2 teaspoons cumin
- 1 teaspoon thyme
- Salt and black pepper to the taste
- 1 cup brown lentils, rinsed
- 6 cups baby spinach
- 4 cups veggie stock

Directions:

1. Set your instant pot on Sauté mode, add oil and heat it up.
2. Add onions, celery and carrots, stir and cook for 5 minutes.
3. Add garlic, turmeric, cumin, thyme, salt and pepper, stir and cook for 1 minute more.
4. Add stock and lentils, stir, cover and cook at High for 12 minutes.
5. Release the pressure for 10 minutes, uncover the pot, add spinach, more salt and pepper, stir, divide into bowls and serve.

Enjoy!

Nutrition:

- Calories 100
- Fat 2
- Fiber 5
- Carbs 16
- Protein 7

Delicious Cabbage Stew

This is so simple to make as long as you have and instant pot at hand!

Preparation time: 10 minutes
Cooking time: 25 minutes
Servings: 4
Ingredients:

- 2 tablespoons extra virgin olive oil
- 2 pounds pork meat, ground
- Salt and black pepper to the taste
- 1 small yellow onion, chopped
- 1 red chili, chopped
- 1 cabbage head, shredded
- 2 tablespoons butter
- 2 tablespoons water

Directions:

1. Set your instant pot on Sauté mode, add oil and heat it up.
2. Add pork, salt and pepper, stir and brown on all side for 6 minutes.
3. Add cabbage, onion, and chili and stir.
4. Also, add butter and water, stir, cover and cook at High for 13 minutes.
5. Release pressure, uncover the pot, divide into bowls and serve.

Enjoy!

Nutrition:

- Calories 140
- Fat 1
- Fiber 2
- Carbs 30
- Protein 3

Simple Turkey Stew

You will never find something as delicious as this stew!

Preparation time: 10 minutes
Cooking time: 35 minutes
Servings: 4
Ingredients:

- 1 tablespoon avocado oil
- 1 yellow onion, chopped
- 3 celery stalks, chopped
- 2 carrots, chopped
- Salt and black pepper to the taste
- 2 cups potatoes, chopped
- 3 cups turkey meat, already cooked and shredded
- 15 ounces canned tomatoes, chopped
- 5 cups turkey stock
- 1 tablespoon cranberry sauce
- 1 teaspoon dried garlic, minced

Directions:

1. Set your instant pot on Sauté mode, add oil and heat it up.
2. Add carrots, celery and onions, stir and cook for 3 minutes.
3. Add potatoes, tomatoes, stock, garlic, meat and cranberry sauce, stir, cover and cook on Low for 30 minutes.
4. Release the pressure, uncover the pot, add salt and pepper, stir, divide into bowls and serve.

Enjoy!

Nutrition:

- Calories 210
- Fat 4
- Fiber 0
- Carbs 15
- Protein 28

Mushroom And Beef Stew

It's a classic dish with a modern twist!

Preparation time: 10 minutes
Cooking time: 25 minutes
Servings: 6
Ingredients:

- 1 tablespoon olive oil
- 1 red onion, chopped
- 2 pounds beef chuck, cubed
- 1 teaspoon rosemary, chopped
- 1 celery stalk, chopped
- ½ cup red wine
- 1 cup beef stock
- Salt and black pepper to the taste
- 1 ounce dried porcini mushrooms, chopped
- 2 carrots, chopped
- 2 tablespoons flour
- 2 tablespoons butter

Directions:

1. Set your instant pot on Sauté mode, add oil and beef, stir and brown for 5 minutes.
2. Add onion, celery, rosemary, salt, pepper, wine and stock and stir.
3. Add carrots and mushrooms, cover pot and cook at High for 15 minutes.
4. Release the pressure, uncover the pot and set it on Simmer mode.
5. Meanwhile, heat up a pan over medium high heat, add butter and melt it.
6. Add flour and 6 tablespoons of cooking liquid from the stew and stir well.
7. Pour this over stew, stir, cook for 5 minutes, divide into bowls and serve.

Enjoy!
Nutrition:

- Calories 322
- Fat 18
- Fiber 3
- Carbs 12
- Protein 24

Oxtail Stew

This is a rich and flavored stew!

Preparation time: 10 minutes
Cooking time: 40 minutes
Servings: 4
Ingredients:

- 5 pounds oxtails
- 1 yellow onion, chopped
- Salt and black pepper to the taste
- 3 carrots, chopped
- 3 celery stalks, chopped
- 1 garlic clove, chopped
- 1 parsley bunch, chopped
- 2 cups red wine, chopped
- 1 cup tomatoes, chopped
- 1 cup water
- Sugar to the taste

Directions:

1. In your instant pot, mix oxtails with salt, pepper, onion, carrots, celery, garlic, tomatoes, red wine, parsley, water and sugar, stir, cover and cook on Medium for 40 minutes.
2. Release the pressure, uncover the pot, divide oxtail stew into bowls and serve.

Enjoy!

Nutrition:

- Calories 312
- Fat 12
- Fiber 14
- Carbs 15
- Protein 14
- Sugar 1

Lamb Stew

It's an excellent dish!

Preparation time: 10 minutes
Cooking time: 30 minutes
Servings: 4
Ingredients:

- 2 pounds lamb shoulder, cubed
- ¼ cup red wine vinegar
- 1 tablespoon garlic, minced
- 14 ounces canned tomatoes, chopped
- 2 yellow onions, chopped
- 1 tablespoon olive oil
- 2 tablespoons tomato paste
- 1 teaspoon oregano, dried
- 1 teaspoon basil, dried
- Salt and black pepper to the taste
- 2 bay leaves
- 1 red bell pepper, chopped
- 1 green bell pepper, chopped
- 1/3 cup parsley, chopped

Directions:

1. Set the pot on Sauté mode, add oil and heat it up.
2. Add onions and garlic, stir and cook for 2 minutes.
3. Add vinegar, stir and cook for 2 minutes.
4. Add lamb, tomatoes, tomato paste, oregano, basil, salt, pepper and bay leaves, stir, cover pot and cook at High for 12 minutes.
5. Release the pressure for 10 minutes, uncover the pot, discard bay leaves, add green and red pepper, more salt and pepper if needed, stir, cover and cook on High for 8 more minutes.
6. Release the pressure again, uncover, add parsley, stir and divide into bowls.

Enjoy!
Nutrition:

- Calories 700
- Fat 52
- Fiber 4.4
- Carbs 17
- Protein 40

Different Lamb Stew

If we've caught your attention with that last recipe, then check this one out as well!

Preparation time: 10 minutes
Cooking time: 15 minutes
Servings: 6
Ingredients:

- 2 onions, chopped
- 3 pounds lamb shoulder, cut into medium chunks
- 2 big potatoes, roughly chopped
- Salt and black pepper to the taste
- 2 thyme springs, chopped
- 6 ounces dark beer
- 2 cups water
- 2 carrots, chopped
- ¼ cup parsley, minced

Directions:

1. Put onions and lamb in your instant pot.
2. Add salt, pepper, potatoes, thyme, water, beer and carrots, stir, cover and cook at High for 15 minutes.
3. Release the pressure, uncover the pot, add parsley, more salt and pepper if needed, stir, divide into bowls and serve.

Enjoy!
Nutrition:

- Calories 236
- Fat 8
- Fiber 2.5
- Carbs 22
- Protein 19

Delicious German Stew

This German stew is worth trying as soon as possible!

Preparation time: 10 minutes
Cooking time: 10 minutes
Servings: 4
Ingredients:

- 1 pound kielbasa, cut into medium pieces
- 14 ounces canned tomatoes, chopped
- 2 potatoes, cut into quarters
- 1 small jar sauerkraut
- 1 onion, cut into medium chunks

Directions:

1. In your instant pot, add kielbasa, tomatoes, potatoes, sauerkraut and onion, stir, cover and cook at High for 10 minutes.
2. Release pressure, uncover the pot, divide stew into bowls and serve.

Enjoy!
Nutrition:

- Calories 140
- Fat 4
- Fiber 2
- Carbs 11
- Protein 12

Beef And Root Vegetables Stew

It's so unique and tasty!

Preparation time: 10 minutes
Cooking time: 32 minutes
Servings: 4
Ingredients:

- 1 pound beef meat, cubed
- 2 tablespoons olive oil
- 2 bacon slices, cooked and crumbled
- ½ cup white flour
- Salt and black pepper to the taste
- 1 rutabaga, diced
- 1 cup cipollini onions, peeled
- 4 carrots, chopped
- 4 garlic cloves, minced
- 2 cups beef stock
- 1 tablespoon tomato paste
- ½ cup bourbon
- A bunch of thyme, chopped
- A bunch of rosemary, chopped
- 1 cup peas
- 2 bay leaves

Directions:

1. Mix flour with salt and pepper and place on a plate.
2. Dredge meat in flour mix and leave aside.
3. Set your instant pot on Sauté mode, add oil and heat up.
4. Add meat, brown on all sides and transfer to a bowl.
5. Add garlic, bourbon, stock, thyme, rutabaga, carrots, tomato paste, rosemary and onions, stir and cook fro 2 minutes.
6. Return beef to pot, cover and cook at High for 10 minutes.
7. Release the pressure fast, uncover the pot, add bay leaves, bacon, peas, more salt and pepper, stir and cook on Low for 12 minutes.
8. Release the pressure again, uncover the pot, stir, discard bay leaves, divide into bowls and serve.

Enjoy!

Nutrition:

- Calories 302
- Fat 9
- Fiber 6
- Carbs 33
- Protein 18

Italian Sausage Stew

It is just so tasty!

Preparation time: 10 minutes
Cooking time: 20 minutes
Servings: 6
Ingredients:

- 1 pound Andouille sausage, crumbled
- ½ pound cherry tomatoes, cut into halves
- 1 sweet onion, chopped
- 1 and ½ pounds gold potatoes, cubed
- ¾ pound collard greens, thinly sliced
- 1 cup chicken stock
- Salt and black pepper to the taste
- Juice of ½ lemon

Directions:

1. Set your instant pot on Sauté mode, add sausage, stir and cook for 8 minutes.
2. Add onions and tomatoes, stir and cook 4 minutes more.
3. Add potatoes, stock, salt, pepper and collard greens, stir, cover pot and cook at High for 10 minutes.
4. Release the pressure, uncover the pot, add more salt and pepper and lemon juice, stir, divide into bowls and serve.

Enjoy!

Nutrition:

- Calories 230
- Fat 10
- Fiber 1
- Carbs 24
- Protein 28

Okra Stew

It's simple but the taste is very rich!

Preparation time: 10 minutes
Cooking time: 20 minutes
Servings: 4
Ingredients:

- 1 yellow onion, chopped
- 1 garlic clove, minced
- 1 pound beef meat, cubed
- 1 cardamom pod
- 2 cups chicken stock
- 14 ounces frozen okra
- 12 ounces tomato sauce
- Salt and black pepper to the taste
- ½ cup parsley, chopped
- A drizzle of olive oil
- Juice of ½ lemon

For the marinade:

- ½ teaspoon onion powder
- ½ teaspoon garlic powder
- A pinch of salt
- 1 tablespoon 7- spice mix

Directions:

1. In a bowl, mix meat with 7-spice mix, a pinch of salt, onion and garlic powder, toss to coat and leave aside for now.
2. Set your instant pot on Sauté mode, add some olive oil and heat it up.
3. Add onion, stir and cook 2 minutes.
4. Add garlic and cardamom, stir and cook for 1 minute.
5. Add meat, stir and brown meat for 2 minutes.
6. Add stock, tomato sauce, okra, salt and pepper, stir, cover and cook on Low for 20 minutes.
7. Release the pressure, uncover the pot, add more salt and pepper if needed, lemon juice and parsley, stir, divide into bowls and serve.

Enjoy!
Nutrition:

- Calories 230
- Fat 10
- Fiber 8
- Carbs 15
- Protein 20

Instant Pot Beans And Grains Recipes

Barley And Mushroom Risotto

it's an original and tasty dish you can try today!

Preparation time: 10 minutes
Cooking time: 30 minutes
Servings: 4
Ingredients:

- 2 cups yellow onions, chopped
- 1 tablespoon olive oil
- 1 cup pearl barley
- 1 teaspoon fennel seeds
- 2 tablespoons black barley
- 3 cups chicken stock
- 1/3 cup dry sherry
- 1 and ½ cups water
- 1.5 ounce dried mushrooms
- Salt and black pepper to the taste
- ¼ cup parmesan, grated

Directions:

1. Set your instant pot on Sauté mode, add oil and heat it up.
2. Add fennel and onions, stir and cook for 4 minutes.
3. Add barley and black barley, sherry, mushrooms, stock, water, salt and pepper and stir well.
4. Cover the pot, cook at High for 18 minutes, release the pressure, uncover the pot and set it on Simmer mode.
5. Add more salt and pepper of needed, stir and cook for 5 more minutes.
6. Divide into bowls, add parmesan on top and serve.

Enjoy!

Nutrition:

- Calories 200
- Fat 5
- Fiber 6.1
- Carbs 31
- Protein 7.6

Different Barley Dish

This is a different barley risotto you just have to make for your loved ones!

Preparation time: 10 minutes
Cooking time: 25 minutes
Servings: 4
Ingredients:

- 1 tablespoon extra virgin olive oil
- 1 tablespoon butter
- 1 white onion, chopped
- 1 garlic clove, minced
- 1 and ½ cups pearl barley, rinsed
- 1 celery stalk, chopped
- 1/3 cup mushrooms, chopped
- 4 cups veggie stock
- 2 and ¼ cups water
- Salt and black pepper to the taste
- 3 tablespoons parsley, chopped
- 1 cup parmesan cheese, grated

Directions:

1. Set your instant pot on Sauté mode, add oil and butter and heat them up.
2. Add onion and garlic, stir and cook for 4 minutes.
3. Add celery and barley and toss to coat.
4. Add mushrooms, water, stock, salt and pepper, stir, cover pot and cook at High for 18 minutes.
5. Release the pressure, uncover the pot, add cheese and parsley and more salt and pepper if needed, stir for 2 minutes, divide into bowls and serve.

Enjoy!
Nutrition:

- Calories 170
- Fat 6
- Fiber 4.5
- Carbs 30
- Protein 8

Delicious Barley Salad

It's a light and delicious salad you can serve for lunch!

Preparation time: 10 minutes
Cooking time: 20 minutes
Servings: 4
Ingredients:

- 1 cup hulled barley, rinsed
- 2 and ½ cups water
- ¾ cup jarred spinach pesto
- 1 green apple, chopped
- ¼ cup celery, chopped
- Salt and white pepper to the taste

Directions:

1. Put barley, water, salt and pepper in your instant pot, stir, cover and cook at High for 20 minutes.
2. Release the pressure fast, uncover pot, strain barley and put in a bowl.
3. Add celery, apple, spinach pesto and more salt and pepper, toss to coat and serve right away.

Enjoy!

Nutrition:

- Calories 170
- Fat 7
- Fiber 7
- Carbs 0
- Protein 5

Wheatberry Salad

It's incredible how a simple ingredient can change into a special dish!

Preparation time: 10 minutes
Cooking time: 35 minutes
Servings: 6
Ingredients:

- 1 and ½ cups wheat berries
- 1 tablespoon extra virgin olive oil
- Salt and black pepper to the taste
- 4 cups water

For the salad:

- 1 tablespoon balsamic vinegar
- 1 tablespoon olive oil
- 1 cup cherry tomatoes, cut into halves
- 2 green onions, chopped
- 2 ounces feta cheese, crumbled
- ½ cup kalamata olives, pitted and chopped
- 1 handful basil leaves, chopped
- 1 handful parsley leaves, chopped

Directions:

1. Set your instant pot on Sauté mode, add 1 tablespoon oil and heat it up.
2. Add wheat berries, stir and cook for 5 minutes.
3. Add water, salt and pepper to the taste, cover pot and cook on High for 30 minutes.
4. Release the pressure for 10 minutes, uncover the pot, drain wheat berries and put them in a salad bowl.
5. Add salt and pepper, 1 tablespoon oil, balsamic vinegar, tomatoes, green onions, olives, cheese, basil and parsley, toss to coat and serve right away.

Enjoy!

Nutrition:

- Calories 240
- Fat 11
- Fiber 6.3
- Carbs 31
- Protein 5

Cracked Wheat And Veggies

It's a simple and very tasty dish you can serve for lunch or dinner!

Preparation time: 10 minutes
Cooking time: 15 minutes
Servings: 4
Ingredients:

- ½ cup cracked whole wheat
- 1 and ½ cups water
- 2 tomatoes, chopped
- 2 small potatoes, cubed
- 5 cauliflower florets, chopped
- Salt and black pepper to the taste
- ¼ teaspoon mustard seeds
- ¼ teaspoon cumin seeds
- 1 teaspoon ginger, grated
- 1 tablespoon chana dal
- 2 garlic cloves, minced
- 1 yellow onion, chopped
- 2 curry leaves
- 3 teaspoons vegetable oil
- ¼ teaspoon garam masala
- A few cilantro leaves, chopped for serving

Directions:

1. Set your instant pot on Sauté mode, add oil and heat it up.
2. Add cumin and mustard seeds, stir and cook for 1 minute.
3. Add onion, garlic, chana dal, garam masala, ginger and curry leaves, stir and cook for 2 minutes.
4. Add cauliflower, potatoes and tomatoes, stir and cook for 4 minutes.
5. Add wheat, salt, pepper and water, stir, cover and cook on High for 5 minutes.
6. Release the pressure, uncover the pot, transfer wheat and veggies to plates, sprinkle cilantro on top and serve.

Enjoy!

Nutrition:

- Calories 145
- Fat 2
- Fiber 4
- Carbs 16
- Protein 7

Cracked Wheat Surprise

We think you will be impressed with this dish!

Preparation time: 5 minutes
Cooking time: 17 minutes
Servings: 2
Ingredients:

- 2 cups cracked wheat
- 1 teaspoon fennel seeds
- 2 and ½ cups clarified butter
- 2 cups jaggery
- 3 cloves
- 1 cup milk
- A pinch of salt
- 3 cups water
- A few almonds, chopped

Directions:

1. Set your instant pot on Sauté mode, add butter and heat it up.
2. Add cracked wheat, stir and cook for 5 minutes.
3. Add cloves and fennel seeds, stir and cook for 2 minutes.
4. Add jaggery, a pinch of salt, milk and water, stir, cover and cook at High for 10 minutes.
5. Release the pressure, uncover the pot, divide into bowls and serve with chopped almonds on top.

Enjoy!

Nutrition:

- Calories 120
- Fat 1
- Fiber 1
- Carbs 4
- Protein 8

Tasty Bulgur Salad

It's so fresh and tasty! Try it!

Preparation time: 15 minutes
Cooking time: 12 minutes
Servings: 4
Ingredients:

- Zest from 1 orange
- Juice from 2 oranges
- 2 garlic cloves, minced
- 2 teaspoons canola oil
- 2 tablespoons ginger, grated
- 1 cup bulgur, rinsed
- 1 tablespoon soy sauce
- 2/3 cup scallions, chopped
- 1/3 cup almonds, chopped
- Salt to the taste
- 2 teaspoons brown sugar
- ½ cups water

Directions:

1. Set your instant pot on Sauté mode, add oil and heat it up.
2. Add ginger and garlic, stir and cook for 1 minutes.
3. Add bulgur, sugar, water, and orange juice, stir, cover and cook at High for 5 minutes.
4. Release the pressure naturally, uncover the pot and leave bulgur aside for now.
5. Heat up a pan over medium heat, add almonds, stir and toast them for 3 minutes.
6. Add orange zest, salt, soy sauce and scallions, stir and cook for 1 minute.
7. Add this to bulgur mix, stir with a fork, transfer to a bowl and serve.

Enjoy!

Nutrition:

- Calories 232
- Fat 7
- Fiber 6
- Carbs 38
- Protein 7

Tasty Bulgur Pilaf

It's so flavored! You will love this pilaf!

Preparation time: 10 minutes
Cooking time: 21 minutes
Servings: 6
Ingredients:

- 2 cups red onions, chopped
- 2 tablespoons extra virgin olive oil
- Salt and black pepper to the taste
- 2 teaspoons ginger, grated
- ¼ cup dill, chopped
- 1 garlic clove, minced
- 1 and ½ cups bulgur
- ¼ cup mint, chopped
- ¼ cup parsley, chopped
- 3 tablespoons lemon juice
- ½ teaspoon cumin, ground
- ½ teaspoons turmeric, ground
- 2 cups veggie stock
- 1 and ½ cups carrot, chopped
- ½ cup walnuts, toasted and chopped

Directions:

1. Set your instant pot on Sauté mode, add oil and heat it up.
2. Add onion, stir and cook on Low temperature for 12 minutes.
3. Add garlic, stir and cook for 1 minute.
4. Add cumin, turmeric and bulgur, stir and cook for 1 minute.
5. Add ginger, stock, carrots, salt and pepper, stir, cover and cook at High for 5 minutes.
6. Release the pressure, uncover the pot, add mint, dill, parsley, lemon juice and more salt and pepper if needed and stir gently.
7. Divide among plates and serve with almonds on top.

Enjoy!

Nutrition:

- Calories 270
- Fat 12
- Fiber 8
- Carbs 38
- Protein 7

Simple Buckwheat Porridge

It's a simple dish, but it's very tasty!

Preparation time: 10 minutes
Cooking time: 6 minutes
Servings: 4
Ingredients:

- 3 cups rice milk
- 1 cup buckwheat groats
- 1 banana, sliced
- 1 teaspoon cinnamon
- ¼ cup raisins
- 1 teaspoon cinnamon, ground
- ½ teaspoon vanilla
- Chopped nuts for serving

Directions:

1. Put buckwheat in your instant pot, add milk, raisins, banana, vanilla and cinnamon, stir, cover and cook on High for 6 minutes.
2. Release the pressure for 15 minutes, uncover the pot, stir porridge, divide into bowls and serve with chopped nuts on top.

Enjoy!

Nutrition:

- Calories 400
- Fat 3
- Fiber 13
- Carbs 30
- Protein 13

Couscous With Chicken And Veggies

It's a complete meal for you to serve to your loved ones!

Preparation time: 10 minutes
Cooking time: 15 minutes
Servings: 4
Ingredients:

- 8 chicken thighs, skinless
- 1 and ½ cups mushrooms, cut into halves
- 1 and ½ cups carrots, chopped
- 1 green bell pepper, chopped
- 1 yellow onion, chopped
- 2 garlic cloves, minced
- 15 ounces canned stewed tomatoes, chopped
- Salt and black pepper to the taste
- ¾ cup couscous
- 1 zucchini, chopped
- ½ cup chicken stock
- A handful parsley, chopped

Directions:

1. In your instant pot, mix chicken with mushrooms, carrots, bell pepper, onion, garlic, tomatoes and stock, stir, cover and cook at High for 8 minutes.
2. Release the pressure fast, uncover the pot, add couscous, zucchini, salt and pepper, stir, cover again and cook on Low for 6 minutes.
3. Release the pressure again, uncover the pot, add parsley, stir gently, divide into bowls and serve.

Enjoy!

Nutrition:

- Calories 300
- Fat 10
- Fiber 3
- Carbs 35
- Protein 20

Israeli Couscous

This is probably the best couscous dish you will ever taste!

Preparation time: 10 minutes
Cooking time: 8 minutes
Servings: 4
Ingredients:

- ½ cup red onion, chopped
- ½ teaspoon sesame oil
- ¼ cup red bell pepper, chopped
- 1 cup couscous, rinsed
- 1 and ½ cups veggie stock
- ½ teaspoon cinnamon, ground
- ¼ teaspoon coriander, ground
- Salt and black pepper to the taste
- 2 tablespoons red wine vinegar

Directions:

1. Set your instant pot on Sauté mode, add oil and heat it up.
2. Add bell pepper and onion, stir and cook for 5 minutes.
3. Add couscous, coriander, stock, cinnamon, salt, pepper and vinegar, stir, cover and cook at High for 3 minutes.
4. Release the pressure, uncover the pot, divide couscous into bowls and serve.

Enjoy!

Nutrition:

- Calories 150
- Fat 1
- Fiber 5
- Carbs 33
- Protein 6

Tasty Millet Dish

This is so tasty, and it will be done in no time!

Preparation time: 10 minutes
Cooking time: 25 minutes
Servings: 4
Ingredients:

- 1 cup onion, chopped
- 2 garlic cloves, minced
- ½ cup oyster mushrooms, sliced
- ½ cup green lentils, rinsed
- 1 cup millet
- 2 and ¼ cups veggie stock
- ½ cup bok choy, sliced
- 1 cup snow peas
- ¼ cup parsley and chives, chopped
- 1 cup asparagus, chopped
- 1 tablespoon lemon juice
- Salt and black pepper to the taste

Directions:

1. Set your instant pot on Sauté mode, add onions, garlic and mushrooms, stir and cook for 2 minutes.
2. Add millet and lentils, stir and cook for 1 minute.
3. Add stock, stir, cover and cook at High for 10 minutes.
4. Release the pressure naturally, uncover the pot, add asparagus, bok choy and peas, stir, cover and cook at High for 3 minutes.
5. Release the pressure again, uncover, add lemon juice, salt, pepper and mixed parsley and chives, stir gently, divide into bowls and serve.

Enjoy!

Nutrition:

- Calories 100
- Fat 1.2
- Fiber 7
- Carbs 20
- Protein 10

Creamy Millet Dish

It's such a satisfying meat!

Preparation time: 10 minutes
Cooking time: 20 minutes
Servings: 4
Ingredients:

- 1 cup split mung beans
- 1 bay leaf
- 1 cup carrot, chopped
- 1 cup millet, chopped
- 1 cup celery, chopped
- 4 cardamom pods
- 6 cups water
- 1 and ½ cups fresh peas
- 1 tablespoon lime juice
- ¼ cup cilantro, chopped
- 1 tablespoon ghee
- 1 teaspoon coriander seeds, ground
- 1 teaspoon fennel seeds, ground
- ½ teaspoon cumin seeds, ground
- ½ teaspoon turmeric powder
- Salt and black pepper to the taste
- ½ teaspoon ginger, grated

Directions:

1. Set your instant pot on Sauté mode, add mung beans, stir and cook until they are golden.
2. Add millet, carrot, bay leaf, celery, cardamom, water, salt and pepper, stir, cover and cook at High for 10 minutes.
3. Release pressure, uncover the pot and set it on simmer mode.
4. Heat up a pan with the ghee over medium heat, add coriander, fennel, cumin, turmeric and ginger, stir and cook for 2 minutes.
5. Add this to your instant pot, stir, add more salt and pepper, peas and lime juice, simmer for 5 minutes, divide among plates, sprinkle cilantro and serve.

Enjoy!
Nutrition:

- Calories 231
- Fat 2
- Fiber 8
- Carbs 41
- Protein 11

Tasty Oats And Veggies

It's a great combination! We recommend you to try it soon!

Preparation time: 10 minutes
Cooking time: 15 minutes
Servings: 4
Ingredients:

- 1 cup steel cut oats
- 1 and ½ cups water
- 1 carrots, chopped
- ½ green bell pepper, chopped
- 1 inch ginger, grated
- 1 Thai green chili, chopped
- 2 curry leaves
- ¼ teaspoon mustard seeds
- ½ teaspoon urad dal
- A pinch of asafetida powder
- 1 and ½ tablespoons canola oil
- A pinch of turmeric powder
- Salt to the taste

Directions:

1. Put oats in your instant pot, add water, cover and cook at High for 7 minutes.
2. Heat up a pan with the oil over medium heat, add mustard seeds, urad dal, asafetida powder, turmeric, chili pepper, curry leaf, ginger, carrot and bell pepper, stir and cook for 5 minutes.
3. Release pressure from the pot, uncover, add oats to the pan, also add salt, stir, divide into bowls and serve.

Enjoy!

Nutrition:

- Calories 211
- Fat 6.3
- Fiber 5.6
- Carbs 32
- Protein 7.5

Quinoa And Veggies

It's the best lunch idea!

Preparation time: 10 minutes
Cooking time: 2 minutes
Servings: 4
Ingredients:

- 1 and ½ cups quinoa
- 1 red bell pepper, chopped
- 3 celery stalks, chopped
- Salt to the taste
- 4 cups spinach
- 2 tomatoes, chopped
- 1 and ½ cups chicken stock
- ½ cup black olives, pitted and chopped
- ½ cup feta cheese, crumbled
- 1/3 cup jarred pesto
- ¼ cup almonds, sliced

Directions:

1. In your instant pot, mix quinoa with bell pepper, celery, spinach, stock and salt, stir gently, cover and cook at High for 2 minutes.
2. Release the pressure for 10 minutes, uncover pot, add tomatoes, pesto and olives, stir and transfer to plates.
3. Add cheese and almonds on top, toss to coat and serve.

Enjoy!

Nutrition:

- Calories 249
- Fat 7
- Fiber 5.4
- Carbs 20
- Protein 7.4

Mexican Cranberry Beans

It's time for a fiesta! This dish is what you need!

Preparation time: 10 minutes
Cooking time: 20 minutes
Servings: 6
Ingredients:

- 1 pound cranberry beans, soaked for 8 hours and drained
- 3 and ¼ cups water
- 4 garlic cloves, minced
- 1 yellow onion, chopped
- 1 and ½ teaspoons cumin
- 1/3 cup cilantro, chopped
- 1 tablespoon chili powder
- 1 teaspoon oregano, dried
- Salt and black pepper to the taste
- Cooker rice for serving

Directions:

1. Put beans in your instant pot, add the water, garlic and onion, cover and cook at High for 20 minutes.
2. Release the pressure, uncover the pot, add cumin, cilantro, oregano, chili powder, salt and pepper, stir well, mash a bit using a potato mashes, divide among plates on top of rice and serve.

Enjoy!

Nutrition:

- Calories 100
- Fat 1
- Fiber 4
- Carbs 10
- Protein 6

Cranberry Beans And Pasta

Are you trying to impress your loved one with a tasty dinner dish? Then this is what you need!

Preparation time: 10 minutes
Cooking time: 20 minutes
Servings: 8
Ingredients:

- 2 cups dried cranberry beans, soaked for 8 hours and drained
- 7 garlic cloves, minced
- 6 cups water
- 2 celery ribs, chopped
- 1 yellow onion, chopped
- 1 teaspoon rosemary, chopped
- ¼ teaspoon red pepper flakes
- 26 ounces canned tomatoes, chopped
- 3 teaspoons basil, dried
- ½ teaspoon smoked paprika
- 2 teaspoons oregano, dried
- Salt and black pepper to the taste
- 2 cups small pasta
- 3 tablespoons nutritional yeast
- 10 ounces kale leaves

Directions:

1. Set your instant pot on Sauté mode, add onion, celery, garlic, pepper flakes, rosemary and a pinch of salt, stir and brown for 2 minutes.
2. Add tomatoes, basil, oregano and paprika, stir and cook for 1 minute.
3. Add beans, 6 cups water, cover pot and cook at High for 10 minutes.
4. Release the pressure, uncover the pot, add pasta, yeast, kale, salt and pepper, stir and set the pot on Sauté mode again.
5. Cook for 5 minutes more, divide into bowls and serve.

Enjoy!

Nutrition:

- Calories 330
- Fat 14
- Fiber 10
- Carbs 32
- Protein 18

Delicious Cranberry Beans Mix

Today, you get to taste something amazing!

Preparation time: 10 minutes
Cooking time: 15 minutes
Servings: 6
Ingredients:

- 1 and ½ cups cranberry beans, soaked for 8 hours and drained
- 4-inch kombu piece, sliced
- 4 bacon slices, chopped
- Salt and black pepper to the taste
- 8 cups kale, chopped
- 4 ounces shiitake mushrooms, chopped
- ½ teaspoon garlic powder
- 1 teaspoon extra virgin olive oil

Directions:

1. Put beans in your instant pot, add 2 inches water, salt, pepper, kombu, cover and cook at High for 8 minutes.
2. Release the pressure uncover the pot, transfer beans and cooking liquid to a pot and leave aside for now.
3. Set your pot on Sauté mode, add oil and heat it up.
4. Add garlic powder, bacon, mushrooms, salt, pepper and ¾ cup cooking liquid from the pot, stir well and cook for 1 minute.
5. Cover pot, cook at High for 3 minutes and release pressure.
6. Add beans and kale, stir and divide into bowls.

Enjoy!

Nutrition:

- Calories 228
- Fat 2
- Fiber 14
- Carbs 41
- Protein 9

Cranberry Bean Chili

If you are a vegetarian, then this is a dish you should try!

Preparation time: 10 minutes
Cooking time: 40 minutes
Servings: 8
Ingredients:

- 1 pound cranberry beans, soaked in water for 7 hours and drained
- 5 cups water
- 14 ounces canned tomatoes and green chilies, chopped
- ¼ cup millet
- ½ cup bulgur
- 1 and ½ teaspoons cumin, ground
- 2 tablespoons tomato paste
- 1 teaspoon chili powder
- 1 teaspoon garlic, minced
- ½ teaspoon liquid smoke
- 1 teaspoon oregano, dried
- ½ teaspoon ancho chili powder
- Salt and black pepper to the taste
- Hot sauce for serving
- Pickled jalapenos for serving

Directions:

1. Put beans and 3 cups water in your instant pot, cover and cook at High for 25 minutes.
2. Release the pressure fast, add the rest of the water, tomatoes and chilies, millet, bulgur, cumin, tomato paste, chili powder, garlic, liquid smoke, oregano, ancho chili powder, salt and pepper, stir, cover and cook on High for 10 minutes more.
3. Release the pressure again, uncover, divide into bowls and serve with hot sauce on top and pickled jalapenos on the side.

Enjoy!
Nutrition:

- Calories 200
- Fat 13
- Fiber 4
- Carbs 14
- Protein 15

Lentils Tacos

You need to try them! They taste superb!

Preparation time: 10 minutes
Cooking time: 15 minutes
Servings: 4
Ingredients:

- 4 ounces tomato sauce
- ½ teaspoon cumin
- 1 teaspoon salt
- 1 teaspoon garlic powder
- 1 teaspoon chili powder
- 1 teaspoon onion powder
- 4 cups water
- 2 cups brown lentils
- Taco shells for serving

Directions:

1. In your instant pot, mix lentils with water, tomato sauce, cumin, garlic powder, chili powder and onion powder, stir, cover and cook at High for 15 minutes.
2. Release the pressure, uncover the pot, divide lentils mix into taco shells and serve.

Enjoy!

Nutrition:

- Calories 157
- Fat 4
- Fiber 8
- Carbs 24
- Protein 6.4

Italian Lentils Dinner

Discover how to make this delicious Italian dinner!

Preparation time: 10 minutes
Cooking time: 15 minutes
Servings: 4
Ingredients:

- ½ cup brown rice, soaked overnight and drained
- ¾ cup green lentils, soaked overnight and drained
- 2 and ½ cups chicken stock
- 1 cup tomato sauce
- ¾ cup onion, chopped
- 1 cup green and red bell pepper, chopped
- 2 cups chicken, already cooked and shredded
- 3 carrots, chopped
- A handful greens
- Salt and black pepper to the taste
- 3 teaspoons Italian seasoning
- 2 garlic cloves, crushed
- 1 cup mozzarella cheese, shredded

Directions:

1. In your instant pot, mix lentils with rice, salt, pepper, stock, tomato sauce, onion, red and green pepper, chicken, carrots, greens, Italian seasoning and garlic, stir, cover and cook on High for 15 minutes.
2. Release the pressure, uncover pot, add cheese, stir, divide among bowls and serve.

Enjoy!

Nutrition:

- Calories 186
- Fat 2
- Fiber 3.3
- Carbs 28
- Protein 14.4

Lentils And Tomato Sauce

This is something you will like very much!

Preparation time: 10 minutes
Cooking time: 20 minutes
Servings: 4
Ingredients:

- 1 tablespoon olive oil
- 1 green bell pepper, chopped
- 1 yellow onion, chopped
- 1 celery stalk, chopped
- 1 and ½ cups tomatoes, chopped
- Salt and black pepper to the taste
- 1 teaspoon curry powder
- 2 cups water
- 1 and ½ cups lentils

Directions:

1. Set your instant pot on Sauté mode, add the oil and heat it up.
2. Add celery, bell pepper, onion and tomatoes, stir and cook for 4 minutes.
3. Add curry, salt, pepper, lentils and water, stir, cover and cook at High for 15 minutes.
4. Release the pressure, uncover the pot, divide lentils among bowls and serve.

Enjoy!

Nutrition:

- Calories 105
- Fat 3
- Fiber 4.6
- Carbs 1.7
- Protein 6

Indian Lentils

These are amazing and very delicious!

Preparation time: 10 minutes
Cooking time: 20 minutes
Servings: 4
Ingredients:

- 3 teaspoons butter
- 1 teaspoon extra virgin olive oil
- 1 cup red lentils
- 1 yellow onion, chopped
- 2 teaspoons cumin
- ¼ teaspoon coriander
- ¼ teaspoon garlic powder
- ¼ teaspoon turmeric
- ¼ teaspoon Aleppo pepper
- ¼ teaspoon red pepper flakes
- Salt and black pepper to the taste
- 3 cups chicken stock

Directions:

1. Set your instant pot on Sauté mode, add butter and oil and heat up.
2. Add onions, stir and cook for 4 minutes.
3. Add cumin, coriander, garlic powder, turmeric, Aleppo pepper and pepper flakes, stir and cook for 2 minutes.
4. Add lentils and stock, stir, cover and cook at High for 15 minutes.
5. Release the pressure, uncover pot, divide into bowls and serve.

Enjoy!

Nutrition:

- Calories 198
- Fat 6
- Fiber 8.7
- Carbs 26
- Protein 10.4

Lentils Salad

Try this fresh salad! It's great!

Preparation time: 10 minutes
Cooking time: 8 minutes
Servings: 4
Ingredients:

- 2 cups chicken stock
- 1 cup lentils
- 1 bay leaf
- ½ teaspoon thyme, dried
- ¼ cup red onion, chopped
- ½ cup celery, chopped
- ¼ cup red bell pepper, chopped
- 2 tablespoons extra virgin olive oil
- 1 tablespoon garlic, minced
- ½ teaspoon oregano, dried
- Juice of 1 lemon
- 2 tablespoons parsley, chopped
- Salt and black pepper to the taste

Directions:

1. Put lentils in your instant pot.
2. Add bay leaf, stock and thyme, stir, cover and cook at High for 8 minutes.
3. Release pressure, uncover the pot, drain lentils and put them in a bowl.
4. Add celery, onion, bell pepper, garlic, parsley, oregano, lemon juice, olive oil, salt and pepper to the taste, toss to coat and serve.

Enjoy!

Nutrition:

- Calories 165
- Fat 5
- Fiber 10
- Carbs 20
- Protein 9

Chickpeas Curry

It's a vegetarian curry everyone will love!

Preparation time: 10 minutes
Cooking time: 21 minutes
Servings: 6
Ingredients:

- 4 teaspoons cumin seeds
- 8 teaspoons olive oil
- 4 teaspoons garlic, minced
- 1 yellow onion, finely chopped
- 2 teaspoons garam masala
- 2 teaspoons coriander, ground
- 2 teaspoons turmeric, ground
- 3 cups chickpeas, already cooked, drained and rinsed
- 28 ounces canned tomatoes, chopped
- 3 potatoes, cubed
- ½ cup water
- Salt and black pepper to the taste
- Basmati rice, already cooked for serving
- Some cilantro, chopped for serving

Directions:

1. Set your instant pot on Sauté mode, add oil and heat it up.
2. Add cumin seeds, stir and cook for 30 seconds.
3. Add onion, stir and cook for 5 minutes.
4. Add garlic, garam masala, coriander, turmeric, tomatoes, potatoes, chickpeas, water, salt and pepper, stir, cover and cook at High for 15 minutes.
5. Release the pressure, uncover the pot, divide chickpeas curry on plates and serve with rice on the side and cilantro on top.

Enjoy!
Nutrition:

- Calories 384
- Fat 8.3
- Fiber 12
- Carbs 69
- Protein 11.5

Chickpeas And Dumplings

It's a very interesting combination we recommend you to try!

Preparation time: 10 minutes
Cooking time: 17 minutes
Servings: 4
Ingredients:

- 4 carrots, chopped
- 1 yellow onion, chopped
- 4 red baby potatoes, chopped
- 2 garlic cloves, minced
- 28 ounces veggie stock
- 1 veggie bouillon cube
- 2 cans chickpeas
- Salt and black pepper to the taste
- A pinch of cayenne pepper
- 2 green onions, chopped
- 2 celery stalks, chopped
- 1 and ¾ teaspoons baking powder
- ¾ cup white flour
- ½ teaspoon dill, dried
- ½ cup milk

Directions:

1. Set your instant pot on Sauté mode, add onion and garlic and a splash of stock, stir and cook for 3 minutes.
2. Add potatoes, carrots, chickpeas, stock, bouillon cube, salt, pepper and cayenne pepper, stir, cover and cook at High for 7 minutes.
3. Release the pressure, uncover the pot, add celery and green onions, stir and leave aside.
4. Meanwhile, in a bowl, mix flour with baking powder, a pinch of salt, dill and milk and stir very well.
5. Shape 10 dumplings, heat up soup on Simmer mode, drop dumplings into the pot, cover it and cook on Steam mode for 10 minutes.
6. Uncover pot, add more salt and pepper if needed, stir, divide into bowls and serve.

Enjoy!

Nutrition:

- Calories 300
- Fat 5
- Fiber 10
- Carbs 56
- Protein 12

Chickpeas And Garlic

It's more than simple to make this dish!

Preparation time: 10 minutes
Cooking time: 35 minutes
Servings: 4
Ingredients:

- 2 bay leaves
- 4 garlic cloves
- 2 cups chickpeas, rinsed
- Water
- 2 tomatoes, chopped
- 2 small cucumbers, chopped
- 1 teaspoon olive oil
- Salt and black pepper to the taste

Directions:

1. Put chickpeas in your instant pot.
2. Add water, garlic and bay leaves, stir, cover and cook at High for 35 minutes.
3. Release the pressure naturally for 10 minutes, uncover pot, drain water and put chickpeas and garlic in a bowl.
4. Add cucumber, tomatoes, salt, pepper and oil, toss to coat and serve.

Enjoy!

Nutrition:

- Calories 110
- Fat 7
- Fiber 0.6
- Carbs 17
- Protein 8

Chickpea And Pesto Delight

It's so savory and great!

Preparation time: 10 minutes
Cooking time: 20 minutes
Servings: 4
Ingredients:

For the pesto:
- ¼ cup extra virgin olive oil
- 1 and ½ cups basil
- 1 garlic clove, minced
- ¼ cup parmesan cheese, grated
- 1 tablespoon pine nuts, roasted

For the chickpeas:

- 12 ounces chickpeas, soaked for 8 hours
- 1 yellow onion, chopped
- 2 tablespoons extra virgin olive oil
- 2 carrots, chopped
- 14 ounces canned tomatoes
- 4 cups chicken stock
- ¼ cup parmesan, grated

Directions:

1. In your blender, mix basil with ¼ cup cheese, 1 garlic clove, pine nuts, ¼ cup oil and some salt and blend very well.
2. Transfer to a bowl and leave aside for now.
3. Set your instant pot on Sauté mode, add 2 tablespoons oil and heat it up.
4. Add onion and some salt, stir and cook for 3 minutes.
5. Add carrots, chickpeas, tomatoes, stock, salt and pepper to the taste, stir, cover and cook at High for 10 minutes.
6. Release the pressure fast, uncover the pot and transfer chickpeas mix into bowls.
7. Add pesto on top, sprinkle ¼ cup parmesan and serve.

Enjoy!

Nutrition:
- Calories 100
- Fat 3.5
- Fiber 3
- Carbs 13
- Protein 3.2

Kidney Beans Etouffee

This is an exceptional dish! You'll see!

Preparation time: 10 minutes
Cooking time: 30 minutes
Servings: 4
Ingredients:

- 1 tablespoon vegetable oil
- 2 cups bell pepper, chopped
- 1 cup yellow onion, chopped
- 2 teaspoons garlic, chopped
- 1 cup water
- 3 bay leaves
- 1 cup red kidney beans, soaked for 12 hours and drained
- 2 teaspoons smoked paprika
- 1 and ½ teaspoons thyme, dried
- A pinch of cayenne pepper
- 2 teaspoons marjoram, dried
- 1 teaspoon oregano, dried
- 14 ounces canned tomatoes, crushed
- ½ teaspoon liquid smoke
- Salt and black pepper to the taste
- Already cooked rice for serving

Directions:

1. Set your instant pot on Sauté mode, add oil and heat it up.
2. Add onion, stir and cook for 5 minutes.
3. Add bell pepper and garlic, stir and cook 5 more minutes.
4. Add beans, bay leaves, water, thyme, paprika, cayenne and marjoram, stir, cover and cook on High for 15 minutes.
5. Release the pressure, uncover the pot, discard bay leaves, add oregano, tomatoes, liquid smoke, salt and pepper to the taste, stir, cover the pot again and cook at High for 3 more minutes.
6. Release the pressure naturally, uncover the pot and divide beans mix among plates on top of already cooked rice.

Enjoy!
Nutrition:

- Calories 189
- Fat 3
- Fiber 10
- Carbs 32
- Protein 11.3

Kidney Beans Curry

This is called Rajma and it's a real comfort food!

Preparation time: 10 minutes
Cooking time: 1 hour and 10 minutes
Servings: 8
Ingredients:

- 2 cups red kidney beans, soaked for 8 hours and drained
- 1 inch piece ginger, chopped
- 1 yellow onion, chopped
- 4 garlic cloves, chopped
- 2 tablespoons vegetable oil
- 2 teaspoons ghee
- 2 red chili peppers, dried and crushed
- Salt and black pepper to the taste
- 6 cloves
- 1 teaspoon cumin seeds
- 1 teaspoons turmeric, ground
- 1 teaspoon cumin, ground
- 1 teaspoon coriander, ground
- 2 tomatoes chopped
- 2 cups water
- 1 teaspoon sugar
- 1 teaspoon red pepper, ground
- 2 teaspoons garam masala
- ¼ cup cilantro, chopped

Directions:

1. Grind ginger, garlic and onion using a mortar and pestle and transfer paste to a bowl.
2. Set your instant pot on Sauté mode, add ghee and oil and heat it up.
3. Add red chili pepper, cloves and cumin seeds, stir and fry for 3 minutes.
4. Add onion paste, stir and cook for 3 more minutes.
5. Add coriander, cumin and turmeric, stir and cook for 30 seconds.
6. Add tomatoes, stir and cook 5 minutes.
7. Add beans, 2 cups water, salt, pepper and sugar, stir, cover and cook at High for 40 minutes.
8. Switch instant pot to Low and cook for 10 minutes more.
9. Release the pressure, uncover the pot, add red pepper, garam masala and cilantro, stir, divide among plates and serve.

Enjoy!
Nutrition:

- Calories 224
- Fat 4
- Fiber 7
- Carbs 30
- Protein 12

Special Kidney Beans Dish

It's a special and surprising dish!

Preparation time: 10 minutes
Cooking time: 25 minutes
Servings: 8
Ingredients:

- 1 pound red kidney beans, soaked for 8 hours and drained
- 2 yellow onions, chopped
- 8 ounces smoked Cajun Tasso, chopped
- 1 celery rib, chopped
- 2 tablespoons garlic, minced
- 1 green bell pepper, chopped
- 2 teaspoons thyme, dried
- 3 tablespoons extra virgin olive oil
- 2 bay leaves
- Cajun seasoning to the taste
- 4 green onions, chopped
- Hot sauce to the taste

Directions:

1. Set your instant pot on Sauté mode, add oil and heat it up.
2. Add Tasso, stir, cook for 5 minutes and transfer to a bowl.
3. Add onions and Cajun seasoning to the pot, stir and cook for 10 minutes.
4. Add garlic, stir and cook 5 minutes.
5. Add bell pepper and celery, stir and cook 5 minutes.
6. Add beans, water to cover everything, bay leaves, thyme, cover and cook at High for 15 minutes.
7. Release the pressure fast, uncover the pot, add Tasso and leave aside for 5 minutes.
8. Divide beans and Tasso mix on plates, garnish with green onions and serve with hot sauce to the taste.

Enjoy!

Nutrition:

- Calories 240
- Fat 3
- Fiber 4
- Carbs 16
- Protein 5

Black Beans And Chorizo

It's delicious and very simple to make!

Preparation time: 10 minutes
Cooking time: 45 minutes
Servings: 6
Ingredients:

- 1 tablespoon vegetable oil
- 6 ounces chorizo, chopped
- 1 yellow onion, cut into half
- 1 pound black beans, soaked for 8 hours and drained
- 6 garlic cloves, minced
- 2 bay leaves
- 1 orange, cut into half
- 2 quarts chicken stock
- Salt to the taste
- Chopped cilantro, chopped for serving

Directions:

1. Set your instant pot on Sauté mode, add oil and heat it up.
2. Add chorizo, stir and cook for 2 minutes.
3. Add onion, beans, garlic, bay leaves, orange, salt and stock, stir, cover and cook at High for 40 minutes.
4. Release the pressure naturally, uncover your pot, discard bay leaves, onion and orange, add more salt and cilantro, stir, divide into bowls and serve.

Enjoy!

Nutrition:

- Calories 230
- Fat 7.7
- Fiber 8
- Carbs 30
- Protein 12.5

Tasty Black Beans

Enjoy this tasty and easy to make dish!

Preparation time: 10 minutes
Cooking time: 30 minutes
Servings: 4
Ingredients:

- 1 pound ham hock
- 4 tablespoons extra virgin olive oil
- 1 yellow onion, chopped
- 1 bay leaf
- 2 garlic cloves, minced
- 2 cups black beans, soaked for 8 hours and drained
- Salt and black pepper to the taste
- 6 cups water

Directions:

1. Set your instant pot on Sauté mode, add 3 tablespoons oil and heat up.
2. Add ham hock and onions, stir and cook for 5 minutes.
3. Add bay leaf and garlic, stir and cook for 1 minute.
4. Add beans and stir well.
5. Add water, the rest of the oil, salt and pepper, stir, cover and cook at High for 25 minutes.
6. Release the pressure, leave aside for 5 minutes, uncover, discard bay leaf, discard ham hock bone, add more salt and pepper if needed, stir, divide into bowls and serve.

Nutrition:

- Calories 500
- Fat 4
- Fiber 21
- Carbs 35
- Protein 32

Spicy Black Beans

This is a real Mexican dish you should try soon!

Preparation time: 10 minutes
Cooking time: 35 minutes
Servings: 8
Ingredients:

- 16 ounces black beans, soaked overnight and drained
- 2 tablespoons chili powder
- 1 yellow onion, chopped
- 4 garlic cloves, minced
- 2 teaspoons cumin, ground
- 1 teaspoon chipotle powder
- 2 teaspoons oregano, dried
- 8 ounces tomato paste
- 2 quarts water
- 4 tablespoons sunflower oil
- Salt to the taste

Directions:

1. In your instant pot, mix beans with garlic, onion, chili powder, chipotle powder, cumin, oregano, tomato paste, water, oil and salt, stir, cover and cook at High for 30 minutes.
2. Release the pressure, uncover the pot and set it on Simmer mode.
3. Add more salt if needed, stir, cook for 3 minutes, divide into bowls and serve.

Enjoy!

Nutrition:

- Calories 180
- Fat 3
- Fiber 7
- Carbs 7
- Protein 10

Chili Lime Black Beans

It's a great combination you need to try soon!

Preparation time: 10 minutes
Cooking time: 42 minutes
Servings: 4
Ingredients:

- 2 cups black beans, soaked for 8 hours and drained
- 2 teaspoons red palm oil
- 1 yellow onion, chopped
- Salt to the taste
- 4 garlic cloves, minced
- 1 tablespoon chili powder
- 1 teaspoon smoked paprika
- 3 cups water
- Juice from 1 lime

Directions:

1. Set your instant pot on Sauté mode, add oil and heat it up.
2. Add garlic and onion, stir and cook for 2 minutes.
3. Add beans, chili powder, paprika, salt and water, stir, cover and cook on High for 40 minutes.
4. Release the pressure naturally, uncover the pot, add lime juice and more salt, stir, divide into bowls and serve.

Enjoy!
Nutrition:

- Calories 200
- Fat 3
- Fiber 5
- Carbs 22
- Protein 7

Tasty Marrow Beans And Lemon

This dish is more delicious than we thought!

Preparation time: 10 minutes
Cooking time: 45 minutes
Servings: 4
Ingredients:

- 2 cups marrow beans, soaked for 8 hours and drained
- 1 cup yellow onion, chopped
- 1 tablespoon extra virgin olive oil
- 1 tablespoon rosemary, chopped
- 4 garlic cloves, minced
- 1 carrot, chopped
- Salt and black pepper to the taste
- 4 cups water
- 1 bay leaf
- 2 tablespoons lemon juice
- Already cooked quinoa for serving

Directions:

1. Set your instant pot on Sauté mode, add oil and heat it up.
2. Add onion, carrot, garlic and rosemary, stir and cook for 3 minutes.
3. Add water, bay leaf, beans and some salt, stir, cover and cook at High for 45 minutes.
4. Release the pressure naturally, uncover the pot, discard bay leaf, add salt and pepper to the taste and lemon juice, stir well and divide into bowls over already cooked quinoa.

Enjoy!

Nutrition:

- Calories 165
- Fat 2
- Fiber 6
- Carbs 28
- Protein 9

White Beans And Shrimp

It's a great combination!

Preparation time: 10 minutes
Cooking time: 35 minutes
Servings: 8
Ingredients:

- 1 pound white beans, soaked for 8 hours and drained
- 1 garlic clove, minced
- 2 yellow onions, chopped
- 1 green bell pepper, chopped
- 1 celery rib, chopped
- 4 parsley springs, chopped
- 2 cups seafood stock
- 2 bay leaves
- 3 tablespoons canola oil
- Creole seasoning to the taste
- 1 pound shrimp, peeled and deveined
- Cooker rice for serving
- Hot sauce for serving

Directions:

1. Set your instant pot on Sauté mode, add oil and heat it up.
2. Add onions and Creole seasoning to the taste, stir and cook for 5 minutes.
3. Add garlic, stir and cook 5 minutes more.
4. Add bell pepper and celery, stir and cook for 5 minutes.
5. Add beans, stock and some water to cover everything in the pot.
6. Add bay leaves and parsley, stir, cover and cook at High for 15 minutes.
7. Release the pressure, uncover the pot, add shrimp, cover pot and leave it aside for 10 minutes.
8. Divide beans and shrimp among plates on top of cooked rice and serve with hot sauce.

Enjoy!

Nutrition:

- Calories 340
- Fat 13
- Fiber 11
- Carbs 38
- Protein 21

Baked Beans

You need to pay attention to this great recipe!

Preparation time: 10 minutes
Cooking time: 55 minutes
Servings: 4
Ingredients:

- 1 pound white beans, soaked for 8 hours and drained
- ½ cup molasses
- 2 garlic cloves, minced
- 1 yellow onion, chopped
- ½ cup maple syrup
- 1 tablespoon mustard powder
- Salt and black pepper to the taste
- 7 cups water
- 1/8 cup balsamic vinegar

Directions:

1. Put the beans and 3 cups water in your instant pot, cover and cook at High for 10 minutes.
2. Release pressure naturally, uncover the pot, drain beans and return them to the pot.
3. Add 4 cups water, molasses, garlic, onion, maple syrup, vinegar, salt and pepper, stir, cover and cook on High for 45 minutes.
4. Release the pressure again, uncover the pot, divide into bowls and serve.

Enjoy!

Nutrition:

- Calories 152
- Fat 5.5
- Fiber 5.4
- Carbs 21
- Protein 5.5

Creamy White Beans

This is a New Orleans style dish!

Preparation time: 10 minutes
Cooking time: 35 minutes
Servings: 8
Ingredients:

- 1 yellow onion, chopped
- 1 pound white beans
- 5 cups water
- 2 celery ribs, chopped
- 2 bay leaves
- 4 garlic cloves, minced
- 1 green bell pepper, chopped
- 1 teaspoon oregano
- 1 teaspoon thyme
- Salt and white pepper to the taste
- 1 tablespoon soy sauce
- 1 tablespoon Tabasco sauce

Directions:

1. Put beans and water in your instant pot.
2. Add onion, celery, garlic, bell pepper, oregano, thyme, salt, white pepper and soy sauce, stir, cover and cook at High for 15 minutes.
3. Release the pressure naturally for 15 minutes, uncover the pot and set it on Simmer mode.
4. Add more salt and pepper to the taste and Tabasco sauce, stir and cook for 20 minutes.
5. Divide into bowls and serve.

Enjoy!

Nutrition:

- Calories 170
- Fat 0.6
- Fiber 10
- Carbs 31
- Protein 10.5

Mung Beans Dish

We were impressed with the taste! Try it and see for yourself!

Preparation time: 10 minutes
Cooking time: 17 minutes
Servings: 4
Ingredients:

- ¾ cup mung beans, soaked for 15 minutes and drained
- 1 small red onion, chopped
- ½ teaspoon cumin seeds
- ½ teaspoon coconut oil
- ½ cup brown rice, soaked for 15 minutes and drained
- 28 ounces canned tomatoes, crushed
- 5 garlic cloves, minced
- 1 inch ginger piece, chopped
- 1 teaspoon coriander, ground
- 1 teaspoon turmeric
- ½ teaspoon garam masala
- A pinch of cayenne
- Salt and black pepper to the taste
- 1 teaspoon lemon juice
- 4 cups water

Directions:

1. In your food processor, mix tomatoes with onions, ginger, garlic, coriander, turmeric, cayenne, salt, pepper and garam masala and blend well.
2. Set your instant pot on Sauté mode, add oil and heat up.
3. Add cumin seeds, stir and fry for 2 minutes.
4. Add tomatoes mix, stir and cook for 15 minutes.
5. Add beans, rice, water, salt, pepper and lemon juice, stir, cover and cook at High for 15 minutes.
6. Release the pressure for 10 minutes, uncover the pot, stir again, divide into bowls and serve.

Enjoy!
Nutrition:

- Calories 180
- Fat 1
- Fiber 15
- Carbs 39
- Protein 7

Indian Style Mung Beans

There's nothing more comforting than a tasty dish! Here's one!

Preparation time: 10 minutes
Cooking time: 1 hour
Servings: 4
Ingredients:

- 1 cup mung beans, soaked for 6 hours and drained
- 1 teaspoon cumin seeds
- 2 teaspoons ghee
- A pinch of cayenne pepper
- 2 teaspoons turmeric
- ½ tablespoon coriander, ground
- 1 teaspoon cumin, ground
- 1 tablespoon ginger, grated
- 1 yellow onion, chopped
- 1 tomato, chopped
- 1 and ½ cups water
- 4 jalapeno peppers, chopped
- ¼ cup cilantro, chopped
- Salt and black pepper to the taste

Directions:

1. Set your instant pot on Sauté mode, add ghee and heat it up.
2. Add cumin seeds, stir and cook for 1 minute.
3. Add cayenne, turmeric, coriander, cumin and ginger, stir and cook for 2 minutes.
4. Add jalapenos and onion, stir and cook for 4 minutes.
5. Add beans and water, salt and pepper, stir, cover and cook at High for 20 minutes.
6. Release the pressure, uncover, add tomatoes, more salt and pepper if needed and set the pot on Simmer mode.
7. Stir and simmer for 20 minutes more, add cilantro, divide into bowls and serve.

Enjoy!

Nutrition:

- Calories 210
- Fat 4.3
- Fiber 8.7
- Carbs 33
- Protein 13

Navy Beans And Cabbage

It's so tasty!

Preparation time: 10 minutes
Cooking time: 40 minutes
Servings: 8
Ingredients:

- 6 bacon slices, chopped
- 1 yellow onion, chopped
- 1 and ½ cups navy beans, soaked for 8 hours and drained
- ¼ teaspoon cloves
- 3 cups chicken stock
- 1 bay leaf
- 1 cabbage head, chopped
- 3 tablespoons honey
- 3 tablespoons white wine vinegar
- Salt and black pepper to the taste

Directions:

1. Set your instant pot on Sauté mode, add bacon, stir and brown it for 4 minutes.
2. Add onions, stir and cook for 4 minutes.
3. Add stock, beans, clove and bay leaf, stir, cover and cook at High for 35 minutes.
4. Release the pressure fast, uncover, add vinegar, honey and cabbage, stir, cover and cook at High for 12 minutes more.
5. Release pressure again, uncover, add salt and pepper, stir, divide into bowls and serve.

Enjoy!

Nutrition:

- Calories 150
- Fat 1
- Fiber 9.5
- Carbs 27
- Protein 7

Black Eyed Pea Curry

You will adore this Indian style curry!

Preparation time: 10 minutes
Cooking time: 45 minutes
Servings: 4
Ingredients:

- 1 cup black-eyed peas, soaked for 3 hours and drained
- ½ teaspoon cumin seeds
- 2 tablespoons avocado oil
- 1 bay leaf
- 1 yellow onion, chopped
- 6 garlic cloves, minced
- 1 inch ginger piece, minced
- 1 teaspoon turmeric
- A pinch of cayenne pepper
- 2 tomatoes, chopped
- Salt and black pepper to the taste
- 1 teaspoon garam masala
- 3 cups water
- Cilantro leaves, chopped for serving

Directions:

1. Set your instant pot on Sauté mode, add oil and heat it up.
2. Add cumin seeds, stir and fry for 2 minutes.
3. Add onion and bay leaf, stir and cook 8 minutes.
4. Add ginger, garlic, turmeric, cayenne, salt, pepper and garam masala, stir and cook for 2 minutes.
5. Add peas, tomatoes and water, stir, cover and cook at High for 30 minutes.
6. Release the pressure, uncover the pot, add cilantro, more salt and pepper if needed, stir, divide into bowls and serve.

Enjoy!
Nutrition:

- Calories 200
- Fat 6
- Fiber 12
- Carbs 33
- Protein 12

Tasty Fava Bean Dip

Serve this with some crackers and enjoy!

Preparation time: 10 minutes
Cooking time: 30 minutes
Servings: 6
Ingredients:

- 2 cups fava beans, soaked
- 2 garlic cloves, crushed
- 3 cups water
- 2 teaspoons tahini
- 2 tablespoons vegetable oil
- 2 teaspoons cumin powder
- 1 teaspoon harissa
- Zest from 1 lemon
- Juice of 1 lemon
- Salt and black pepper to the taste
- 1 tablespoon olive oil
- 1 teaspoon paprika

Directions:

1. Set your instant pot on Sauté mode, add vegetable oil and heat it up.
2. Add garlic, stir and cook for 3 minutes.
3. Add fava beans, 3 cups water, stir, cover and cook at High for 12 minutes.
4. Release the pressure naturally for 10 minutes, uncover the pot, drain most of the liquid and set it on Sauté mode again.
5. Add cumin, harissa, tahini, salt and pepper and lemon zest, stir and blend everything using an immersion blender.
6. Add paprika, lemon juice and olive oil and stir gently.
7. Divide into bowls and serve.

Enjoy!

Nutrition:

- Calories 60
- Fat 1
- Fiber 0
- Carbs 9
- Protein 3

Fava Bean Puree

This is a perfect appetizer for your next party!

Preparation time: 10 minutes
Cooking time: 25 minutes
Servings: 6
Ingredients:

- 1 pound fava bean, rinsed
- 1 cup yellow onion, chopped
- 4 and ½ cups water
- 1 bay leaf
- ¼ cup extra virgin olive oil
- 1 garlic clove, minced
- 2 tablespoons lemon juice
- Salt to the taste

Directions:

1. Put fava beans in your instant pot, add 4 cups water, some salt and bay leaf, cover and cook at High for 18 minutes.
2. Release the pressure naturally, uncover the pot, drain beans and discard bay leaf.
3. Return beans to the pot, add ½ cup water, garlic, onion and salt, stir, cover and cook 5 minutes.
4. Release the pressure again, uncover pot, transfer beans mix to your food processor, add olive oil and lemon juice and blend well.
5. Divide into bowls and serve cold.

Enjoy!

Nutrition:

- Calories 330
- Fat 4
- Fiber 1
- Carbs 30
- Protein 10

Full Mudammas

It's a fava beans delight!

Preparation time: 10 minutes
Cooking time: 25 minutes
Servings: 2
Ingredients:

- 2 cups already cooked fava beans
- 4 roasted garlic cloves, chopped
- 1 small red onion, chopped
- 1 tablespoon olive oil
- 1 teaspoon cumin
- ½ cup water
- Salt and black pepper to the taste
- Juice from 2 lemons
- 1 egg, hard boiled, peeled and sliced
- 1 tomato, finely chopped
- 1 yellow onion, cut into thin rings
- A pinch of red chili flakes
- A pinch of paprika

Directions:

1. Set your instant pot on Sauté mode, add oil and heat it up.
2. Add red onion, stir and cook for 3 minutes.
3. Add cumin and garlic, stir and cook for 1 minute. Add beans, salt, pepper and water, stir, cover and cook at High for 15 minutes.
4. Release the pressure, uncover the pot, set it on Simmer mode and cook for 10 more minutes.
5. Transfer to a bowl, add more salt, pepper and lemon juice and mash using a potato masher.
6. Garnish with egg slices, tomato pieces, yellow onion rings, red chili flakes and paprika sprinkled on top.
7. Serve hot!

Enjoy!

Nutrition:

- Calories 154
- Fat 1.4
- Fiber 3
- Carbs 30
- Protein 8.6

Tasty Butter Beans

We guarantee these are amazing and super tasty!

Preparation time: 10 minutes
Cooking time: 1 hour
Servings: 8
Ingredients:

- 1 pound butter beans, soaked for 8 hours and drained
- 1 pound bacon, chopped
- 4 cups water
- 1 garlic clove, minced
- 1 jalapeno pepper, chopped
- ½ teaspoon cumin, ground
- 12 ounces beer
- Salt and black pepper to the taste

Directions:

1. Set your instant pot on Sauté mode, add bacon and brown it for 10 minutes.
2. Transfer bacon to paper towels, drain grease, put in a bowl and leave aside.
3. Add the water, cumin and beer to your pot and stir.
4. Add beans, stir, cover and cook at High for 30 minutes.
5. Release the pressure, uncover the pot, add garlic, bacon, jalapeno, salt and pepper, stir, cover again and cook at High for 3 minutes more.
6. Release pressure again, uncover, transfer to bowls and serve.

Enjoy!

Nutrition:

- Calories 156
- Fat 4
- Fiber 3
- Carbs 6
- Protein 1

Split Pea Curry

This is a vegetarian dish you will enjoy for sure!

Preparation time: 10 minutes
Cooking time: 35 minutes
Servings: 4
Ingredients:

- 7 ounces split peas
- 1 tablespoon olive oil
- 2 yellow onions, chopped
- 2 bell peppers, chopped
- 4 tablespoons curry paste
- 2 teaspoons black onion seeds
- 15 ounces canned tomatoes, chopped
- 15 ounces canned coconut milk
- A bunch of coriander leaves, chopped
- Zest and juice of 1 lime
- Salt and black pepper to the taste
- 5 ounces coconut yogurt
- Naan bread for serving

Directions:

1. Set your instant pot on Sauté mode, add oil and heat it up.
2. Add onions and bell peppers, stir and cook for 10 minutes.
3. Add curry paste and black onion seeds, stir and cook for 1 minute.
4. Add split peas, coconut milk, tomatoes and coriander.
5. Also, add some salt and pepper, stir, cover and cook at High for 25 minutes.
6. Release pressure, uncover the pot, add more salt and pepper if needed, lime zest and juice and coconut yogurt and stir.
7. Divide into bowls and serve with naan bread on the side.

Enjoy!

Nutrition:

- Calories 435
- Fat 18
- Fiber 8
- Carbs 47
- Protein 16

Split Pea And Squash Curry

Try this curry as well!

Preparation time: 10 minutes
Cooking time: 25 minutes
Servings: 4
Ingredients:

- 1 cup split peas, soaked in water for a few hours and drained
- ¼ teaspoon fenugreek seeds
- ¼ teaspoon udad dhal
- 1 tablespoon peanut oil
- ½ teaspoon mustard seeds
- A pinch of hing
- 1 tablespoon ginger, minced
- 1 garlic clove, minced
- ½ cup onion, chopped
- 2 cups squash, peeled and chopped
- 1/3 cup tomato, cut into chunks
- 2 cups water
- Salt and pepper to the taste
- ½ teaspoon turmeric
- 1 teaspoon cumin, ground
- 1 teaspoon coriander, ground
- 2 teaspoons garam masala
- ½ cup cilantro, chopped

Directions:

1. Set your instant pot on Sauté mode, add oil and heat it up.
2. Add udad dhal, mustard seeds and fenugreek, stir and fry for 1 minute.
3. Add hing, onions, ginger, garlic, stir and cook for 3 minutes more.
4. Add split peas, water, tomato, turmeric, salt, pepper, coriander, cumin, squash and half of the cilantro, stir, cover and cook at High for 10 minutes.
5. Release the pressure naturally, uncover the pot, add the rest of the cilantro and garam masala, stir, divide into bowls and serve.

Enjoy!

Nutrition:

- Calories 275
- Fat 2.7
- Fiber 12.5
- Carbs 53
- Protein 12

Tasty Pea And Pineapple Curry

It's a very hearty Indian dish!

Preparation time: 10 minutes
Cooking time: 35 minutes
Servings: 4
Ingredients:

- 1 cup peas, soaked in water for a few hours and drained
- 4 cups water
- 3 tablespoons extra virgin olive oil
- 1 yellow onion, chopped
- 1 cup brown lentils
- 1 teaspoon curry powder
- ½ teaspoon turmeric
- ¼ teaspoon cinnamon
- ½ teaspoon cumin
- 2/3 cup canned pineapple, cut into chunks
- ¼ cup cashew butter

Directions:

1. In a bowl, mix cashew butter with some water, stir very well and leave aside for now.
2. Put lentils and beans in you instant pot, add 3 and ½ cups water, stir, cover and cook at High for 25 minutes.
3. Release the pressure, drain peas and lentils and put them in a bowl.
4. Set your instant pot on Sauté mode, add oil and heat it up.
5. Add turmeric, cumin, curry powder and cinnamon, stir and cook for 3 minutes.
6. Add onions, stir and cook for 4 minutes.
7. Set the pot on Simmer mode, add peas and lentils, cashew butter, pineapple and ½ cup water, stir, simmer for 5 minutes, divide into bowls and serve.

Enjoy!

Nutrition:

- Calories 333
- Fat 11
- Fiber 17
- Carbs 43
- Protein 16

Instant Pot Sauce Recipes

Simple Spaghetti Sauce

You will love this simple and very tasty sauce!

Preparation time: 10 minutes
Cooking time: 40 minutes
Servings: 6
Ingredients:

- 1 and 2/3 pounds beef, ground
- 2 carrots, chopped
- 4 garlic cloves, minced
- 2 celery ribs, chopped
- 28 ounces canned tomatoes, crushed
- 1 yellow onion, chopped
- 2 bay leaves
- 1 tablespoon olive oil
- A pinch of basil, dried
- A pinch of oregano, dried
- A splash of red wine
- Salt and black pepper to the taste

For the chicken stock mix:

- 1 cup chicken stock
- 2 tablespoons soy sauce
- 3 tablespoons tomato paste
- 2 tablespoons fish sauce
- 1 tablespoon Worcestershire sauce

Directions:

1. Set your instant pot on Sauté mode, add beef, salt, pepper and the oil, stir and brown for 7 minutes.
2. Transfer beef to a bowl when it's brown and leave it aside for now.
3. In a bowl, mix stock with fish sauce, soy sauce, tomato paste and Worcestershire sauce and stir well.
4. Heat up you instant pot again, add onions, garlic, bay leaves, basil and oregano, stir and cook for 5 minutes.
5. Add celery, carrots, salt and pepper, stir and cook for 3 minutes.
6. Add red wine, chicken stock mix, beef and crushed tomatoes on top.
7. Cover pot and cook at High for 10 minutes.
8. Release pressure, uncover, add more salt and pepper if needed, set the pot on Simmer mode and cook the sauce for 4 minutes more.
9. Serve with your favorite pasta.

Enjoy!
Nutrition:

- Calories 281
- Fat 16
- Fiber 5
- Carbs 20
- Protein 17

Tasty Marinara Sauce

It's an Italian-style sauce you will like for sure!

Preparation time: 10 minutes
Cooking time: 20 minutes
Servings: 8
Ingredients:

- 56 ounces canned tomatoes, crushed
- 3 garlic cloves, minced
- ½ cup red lentils
- 1 cup sweet potato, finely chopped
- Salt and black pepper to the taste
- 1 and ½ cups water

Directions:

1. Set your instant pot on Sauté mode, add lentils, sweet potatoes, salt, pepper and garlic, stir and cook them for 2 minutes.
2. Add water and tomatoes, stir, cover pot and cook at High for 13 minutes.
3. Release the pressure, uncover the pot, puree everything using an immersion blender, add more salt and pepper if needed, set the pot on Simmer mode and cook the sauce for 4 minutes more.

Enjoy!
Nutrition:

- Calories 60
- Fat 2
- Fiber 2
- Carbs 9
- Protein 2

Delicious Applesauce

It's so amazing and delicious!

Preparation time: 10 minutes
Cooking time: 8 minutes
Servings: 4
Ingredients:

- 8 apples, cored and chopped
- 2 drops cinnamon oil
- 1 cup water
- 1 teaspoon cinnamon powder

Directions:

1. Put apples in your instant pot, add the water, cover pot and cook at High for 8 minutes.
2. Release the pressure, uncover the pot, add oil and cinnamon and puree using an immersion blender.
3. Serve cold.

Enjoy!
Nutrition:

- Calories 70
- Fat 1
- Fiber 1.2
- Carbs 17
- Protein 0.3

Cranberry Sauce

It's a very elegant sauce you can use both for meat dishes or desserts!

Preparation time: 10 minutes
Cooking time: 15 minutes
Servings: 4
Ingredients:

- 2 and ½ teaspoons orange zest
- 12 ounces cranberries
- ¼ cup orange juice
- 2 tablespoons maple syrup
- A pinch of salt
- 1 cup sugar

Directions:

1. In your instant pot, mix orange juice with maple syrup and stir well.
2. Add orange zest and almost all cranberries, stir, cover and cook at High for 2 minutes.
3. Release the pressure, uncover the pot and set it on Sauté mode.
4. Add the rest of the cranberries, a pinch of salt and the sugar, stir and cook until sugar dissolves.
5. Serve cold.

Enjoy!
Nutrition:

- Calories 151
- Fat 0.4
- Fiber 1
- Carbs 39
- Protein 0.4

Ancho Chili Sauce

This is definitely one of our favorite sauces!

Preparation time: 10 minutes
Cooking time: 10 minutes
Servings: 8
Ingredients:

- 5 ancho chilies, dried, seedless and chopped
- 2 garlic cloves, crushed
- Slat and black pepper to the taste
- 1 and ½ cups water
- 1 and ½ teaspoons sugar
- ½ teaspoon oregano, dried
- ½ teaspoon cumin, ground
- 2 tablespoons apple cider vinegar

Directions:

1. In your instant pot mix water chilies, garlic, salt, pepper, sugar, cumin and oregano, stir, cover and cook at High for 8 minutes.
2. Release the pressure for 5 minutes, uncover the pot and pour sauce into a blender.
3. Add vinegar, blend well and transfer everything to a bowl.

Enjoy!
Nutrition:

- Calories 50
- Fat 2
- Fiber 0
- Carbs 2

Orange And Ginger Sauce

It's very healthy and delicious, and it's perfect for some fish fillets!

Preparation time: 5 minutes
Cooking time: 7 minutes.
Servings: 4
Ingredients:

- 1 cup fish stock
- Salt and black pepper to the taste
- 1 tablespoon olive oil
- 4 spring onions, chopped
- 1 inch ginger piece, chopped
- Zest and juice from 1 orange

Directions:

1. In your instant pot, mix fish stock with salt, pepper, olive oil, spring onions, ginger, orange juice and zest and stir well.
2. Cover pot and cook at High for 7 minutes.
3. Release pressure, uncover the pot and serve your sauce.

Enjoy!
Nutrition:

- Calories 100
- Fat 1
- Fiber 1
- Carbs 2
- Protein 4

BBQ Sauce

It's quick and easy and very flavored!

Preparation time: 10 minutes
Cooking time: 10 minutes
Servings: 8
Ingredients:

- 1 tablespoon sesame seed oil
- ½ cup tomato puree
- 1 yellow onion, chopped
- ½ cup water
- 4 tablespoons white wine vinegar
- 4 tablespoons honey
- 1 teaspoon salt
- ½ teaspoon granulated garlic
- 1 teaspoon liquid smoke
- 1 teaspoon Tabasco sauce
- 1/8 teaspoon cumin powder
- 1/8 teaspoon clove powder
- 5 ounces plums, dried and seedless

Directions:

1. Set your instant pot on Sauté mode, add oil and heat it up.
2. Add onion, stir and cook for 5 minutes.
3. Add tomato puree, honey, water, vinegar, salt, garlic, Tabasco sauce, liquid smoke, cumin and clove powder and stir everything very well.
4. Add plums and stir again well.
5. Cover pot and cook at High for 10 minutes.
6. Release the pressure, uncover the pot, blend everything with an immersion blender, transfer sauce to a bowl and serve.

Enjoy!

Nutrition:

- Calories 20
- Fat 0.4
- Fiber 0.4
- Carbs 3.5
- Protein 0.1

Giblet Gravy

This is perfect for a very special meal!

Preparation time: 10 minutes
Cooking time: 1 hour and 30 minutes
Servings: 2
Ingredients:

- Turkey neck, gizzard, but and heart
- 1 tablespoon vegetable oil
- ½ cup dry vermouth
- 1 yellow onion, chopped
- 1-quart turkey stock
- 1 bay leaf
- 4 tablespoons butter
- 2 thyme springs
- 4 tablespoons white flour
- Salt and black pepper to the taste

Directions:

1. Set your instant pot on Sauté mode, add oil and heat it up.
2. Add turkey pieces and onion, stir and cook for 3 minutes.
3. Stir again and cook for 3 more minutes.
4. Add vermouth, stock, bay leaf and thyme and stir.
5. Cover pot and cook at High for 36 minutes.
6. Release the pressure for 20 minutes, strain stock, reserve turkey gizzard, and heart, leave them to cool down, remove gristle and chop it along with the heart.
7. Heat up a pan with the butter over medium heat, add flour, stir and cook for 3 minutes.
8. Add strained stock, stir well, increase heat to medium high and simmer for 20 minutes.
9. Add salt and pepper, heart and gizzard, stir well and serve.

Enjoy!

Nutrition:

- Calories 181
- Fat 10
- Fiber 1
- Carbs 11.4
- Protein 10.5

Zucchini Pesto

It's a special pesto you can make in your instant pot!

Preparation time: 10 minutes
Cooking time: 10 minutes
Servings: 4
Ingredients:

- 1 yellow onion, chopped
- 1 tablespoon extra virgin olive oil
- 1 and ½ pounds zucchini, chopped
- Salt to the taste
- ½ cup water
- 1 bunch basil, chopped
- 2 garlic cloves, minced

Directions:

1. Set your instant pot on Sauté mode, add oil and heat it up.
2. Add onion, stir and cook 4 minutes.
3. Add zucchini, salt and water, stir, cover and cook at High for 3 minutes.
4. Release the pressure, uncover the pot, add garlic and basil and blend everything using an immersion blender.
5. Transfer to a bowl and serve.

Enjoy!

Nutrition:

- Calories 71
- Fat 5
- Fiber 2.3
- Carbs 2
- Protein 1.2

Delicious Sauce

You'll be surprised with this delicious sauce!

Preparation time: 10 minutes
Cooking time: 20 minutes
Servings: 8
Ingredients:

- 1 yellow onion, chopped
- 2 tablespoons olive oil
- 5 celery ribs
- 8 carrots, chopped
- 4 beets, chopped
- 1 butternut squash, chopped
- 8 garlic cloves, minced
- 1 cup veggie stock
- ¼ cup lemon juice
- 1 bunch basil, chopped
- 2 bay leaves
- Salt and black pepper to the taste

Directions:

1. Set your instant pot on Sauté mode, add oil and heat it up.
2. Add celery, onion and carrots, stir and cook for 4 minutes.
3. Add beets, squash, garlic, stock, lemon juice, basil, bay leaves, salt and pepper, stir, cover and cook for 12 minutes at High.
4. Release the pressure, uncover the pot, discard bay leaves, puree sauce using an immersion blender, transfer to a bowl and serve.

Enjoy!
Nutrition:

- Calories 79
- Fat 1
- Fiber 0.4
- Carbs 5
- Protein 3

Delicious Cheese Sauce

It's an incredible and very tasty sauce!

Preparation time: 10 minutes
Cooking time: 5 minutes
Servings: 4

Ingredients:

- 2 cups processed cheese, cut into chunks
- 1 cup Italian sausage, cooked and chopped
- 5 ounces canned tomatoes and green chilies, finely chopped
- 4 tablespoons water

Directions:

1. In your instant pot, mix sausage with cheese, tomatoes and chilies and water.
2. Stir, cover and cook at High for 5 minutes.
3. Release pressure, uncover pot, transfer sauce to a bowl and serve with your favorite macaroni.

Enjoy!

Nutrition:

- Calories 110
- Fat 8.5
- Fiber 0.4
- Carbs 4.3
- Protein 4.32

Mushroom Sauce

This is the best mushroom sauce you'll ever have!

Preparation time: 10 minutes
Cooking time: 35 minutes
Servings: 6
Ingredients:

- 1 yellow onion, chopped
- ¼ cup olive oil
- 1 tablespoon flour
- Salt and black pepper to the taste
- 1 tablespoon thyme, chopped
- 3 garlic cloves, minced
- 1 and ¼ cup chicken stock
- ¼ cup dry sherry
- 10 ounces shiitake mushrooms, chopped
- 10 ounces cremini mushrooms, chopped
- 10 ounces Portobello mushrooms, chopped
- 1-ounce parmesan cheese, grated
- ½ cup heavy cream
- 1 tablespoons parsley, finely chopped

Directions:

1. Set your instant pot on Sauté mode, add oil and heat it up.
2. Add onion, salt and pepper, stir and cook for 5 minutes.
3. Add garlic, flour and thyme, stir and cook for 1 minute.
4. Add sherry, stock and all mushrooms, stir, cover and cook at High for 25 minutes.
5. Release pressure quick, uncover the pot, add cream, cheese and parsley, stir and set the pot on Simmer mode.
6. Cook for 5 minutes, transfer to a bowl and serve.

Enjoy!

Nutrition:

- Calories 140
- Fat 5.7
- Fiber 3.1
- Carbs 13
- Protein 7.4

Cauliflower Sauce

This is so creamy and textured!

Preparation time: 10 minutes
Cooking time: 10 minutes
Servings: 6
Ingredients:

- 2 tablespoons butter
- 8 garlic cloves, minced
- 7 cups veggie stock
- 6 cups cauliflower florets
- Salt and black pepper to the taste
- ½ cup milk

Directions:

1. Set your instant pot on Sauté mode, add butter and melt it.
2. Add garlic, salt and pepper, stir, cook for 5 minutes and transfer to a bowl.
3. Add stock and cauliflower to the pot, heat up, cover and cook at High for 7 minutes.
4. Release pressure, transfer cauliflower and 1 cup stock to your blender, add salt, pepper, milk and garlic and puree well for a few minutes.
5. Serve right away with your favorite spaghetti.

Enjoy!

Nutrition:

- Calories 119
- Fat 5
- Fiber 1
- Carbs 10
- Protein 8

Mango Sauce

It's quick and spicy! It's amazing!

Preparation time: 10 minutes
Cooking time: 30 minutes
Servings: 4
Ingredients:

- 1 shallot, chopped
- 1 tablespoon vegetable oil
- ¼ teaspoon cardamom powder
- 2 tablespoons ginger, minced
- ½ teaspoon cinnamon
- 2 mangos, chopped
- 2 red hot chilies, chopped
- 1 apple, cored and chopped
- 2 teaspoons salt
- ¼ cup raisins
- 1 and ¼ cup raw sugar
- 1 and ¼ apple cider vinegar

Directions:

1. Set your instant pot on Sauté mode, add oil and heat it up.
2. Add ginger and shallot, stir and cook for 5 minutes.
3. Add cinnamon, hot peppers and cardamom, stir and cook for 2 minutes.
4. Add mangos, apple, raisins, sugar and cider, stir and cook until sugar melts.
5. Cover the pot and cook at High for 7 minutes.
6. Release the pressure, uncover the pot, transfer to a pan and simmer on medium heat for 15 minutes more, stirring from time to time.
7. Transfer to jars and serve when needed.

Enjoy!

Nutrition:

- Calories 80
- Fat 0.3
- Fiber 1
- Carbs 9
- Protein 0.9

Tabasco Sauce

It's the best!

Preparation time: 10 minutes
Cooking time: 2 minutes
Servings: 6
Ingredients:

- 12 ounces hot peppers, chopped
- 2 teaspoons salt
- 1 and ¼ cups apple cider vinegar

Directions:

1. Put peppers in your instant pot.
2. Add vinegar and salt, stir, cover and cook at High for 2 minutes.
3. Release the pressure for 15 minutes, uncover the pot and puree everything using your immersion blender.
4. Transfer to jars and serve when needed.

Enjoy!
Nutrition:

- Calories 12
- Fat 0.04
- Fiber 0
- Carbs 0.04
- Protein 0.06

Delicious Strawberry Sauce

It's time for something really tasty: a strawberry sauce!

Preparation time: 10 minutes
Cooking time: 2 minutes
Servings: 8
Ingredients:

- 1-ounce orange juice
- 1/8 cup sugar
- 1 pound strawberries, cut into halves
- A pinch of ginger, ground
- ½ teaspoon vanilla extract

Directions:

1. In your instant pot, mix strawberries with sugar, stir and leave them aside for 10 minutes.
2. Add orange juice, stir, cover and cook at High for 2 minutes.
3. Release the pressure for 15 minutes, uncover the pot, add vanilla extract and ginger, puree a but using an immersion blender and leave aside until it's cold enough.
4. Serve your strawberry sauce with some tasty pancakes.

Enjoy!
Nutrition:

- Calories 60
- Fat 0
- Carbs 13
- Protein 1

Tomato Chutney

A mango chutney is delicious, but a tomato one is amazing!

Preparation time: 10 minutes
Cooking time: 10 minutes
Servings: 6
Ingredients:

- 3 pounds tomatoes, peeled and chopped
- 1 cup red wine vinegar
- 1 and ¾ cups sugar
- 1 inch ginger piece, grated
- 3 garlic cloves, minced
- 2 onions, chopped
- ¼ cup raisins
- ¾ teaspoon cinnamon, ground
- ¼ teaspoon cloves
- ½ teaspoon coriander, ground
- ¼ teaspoon nutmeg
- ¼ teaspoon ginger, ground
- 1 pinch paprika
- 1 teaspoon chili powder

Directions:

1. Mix tomatoes and grated ginger in your blender, pulse well and transfer to your instant pot.
2. Add vinegar, sugar, garlic, onions, raisins, cinnamon, cloves, coriander, nutmeg, ground ginger, paprika and chili powder, stir, cover and cook at High for 10 minutes.
3. Release the pressure, uncover the pot, transfer to jars and serve when needed.

Enjoy!

Nutrition:

- Calories 140
- Fat 10
- Fiber 0
- Carbs 10
- Protein 4

Different Tomato Sauce

It's a very interesting sauce with a special taste!

Preparation time: 10 minutes
Cooking time: 15 minutes
Servings: 20
Ingredients:

- 2 pounds tomatoes, peeled and chopped
- 1 apple, cored and chopped
- 1 yellow onion, chopped
- 6 ounces sultanas, chopped
- 3 ounces dates chopped
- Salt to the taste
- 3 teaspoons whole spice
- ½ pint vinegar
- ½ pound brown sugar

Directions:

1. Put tomatoes in your instant pot.
2. Add apple, onion, sultanas, dates, salt, whole spice and half of the vinegar, stir, cover and cook at High for 10 minutes.
3. Release the pressure, uncover the pot, set it on Simmer mode, add the rest of the vinegar and sugar, stir and simmer until sugar dissolves.
4. Transfer to jars and serve when needed.

Enjoy!
Nutrition:

- Calories 70
- Fat 4
- Fiber 1
- Carbs 8
- Protein 1.7

Green Tomato Sauce

This is perfect for winter dishes!

Preparation time: 5 minutes
Cooking time: 10 minutes
Servings: 12
Ingredients:

- 2 pounds green tomatoes, chopped
- 1 white onion, chopped
- ¼ cup currants
- 1 Anaheim chili pepper, chopped
- 4 red chili peppers, chopped
- 2 tablespoons ginger, grated
- ¾ cup brown sugar
- ¾ cup white vinegar

Directions:

1. In your instant pot, mix green tomatoes with onion, currants, Anaheim pepper, chili pepper, ginger, sugar, and vinegar, stir, cover and cook at High for 10 minutes.
2. Release the pressure for 5 minutes, uncover pot, transfer sauce to jars and serve.

Enjoy!

Nutrition:

- Calories 50
- Fat 2
- Fiber 2.4
- Carbs 10
- Protein 1.5

Plum Sauce

It's one of the best sauces you will ever try!

Preparation time: 10 minutes
Cooking time: 15 minutes
Servings: 20
Ingredients:

- 3 pounds plumps, pitted and chopped
- 2 onions, chopped
- 2 apples, cored and chopped
- 4 tablespoons ginger, ground
- 4 tablespoons cinnamon
- 4 tablespoons allspice
- 1 and ½ tablespoons salt
- 1-pint vinegar
- ¾ pound sugar

Directions:

1. Put plumps, apples, and onions in your instant pot.
2. Add ginger, cinnamon, allspice, salt and almost all the vinegar, stir, cover and cook at High for 10 minutes.
3. Release the pressure, uncover the pot, set it on Simmer mode, add the rest of the vinegar and the sugar, stir and cook until sugar dissolves.

Enjoy!
Nutrition:

- Calories 100
- Fat 10
- Fiber 3
- Carbs 23
- Protein 26

Delicious Pineapple Sauce

It's unbelievably tasty!

Preparation time: 10 minutes
Cooking time: 3 minutes
Servings: 4
Ingredients:

- 3 cups pineapple tidbits
- 3 tablespoons rum
- 3 tablespoons butter
- 4 tablespoons brown sugar
- 1 teaspoon cinnamon
- 1 teaspoon allspice
- 1 teaspoon nutmeg
- 1 teaspoon ginger

Directions:

1. Set your instant pot on sauté mode, add butter and melt it.
2. Add sugar, pineapple tidbits, rum, allspice, nutmeg, cinnamon and ginger, stir, cover and cook at High for 3 minutes.
3. Release pressure, uncover the pot, stir sauce one more time and serve.

Enjoy!
Nutrition:

- Calories 160
- Fat 0
- Fiber 0
- Carbs 23
- Protein 0

Simple Onion Sauce

It's a special and refined sauce!

Preparation time: 10 minutes
Cooking time: 30 minutes
Servings: 8
Ingredients:

- 6 tablespoons butter
- 3 pounds yellow onion, thinly chopped
- Salt and black pepper to the taste
- ½ teaspoon baking soda

Directions:

1. Set your instant pot on Sauté mode, add butter and heat it up.
2. Add onions and soda, stir and cook for 3 minutes.
3. Cover your pot and cook at High for 20 minutes.
4. Release the pressure, uncover the pot, set it on Sauté mode again and cook for 5 minutes more stirring often.
5. Serve when needed.

Enjoy!

Nutrition:

- Calories 100
- Fat 0.4
- Fiber 0
- Carbs 9
- Protein 0

Clementine Sauce

It's a sweet and simple sauce!

Preparation time: 10 minutes
Cooking time: 6 minutes
Servings: 4
Ingredients:

- 12 ounces cranberries
- 1 cup water
- Juice and peel from 1 clementine
- 1 cup sugar

Directions:

1. In your instant pot, mix cranberries with clementine juice and peel, water and sugar, stir, cover and cook at High for 6 minutes.
2. Release pressure, uncover the pot and serve your sauce.

Enjoy!

Nutrition:

- Calories 50
- Fat 0
- Fiber 0
- Carbs 0.3
- Protein 0

Delicious Orange Sauce

It's so delicious!

Preparation time: 10 minutes
Cooking time: 7 minutes
Servings: 6
Ingredients:

- ¼ cup white wine vinegar
- 1 teaspoon ginger paste
- 2 tablespoons tomato paste
- 3 tablespoons sugar
- 1 cup orange juice
- 1 teaspoon garlic, finely chopped
- 2 tablespoons agave nectar
- 1 teaspoon sesame oil
- 1 teaspoon chili sauce
- 2 tablespoons soy sauce
- ¼ cup veggie stock
- 2 tablespoons cornstarch

Directions:

1. Set your instant pot on Sauté mode, add oil and heat it up.
2. Add garlic and ginger paste, stir and cook for 2 minutes.
3. Add tomato paste, sugar, orange juice, vinegar, agave nectar, soy and chili sauce, stir, cover and cook at High for 3 minutes more.
4. Release pressure, uncover the pot, add stock and cornstarch, stir, cover again and cook at High for 4 minutes.
5. Release pressure again and serve your sauce.

Enjoy!

Nutrition:

- Calories 80
- Fat 7
- Fiber 1.4
- Carbs 5
- Protein 13

Bread Sauce

Serve this with a chicken or turkey roast!

Preparation time: 10 minutes
Cooking time: 10 minutes
Servings: 12
Ingredients:

- 1 yellow onion, chopped
- 2 garlic cloves, crushed
- 6 cloves
- 26 ounces milk
- 6 bread slices, torn
- 2 bay leaves
- Salt to the taste
- 2 tablespoons butter
- A splash of double cream

Directions:

1. Set your instant pot on Simmer mode, add milk and heat it up.
2. Add garlic, cloves, onion, bay leaves and salt, stir well and cook for 3 minutes.
3. Add bread, stir, cover and cook at High for 4 minutes.
4. Release the pressure, uncover pot, transfer sauce to a blender, add butter and cream, discard bay leaf and blend well.
5. Return sauce to the pot set it on Simmer mode and simmer sauce for 3 minutes more.

Enjoy!

Nutrition:

- Calories 113
- Fat 5
- Fiber 2.4
- Carbs 11
- Protein 3

Chili Jam

This goes just right with a tasty roast!

Preparation time: 10 minutes
Cooking time: 40 minutes
Servings: 12
Ingredients:

- 4 garlic cloves, minced
- 2 red onions, finely chopped
- 4 red chili peppers, seeded and chopped
- 17 ounces cranberries
- 4 ounces sugar
- A drizzle of olive oil
- Salt and black pepper to the taste
- 2 tablespoons red wine vinegar
- 3 tablespoons water

Directions:

1. Set your instant pot on Sauté mode, add oil and heat it up.
2. Add onions, garlic and chilies, stir and cook for 8 minutes.
3. Add cranberries, vinegar, water and sugar, stir, cover pot and cook at High for 14 minutes.
4. Release the pressure, uncover the pot, mash sauce using an immersion blender, set the pot on Simmer mode and cook the sauce for 15 minutes.
5. Add salt and pepper to the taste, transfer to jars and serve when needed.

Enjoy!

Nutrition:

- Calories 20
- Fat 0.2
- Fiber 0.4
- Carbs 4
- Protein 0.2

Amazing Sriracha Sauce

You must try this sauce soon!

Preparation time: 10 minutes
Cooking time: 17 minutes
Servings: 6
Ingredients:

- 4 ounces red chilies, seeded and chopped
- 3 tablespoons palm sugar
- 3 ounces bird's eye chilies
- 12 garlic cloves, minced
- 5 ounces distilled vinegar
- 5 ounces water

Directions:

1. In your instant pot, mix water with palm sugar and stir.
2. Add all chilies and garlic, stir, cover and cook at High for 7 minutes.
3. Release pressure, uncover the pot, blend sauce using an immersion blender, add vinegar, stir, set the pot on Simmer mode and cook the sauce for 10 minutes.
4. Serve when needed.

Enjoy!
Nutrition:

- Calories 90
- Fat 0.4
- Fiber 0.3
- Carbs 19
- Protein 2.4

Grapes Sauce

It's easy to make and it will taste really good!

Preparation time: 10 minutes
Cooking time: 10 minutes
Servings: 6
Ingredients:

- 6 ounces black grapes
- ½ cup water
- 2 and ½ tablespoons sugar
- 1 cup corn flour
- A splash of lemon juice

Directions:

1. Put grapes in your instant pot, add water to cover, cook at High for 7 minutes, release pressure, leave mix aside to cool down, blend using an immersion blender, strain sauce and leave aside for now.
2. Heat up a pan over medium heat, add grapes mix, sugar, the water and corn flour, stir and boil until it thickens.
3. Add lemon juice, stir, take off heat and serve.

Enjoy!
Nutrition:

- Calories 60
- Fiber 0.3
- Carbs 0
- Protein 3

Pomegranate Sauce

It's a very elegant sauce you should try!

Preparation time: 10 minutes
Cooking time: 25 minutes
Servings: 4
Ingredients:

- 5 cups pomegranate juice
- ½ cup lemon juice
- 1 cup white sugar

Directions:

1. In your instant pot, mix pomegranate juice with sugar and lemon juice, stir, cover and cook at High for 25 minutes.
2. Release pressure, uncover the pot, divide sauce into jars and serve when needed.

Enjoy!

Nutrition:

- Calories 136
- Fat 0.4
- Fiber 0.8
- Carbs 35
- Protein 1.2

Apricot Sauce

Apricots are awesome, and this sauce is great!

Preparation time: 10 minutes
Cooking time: 20 minutes
Servings: 6
Ingredients:

- 3 ounces apricots, dried and cut into halves
- 2 cups water
- 2/3 cup sugar
- 1 teaspoon vanilla extract

Directions:

1. In your instant pot mix apricots with water, sugar and vanilla, stir, cover and cook on Medium for 20 minutes.
2. Release pressure, uncover pot, transfer sauce to your blender and pulse well.
3. Divide into jars and serve with a poultry dish.

Enjoy!

Nutrition:

- Calories 100
- Fat 0.6
- Fiber 0
- Carbs 10
- Protein 1

Mustard Sauce

It's simply the most delicious mustard sauce ever!

Preparation time: 10 minutes
Cooking time: 7 minutes
Servings: 4
Ingredients:

- 6 ounces mushrooms, chopped
- 3 tablespoon olive oil
- 3.5 ounces dry sherry
- 1 thyme spring
- 1 garlic clove, minced
- 3.5 ounces beef stock
- 1 tablespoon balsamic vinegar
- 1 tablespoon mustard
- 2 tablespoon crème fraiche
- 2 tablespoons parsley, finely chopped

Directions:

1. Set your instant pot on Sauté mode, add oil and heat it up.
2. Add garlic, thyme and mushrooms, stir and cook for 5 minutes.
3. Add sherry, vinegar and stock, stir, cover and cook at High for 3 minutes.
4. Release pressure, uncover the pot, discard thyme, add crème fraiche, mustard, and parsley, stir, set the pot on Simmer mode and cook the sauce for 3 minutes.
5. Serve right away.

Enjoy!

Nutrition:

- Calories 67
- Fat 0.4
- Fiber 0.2
- Carbs 4
- Protein 1

Eggplant Sauce

It's one of our favorite sauces!

Preparation time: 10 minutes
Cooking time: 20 minutes
Servings: 6
Ingredients:

- 1 pound ground meat
- 28 ounces canned tomatoes, chopped
- 5 garlic cloves, minced
- 5 ounces canned tomato paste
- 1 sweet onion, chopped
- 1 eggplant, chopped
- ½ cup olive oil
- ½ teaspoon turmeric
- 1 cup bone stock
- 1 tablespoon apple cider vinegar
- ½ teaspoon dill, dried
- Salt and black pepper to the taste
- ¼ cup parsley, chopped

Directions:

1. Set your instant pot on Sauté mode, add meat, brown for a few minutes and transfer to a bowl.
2. Heat up the oil in your instant pot, add onion and some salt and cook for 2 minutes.
3. Add eggplant and garlic, stir and cook for 1 minute.
4. Add vinegar, stir and cook for 2 minutes.
5. Add tomato paste, tomatoes, meat, salt, pepper, parsley, dill, turmeric and stock, stir, cover and cook at High for 15 minutes.
6. Release pressure, uncover the pot, add more salt and pepper and a splash of lemon juice, stir well and serve.

Enjoy!

Nutrition:

- Calories 142
- Fat 11
- Fiber 4.4
- Carbs 10
- Protein 2.1

Broccoli Sauce

It's so creamy and simple at the same time!

Preparation time: 10 minutes
Cooking time: 6 minutes
Servings: 4
Ingredients:

- 6 cups water
- 3 cups broccoli florets
- 2 garlic cloves, minced
- Salt and black pepper to the taste
- 1/3 cup coconut milk
- 1 tablespoon white wine vinegar
- 1 tablespoons nutritional yeast
- 1 tablespoon olive oil

Directions:

1. Put the water in your instant pot.
2. Add broccoli, salt, pepper and garlic, stir, cover and cook at High for 6 minutes.
3. Release pressure, uncover pot, strain broccoli and garlic and transfer to a food processor.
4. Add coconut milk, vinegar, yeast, olive oil, salt and pepper and blend very well.
5. Serve over pasta.

Enjoy!

Nutrition:

- Calories 128
- Fat 10
- Fiber 1.4
- Carbs 6
- Protein 5.4

Carrot Sauce

Just make sure you serve this sauce hot!

Preparation time: 10 minutes
Cooking time: 15 minutes
Servings: 6
Ingredients:

- 4 tablespoons butter
- 2 cups carrot juice
- A pinch of cinnamon
- Salt and black pepper to the taste
- A pinch of cayenne pepper
- 1 tablespoon mixed chervil, chives and tarragon

Directions:

1. Put carrot juice in your instant pot, set the pot on Simmer mode and bring to a boil.
2. Add butter, salt, pepper, cayenne and cinnamon, stir, cover and cook at High for 5 minutes.
3. Release pressure, uncover the pot, add mixed herbs, stir and serve.

Enjoy!

Nutrition:

- Calories 149
- Fat 7
- Fiber 4
- Carbs 19
- Protein 2
- Sugars 8

Cherry Sauce

It's very easy to make using an instant pot!

Preparation time: 10 minutes
Cooking time: 5 minutes
Servings: 4
Ingredients:

- 1 tablespoon lemon juice
- ¼ cup water
- 1 teaspoon kirsch
- A pinch of salt
- 1 tablespoon sugar
- 2 tablespoons cornstarch
- 2 cups cherries

Directions:

1. In your instant pot, mix water with lemon juice, salt, sugar, kirsch and cornstarch.
2. Add cherries, stir, cover and cook at High for 5 minutes.
3. Release pressure, uncover pot, transfer sauce to a bowl and serve after it's cold.

Enjoy!

Nutrition:

- Calories 60
- Fat 0
- Fiber 0
- Carbs 13
- Protein 0

Dates Sauce

Did you know you could make such an amazing sauce using your instant pot?

Preparation time: 10 minutes
Cooking time: 9 minutes
Servings: 6
Ingredients:

- 2 cups apple juice
- 2 cups dates, dried
- 1 tablespoon lemon juice

Directions:

1. In your instant pot, mix apple juice with lemon juice and dates, stir, cover and cook at High for 9 minutes.
2. Release pressure, uncover the pot, blend using an immersion blender and transfer to a container.
3. Serve when needed!

Enjoy!

Nutrition:

- Calories 30
- Fat 0
- Fiber 1
- Carbs 5
- Protein 0
- Sugar 5

Elderberry Sauce

Pay attention and find out how to make this amazing sauce!

Preparation time: 10 minutes
Cooking time: 10 minutes
Servings: 20
Ingredients:

- 4 cups water
- 1 cup elderberries
- 1 inch ginger piece, grated
- 1 cinnamon stick
- 1 vanilla bean, split
- 5 cloves
- 1 cup honey

Directions:

1. In your instant pot, mix elderberries with water, ginger, cinnamon, vanilla and cloves, stir, cover and cook at High for 10 minutes.
2. Release pressure, strain sauce and keep in jars.

Enjoy!

Nutrition:

- Calories 55
- Fat 0
- Fiber 0
- Carbs 13
- Protein 0

Fennel Sauce

It's so flavored!

Preparation time: 10 minutes
Cooking time: 10 minutes
Servings: 6
Ingredients:

- 1 fennel bulb, cut into pieces
- 2 pints grape tomatoes, cut into halves
- ¼ cup dry white wine
- 5 thyme springs
- 3 tablespoons olive oil
- A pinch of sugar
- Salt and black pepper to the taste

Directions:

1. Set your instant pot in Sauté mode, add oil and heat it up.
2. Add fennel, tomatoes, thyme, sugar, salt and pepper, stir and sauté for 5 minutes.
3. Add white wine, cover pot and cook for 4 minutes more.
4. Release pressure, uncover, discard thyme, stir sauce well and serve.

Enjoy!

Nutrition:

- Calories 76
- Fat 0.6
- Fiber 0.6
- Carbs 4
- Protein 5

Pear Sauce

It's the perfect fall sauce!

Preparation time: 10 minutes
Cooking time: 15 minutes
Servings: 5 pints
Ingredients:

- 10 cups pears, sliced
- 2 teaspoons cinnamon
- 1 cup pear juice
- ½ teaspoon nutmeg

Directions:

1. Put pear pieces in your instant pot, add cinnamon, nutmeg and pear juice.
2. Stir, cover pot and cook at High for 10 minutes.
3. Release pressure, uncover the pot, blend using an immersion blender and serve when needed.

Enjoy!

Nutrition:

- Calories 80
- Fat 0.1
- Fiber 0
- Carbs 20
- Protein 0.1

Guava Sauce

It's an incredible sauce. Try it soon!

Preparation time: 10 minutes
Cooking time: 20 minutes
Servings: 6
Ingredients:

- 1 can guava shells and syrup
- 2 onions, chopped
- ¼ cup vegetable oil
- Juice from 2 lemons
- 2 garlic cloves, chopped
- 1 inch ginger piece, minced
- ½ teaspoon nutmeg
- 2 bird chilies, chopped

Directions:

1. Put guava shells and syrup in your blender, pulse well and leave aside.
2. Set your instant pot on Sauté mode, add oil and heat it up.
3. Add onion and garlic, stir and cook for 4 minutes.
4. Add guava mix, ginger, lemon juice, chilies and nutmeg, stir, cover and cook on High for 15 minutes.
5. Release pressure, uncover the pot and serve sauce with fish.

Enjoy!

Nutrition:

- Calories 85
- Fat 2.3
- Fiber 8
- Carbs 22
- Protein 3

Melon Sauce

This is something special! It's a unique sauce!

Preparation time: 5 minutes
Cooking time: 10 minutes
Servings: 6
Ingredients:

- Flesh from 1 small melon
- 1-ounce sugar
- 1 cup sweet wine
- 1 tablespoon butter
- 1 teaspoon starch
- Juice of 1 lemon

Directions:

1. Put melon and sweet wine in your instant pot, cover and cook at High for 7 minutes.
2. Release pressure, transfer sauce to a blender, add lemon juice, sugar, butter and starch and blend very well.
3. Return this sauce to your instant pot, set it on Simmer mode and cook sauce until it thickens for 3 minutes.
4. Serve right away.

Enjoy!
Nutrition:

- Calories 68
- Fat 0.3
- Carbs 1
- Protein 1

Peach Sauce

It's so flavored!

Preparation time: 5 minutes
Cooking time: 3 minutes
Servings: 6
Ingredients:

- 10 ounces peaches, stoned and chopped
- 1/8 teaspoon nutmeg, ground
- 2 tablespoons cornstarch
- 3 tablespoons sugar
- ½ cup water
- A pinch of salt
- 1/8 teaspoon cinnamon
- 1/8 teaspoon almond extract

Directions:

1. In your instant pot, mix peaches with nutmeg, cornstarch, sugar, cinnamon and salt, stir, cover and cook at High for 3 minutes.
2. Release pressure, uncover the pot, add almond extract, stir and serve sauce.

Enjoy!
Nutrition:

- Calories 100
- Fat 1
- Fiber 0.6
- Carbs 4
- Protein 6

Peach And Whiskey Sauce

This is a special dessert sauce you must try!

Preparation time: 10 minutes
Cooking time: 10 minutes
Servings: 6
Ingredients:

- 1 cup brown sugar
- 3 cups peaches, pureed
- 6 tablespoons whiskey
- 1 cup white sugar
- 2 teaspoons lemon zest, grated

Directions:

1. In your instant pot mix peaches with brown and white sugar, whiskey and lemon zest, stir, cover and cook at High for 10 minutes.
2. Release pressure, uncover the pot, stir sauce and transfer it to jars.
3. Serve when needed.

Enjoy!

Nutrition:

- Calories 100
- Fat 0.7
- Fiber 0.6
- Carbs 7
- Protein 7

Leeks Sauce

Try this magnificent sauce today!

Preparation time: 5 minutes
Cooking time: 7 minutes
Servings: 8
Ingredients:

- 2 leeks, thinly sliced
- 2 tablespoons butter
- 1 cup whipping cream
- 3 tablespoons lemon juice
- Salt and pepper to the taste

Directions:

1. Set your instant pot on Sauté mode, add butter and melt it.
2. Add leeks, stir and cook for 2 minutes.
3. Add lemon juice, stir, cover and cook at High for 3 minutes.
4. Release pressure, uncover pot, transfer sauce to your blender, add whipping cream and blend everything.
5. Return sauce to the pot, set on Simmer mode, add salt and pepper to the taste, stir and cook for 2 minutes.
6. Serve with fish.

Enjoy!

Nutrition:

- Calories 140
- Fat 13
- Fiber 0.4
- Carbs 5
- Protein 1

Parsley Sauce

It's time for a very flavored sauce!

Preparation time: 10 minutes
Cooking time: 7 minutes
Servings: 6
Ingredients:

- 2 cups chicken stock
- 1 yellow onion, finely chopped
- 2 tablespoons butter
- 2 tablespoons flour
- ¾ cup whole milk

- 4 tablespoons parsley, chopped
- 1 egg yolk
- ¼ cup heavy cream
- Salt and white pepper to the taste

Directions:

1. Put stock and onion in your instant pot, set the pot on Simmer mode and bring to a boil.
2. Heat up a pan with the butter over medium heat, add flour and stir well to combine.
3. Pour this mix and whole milk over stock and stir very well.
4. Bring to a boil, add parsley, stir, cover and cook at High for 2 minutes.
5. Release pressure, uncover the pot and set it back on Simmer mode.
6. In a bowl, mix cream with egg yolk and some of the sauce from the pot.
7. Stir this well, pour over sauce and whisk.
8. Add salt and pepper to the taste, stir again, cook for a couple of minutes until it thickens and serve with chicken and some rice.

Enjoy!

Nutrition:

- Calories 70
- Fat 2.5
- Fiber 0.5

- Carbs 7.3
- Protein 2.5

Cilantro Sauce

It is simply so amazing and flavored!

Preparation time: 5 minutes
Cooking time: 6 minutes
Servings: 6
Ingredients:

- 3 garlic cloves, minced
- 1 tablespoon olive oil
- 2 red chilies, minced
- 3 shallots, minced
- 3 scallions, chopped
- 3 tomatoes, chopped
- Salt and black pepper to the taste
- 2 tablespoons cilantro, chopped
- ¼ cup water

Directions:

1. Set your instant pot on Sauté mode, add oil and heat it up.
2. Add garlic, shallots and chilies, stir and cook for 3 minutes.
3. Add scallions, tomatoes, water, salt, pepper and cilantro, stir, cover and cook on High for 3 minutes.
4. Release the pressure, uncover the pot, blend using an immersion blender and serve.

Enjoy!

Nutrition:

- Calories 67
- Fat 1
- Fiber 0.4
- Carbs 1
- Protein 0.5

Chestnut Sauce

You can serve this both as a thick sauce for cakes or as a spread!

Preparation time: 10 minutes
Cooking time: 20 minutes
Servings: 6
Ingredients:

- 11 ounces sugar
- 11 ounces water
- 1 and ½ pounds chestnuts, cut into halves and peeled
- 1/8 cup rum liquor

Directions:

1. In your instant pot, mix sugar with water, rum, and chestnuts.
2. Stir, cover and cook at High for 20 minutes.
3. Release pressure for 10 minutes, uncover the pot and blend everything with an immersion blender.
4. Serve when needed.

Enjoy!
Nutrition:

- Calories 50
- Fat 0
- Fiber 0
- Carbs 10
- Protein 0
- Sugar 12

Quince Sauce

It's the best quince sauce you'll ever try!

Preparation time: 10 minutes
Cooking time: 15 minutes
Servings: 6
Ingredients:

- 2 pounds grated quince
- Juice of 1 lemon
- 10 cloves
- 2 pounds sugar
- ¼ cup water

Directions:

1. In your instant pot, mix quince with sugar and stir well.
2. Add water and stir again.
3. Tie cloves in a cheesecloth and add to the pot as well.
4. Cover and cook at High for 10 minutes.
5. Release pressure for 10 minutes, uncover the pot, stir sauce again and transfer to jars.
6. Serve on top of cakes.

Enjoy!
Nutrition:

- Calories 60
- Fat 0
- Fiber 1
- Carbs 16
- Sugar 9
- Protein 1

Rhubarb Sauce

It's a sweet sauce with just a touch of heat!

Preparation time: 10 minutes
Cooking time: 13 minutes
Servings: 6
Ingredients:

- 8 ounces rhubarb, trimmed and chopped
- 1 tablespoon cider vinegar
- 1 small onion, chopped
- A pinch of cardamom, ground
- 1 garlic clove, minced
- 2 jalapeno peppers, chopped
- 1/3 cup honey
- ¼ cup raisins
- ¼ cup water

Directions:

1. In your instant pot, mix rhubarb with vinegar, onion, cardamom, garlic, jalapenos, honey, water, and raisins, stir, cover and cook at High for 7 minutes.
2. Release the pressure, uncover the pot, set it on Simmer mode and cook for 3 more minutes.
3. Serve when needed.

Enjoy!

Nutrition:

- Calories 90
- Fat 0
- Fiber 1
- Carbs 23
- Protein 1

Corn Sauce

It's a creamy sauce you can use for different meat-based dishes!

Preparation time: 10 minutes
Cooking time: 6 minutes
Servings: 4
Ingredients:

- 1 yellow onion, chopped
- 1 tablespoon olive oil
- 1 teaspoon white flour
- 1 and ¾ cups chicken stock
- ¼ cup white wine
- 1 thyme spring
- 2 cups corn kernels
- Salt and black pepper to the taste
- 2 teaspoons butter
- 1 teaspoon thyme, finely chopped

Directions:

1. Set your instant pot on Sauté mode, add oil and heat it up.
2. Add onion, stir and cook for 3 minutes.
3. Add flour, stir well and cook for 1 minute more.
4. Add wine, stir and cook for 1 minute.
5. Add thyme spring, stock and corn, stir, cover and cook at High for 1 minute.
6. Release pressure, uncover the pot, discard thyme spring, transfer corn sauce to a blender, add salt, pepper, butter and chopped thyme and blend well.
7. Return to pot set it on Sauté mode again and cook 1-2 minutes more.
8. Serve when needed.

Enjoy!

Nutrition:

- Calories 100
- Fat 4.5
- Fiber 2
- Carbs 13
- Protein 3

Instant Pot Dessert Recipes

Pumpkin Chocolate Cake

It's time for a delicious and easy cake!

Preparation time: 10 minutes
Cooking time: 45 minutes
Servings: 12

Ingredients:

- ¾ cup white flour
- ¾ cup whole wheat flour
- A pinch of salt
- 1 teaspoon baking soda
- ¾ teaspoon pumpkin pie spice
- ¾ cup sugar
- 1 banana, mashed
- ½ teaspoon baking powder
- 2 tablespoons canola oil
- ½ cup Greek yogurt
- 8 ounces canned pumpkin puree
- Cooking spray
- 1-quart water
- 1 egg
- ½ teaspoon vanilla extract
- 2/3 cup chocolate chips

Directions:

1. In a bowl, mix white flour with whole wheat flour, salt, baking soda and powder and pumpkin spice and stir.
2. In another bowl, mix sugar with oil, banana, yogurt, pumpkin puree, vanilla and egg and stir using a mixer.
3. Combine the 2 mixtures, add chocolate chips and mix everything.
4. Pour this into a greased Bundt pan, cover pan with paper towels and foil and place in the steamer basket of your instant pot.
5. Add 1-quart water to the pot, cover and cook at High for 35 minutes.
6. Release the pressure for 10 minutes, uncover the pot, leave the cake to cool down, before cutting and serving it.

Enjoy!

Nutrition:

- Calories 270
- Fat 9
- Fiber 1
- Carbs 45
- Protein 3

Chocolate Cheesecake

Surprise your guests with an amazing cheesecake!

Preparation time: 60 minutes
Cooking time: 50 minutes
Servings: 12
Ingredients:

For the crust:
- 4 tablespoons melted butter
- 1 and ½ cups chocolate cookie crumbs

For the filling:
- 24 ounces cream cheese, soft
- 2 tablespoons cornstarch
- 1 cup sugar
- 3 eggs

- 1 tablespoon vanilla extract
- Cooking spray
- 1 cup water
- ½ cup Greek yogurt
- 4 ounces white chocolate
- 4 ounces milk chocolate
- 4 ounces bittersweet chocolate

Directions:

1. In a bowl mix cookie crumbs with butter and stir well.
2. Spray a spring form pan with some cooking oil, line with parchment paper, press crumbs and butter mix on the bottom and keep in the freezer for now.
3. In a bowl, mix cream cheese with cornstarch and sugar and stir using your mixer.
4. Add eggs, yogurt, and vanilla, stir again to combine everything and divide into 3 bowls.
5. Put milk chocolate in a heatproof bowl and heat up in the microwave for 30 seconds.
6. Add this into one of the bowls with the batter you've made earlier and stir well.
7. Put dark and white chocolate in 2 heatproof bowls and heat them up in the microwave for 30 seconds.
8. Add these to the other 2 bowls with cheesecake batter, stir and introduce them all in the fridge for 30 minutes.
9. Take bowls out of the fridge and layer your cheesecake.
10. Pour the dark chocolate batter in the center of the crust.
11. Add white chocolate batter on top and spread evenly and end with milk chocolate batter.
12. Put the pan in the steamer basket of your pot, add 1 cup water in the pot, cover and cook at High for 45 minutes.
13. Release pressure for 10 minutes, take the cake out of the pot, leave aside to cool down and serve.

Enjoy!

Nutrition:
- Calories 470
- Fat 31
- Fiber 2
- Carbs 45
- Protein 8

Apple Bread

It's such a delicious dessert idea!

Preparation time: 10 minutes
Cooking time: 1 hour and 10 minutes
Servings: 6
Ingredients:

- 3 cups apples, cored and cubed
- 1 cup sugar
- 1 tablespoon vanilla
- 2 eggs
- 1 tablespoon apple pie spice
- 2 cups white flour
- 1 tablespoon baking powder
- 1 stick butter
- 1 cup water

Directions:

1. In a bowl mix egg with 1 butter stick, apple pie spice and sugar and stir using your mixer.
2. Add apples and stir again well.
3. In another bowl, mix baking powder with flour and stir.
4. Combine the 2 mixtures, stir and pour into a spring form pan.
5. Place in the steamer basket of your instant pot, add 1 cup water to the pot, cover and cook at High for 1 hour and 10 minutes.
6. Release pressure, fast, leave bread to cool down, cut and serve it.

Enjoy!

Nutrition:

- Calories 89
- Fat 3
- Fiber 1
- Carbs 17
- Protein 0

Banana Bread

if you've enjoyed the apple bread, then you must also like this banana bread!

Preparation time: 10 minutes
Cooking time: 30 minutes
Servings: 6
Ingredients:

- ¾ cup coconut sugar
- 1/3 cup ghee, soft
- 1 teaspoon vanilla
- 1 egg
- 2 bananas, mashed
- 1 teaspoon baking powder
- 1 and ½ cups flour
- A pinch of salt
- ½ teaspoons baking soda
- 1/3 cup cashew milk
- 1 and ½ teaspoons cream of tartar
- 2 cups water
- Cooking spray

Directions:

1. In a bowl, mix milk with cream of tartar and stir well.
2. Add sugar, ghee, egg, vanilla and bananas and stir everything.
3. In another bowl, mix flour with salt, baking powder and soda.
4. Combine the 2 mixtures, stir well, pour this into a cake pan which you've greased with some cooking spray and arrange pan in the steamer basket of your instant pot.
5. Add the water to your pot, cover and cook at High for 30 minutes.
6. Release the pressure, uncover pot, take bread out, leave aside to cool down, slice and serve it.

Enjoy!

Nutrition:

- Calories 325
- Fat 2
- Fiber 1.1
- Carbs 44
- Protein 4.5

Chocolate Lava Cake

Pay attention and learn how to make a delicious lava cake using your instant pot!

Preparation time: 10 minutes

Cooking time: 6 minutes

Servings: 3

Ingredients:

- 1 egg
- 4 tablespoons sugar
- 2 tablespoons olive oil
- 4 tablespoons milk
- 4 tablespoons flour
- A pinch of salt
- 1 tablespoon cocoa powder
- ½ teaspoon baking powder
- ½ teaspoon orange zest
- 1 cup water

Directions:

1. In a bowl, mix the egg with sugar, oil, milk, flour, salt, cocoa powder, baking powder and orange zest and stir very well.
2. Pour this into greased ramekins and place them in the steamer basket of your instant pot.
3. Add 1 cup water to the pot, cover and cook at High for 6 minutes.
4. Release pressure, uncover the pot, take lava cakes out and serve them after they cool down a bit.

Enjoy!

Nutrition:

- Calories 200
- Fat 5
- Fiber 1
- Carbs 24
- Protein 2

Tasty Apple Crisp

It's very easy to make and it tastes great!

Preparation time: 10 minutes
Cooking time: 8 minutes
Servings: 4
Ingredients:

- 2 teaspoons cinnamon
- 5 apples, cored and cut into chunks
- ½ teaspoon nutmeg
- 1 tablespoon maple syrup
- ½ cup water
- 4 tablespoons butter
- ¼ cup flour
- ¾ cup old fashioned rolled oats
- ¼ cup brown sugar
- A pinch of salt

Directions:

1. Put the apples in your instant pot.
2. Add cinnamon, nutmeg, maple syrup and water.
3. In a bowl, mix butter with oats, sugar, salt and flour and stir well.
4. Drop spoonfuls of oats mix on top of apples, cover pot and cook at High for 8 minutes.
5. Release the pressure and serve warm.

Enjoy!

Nutrition:

- Calories 180
- Fat 7
- Fiber 2.5
- Carbs 30
- Protein 1.4
- Sugar 14

Tasty And Simple Candied Lemon Peel

This might sound like something strange but it's a delicious sweet snack!

Preparation time: 20 minutes
Cooking time: 20 minutes
Servings: 80 pieces
Ingredients:

- 5 big lemons
- 2 and ¼ cups white sugar
- 5 cups water

Directions:

1. Wash lemons, slice them in half, reserve juice for another use, slice each half into quarters, take out the pulp and cut peel into thin strips.
2. Put strips in your instant pot, add 4 cups water, cover and cook at High for 3 minutes.
3. Release pressure fast, uncover the pot, strain peel, rinse and put in a bowl.
4. Clean your instant pot and add 2 cups sugar and 1 cup water in it.
5. Add lemon strips, stir, set pot on Simmer mode and cook for 5 minutes.
6. Cover pot, cook at High for 10 more minutes and release pressure naturally for 20 minutes
7. Strain peels again, spread them on a cutting board and leave them to cool down for 10 minutes.
8. Keep them in jars until you serve them.

Enjoy!

Nutrition:

- Calories 7
- Fat 0
- Fiber 0.2
- Carbs 2
- Protein 0

Delicious Baked Apples

Can you make some tasty baked apples in your instant pot? We will show you that it's possible!

Preparation time: 10 minutes
Cooking time: 10 minutes
Servings: 6
Ingredients:

- 6 apples, cored
- 1 cup red wine
- ¼ cup raisins
- 1 teaspoon cinnamon powder
- ½ cup raw sugar

Directions:

1. Put the apples in your instant pot.
2. Add wine, raisins, sugar and cinnamon, cover pot and cook at High for 10 minutes.
3. Release pressure naturally, uncover pot, transfer apples and their cooking juice to plates and serve.

Enjoy!
Nutrition:

- Calories 188
- Fat 0.4
- Fiber 3.5
- Carbs 34
- Protein 0.5

Chocolate Fondue

If you want to impress your loved one, then try this special dessert! It's so easy to make!

Preparation time: 10 minutes
Cooking time: 2 minutes
Servings: 4
Ingredients:

- 3.5 ounces crème fraiche
- 3.5 ounces dark chocolate, cut into chunks
- 1 teaspoon liquor
- 1 teaspoon sugar
- 2 cups water

Directions:

1. In a heat proof container, mix chocolate chunks with sugar, crème fraiche and liquor.
2. Put the water in your instant pot, add the container in the steamer basket, cover pot and cook at High for 2 minutes.
3. Release the pressure naturally, uncover pot, take container out, stir well your fondue and serve it right away with some fresh fruits.

Nutrition:

- Calories 210
- Fat 20
- Fiber 3
- Carbs 6.5
- Protein 2

Special Holiday Pudding

This is just perfect for the winter holiday!

Preparation time: 10 minutes
Cooking time: 40 minutes
Servings: 4
Ingredients:

- 4 ounces dried cranberries, soaked in hot water for 30 minutes, drained and chopped
- A drizzle of olive oil
- 2 cups water
- 4 ounces dried apricots, chopped
- 1 cup white flour
- 3 teaspoons baking powder
- 1 cup raw sugar
- 1 teaspoon ginger powder
- A pinch of cinnamon powder
- A pinch of salt
- 15 tablespoons butter
- 3 tablespoons maple syrup
- 4 eggs
- 1 carrot, grated

Directions:

1. Grease a heatproof pudding mould with a drizzle of oil and leave aside for now.
2. In a blender, mix flour with baking powder, sugar, cinnamon, salt and ginger and pulse a few times.
3. Add butter and pulse again.
4. Add maple syrup and eggs and pulse again.
5. Add dried fruits and carrot and fold them into the batter.
6. Spread this mix into the pudding mold, place this in the steamer basket of your instant pot and add 2 cups water in the pot as well.
7. Set the pot on Sauté mode and steam your pudding for 10 minutes.
8. Cover your pot, cook pudding at High for 30 minutes.
9. Release the pressure naturally for 10 minutes, leave pot aside for another 10 minutes, uncover, take pudding out and leave it aside to cool down before serving it.

Enjoy!

Nutrition:

- Calories 310
- Fat 15
- Fiber 2
- Carbs 27.9
- Protein 3.6

Pumpkin Pie

Taste this divide dessert!

Preparation time: 10 minutes
Cooking time: 20 minutes
Serving: 8
Ingredients:

- 2 pounds butternut squash, peeled and chopped
- 2 eggs
- 2 cups water
- 1 cup whole milk
- ¾ cup maple syrup
- 1 teaspoon cinnamon powder
- ½ teaspoon powdered ginger
- ¼ teaspoon powdered cloves
- A pinch of salt
- 1 tablespoon cornstarch
- Whipped cream for serving
- Chopped pecans

Directions:

1. Put squash cubes in the steamer basket of your instant pot, add 1 cup water, cover pot, cook at High for 4 minutes, release pressure, take squash and transfer to a strainer, cool it down and mash it a bit in a bowl.
2. Add maple syrup, milk, eggs, cinnamon, ginger, cloves, salt and cloves and stir very well.
3. Pour this into ramekins, place them in the steamer basket of your pot, add 1 cup water to the pot, cover and cook at High for 10 minutes.
4. Release the pressure, uncover the pot, take ramekins out, garnish with whipped cream and chopped pecans and serve.

Enjoy!
Nutrition:

- Calories 143
- Fat 3
- Fiber 2.1
- Carbs 19
- Protein 3.3

Delicious Tapioca Pudding

It's a very delicious and light pudding you should try!

Preparation time: 10 minutes

Cooking time: 8 minutes

Servings: 6

Ingredients:

- 1 and ¼ cups milk
- 1/3 cup tapioca pearls, rinsed
- ½ cup water
- ½ cup sugar
- Zest from ½ lemon
- 1 cup water

Directions:

1. In a heat proof bowl mix tapioca with milk, sugar, ½ cup water and lemon zest and stir well.
2. Put this in the steamer basket of your instant pot, add 1 cup water to the pot, cover and cook at High for 8 minutes.
3. Release the pressure, leave it aside for 5 minutes more, uncover the pot, take pudding out and serve it warm.

Enjoy!

Nutrition:

- Calories 180
- Fat 2.5
- Fiber 0.1
- Carbs 90
- Protein 2.5

Upside Down Apple Cake

It's a delightful dessert you will love!

Preparation time: 10 minutes
Cooking time: 20 minutes
Servings: 8
Ingredients:

- 1 apple, sliced
- 1 apple, chopped
- 2 cup water
- 1 cup ricotta cheese
- ¼ cup raw sugar
- 1 tablespoon lemon juice
- 1 egg
- 1 teaspoon vanilla extract
- 3 tablespoons olive oil
- 1 cup white flour
- 2 teaspoons baking powder
- 1/8 teaspoon cinnamon powder
- 1 teaspoon baking soda

Directions:

1. Put chopped and sliced apple in a bowl, add lemon juice, toss to coat and leave aside for now.
2. Line a heatproof dish with some parchment paper, grease with some oil and dust with some flour.
3. Sprinkle some sugar on the bottom and arrange sliced apple on top.
4. In a bowl, mix the egg with cheese, sugar, vanilla extract and oil and stir well.
5. Add flour, baking powder and soda and cinnamon and stir again.
6. Add chopped apple, toss to coat and pour everything into the pan.
7. Place the pan in the steamer basket of your instant pot, add the water to the pot, cover and cook at High for 20 minutes.
8. Release the pressure, uncover the pot, turn cake on a plate and serve warm.

Enjoy!

Nutrition:

- Calories 241
- Fat 10
- Fiber 2
- Carbs 20
- Protein 5.8

Special Brownie Cake

This will really surprise you!

Preparation time: 10 minutes
Cooking time: 50 minutes
Servings: 6
Ingredients:

- 1 cup borlotti beans, soaked for 8 hours and drained
- 4 cups water

For the cake:

- 1/8 teaspoon almond extract
- ½ cup cocoa powder
- ½ cup raw sugar

- 3 tablespoons extra virgin olive oil
- A pinch of salt
- 2 eggs
- 2 teaspoons baking powder
- ¼ cup almonds, sliced

Directions:

1. Put beans and water in your instant pot, cover, cook at High for 12 minutes, release pressure, uncover pot, strain beans, transfer them to a blender and puree them.
2. Discard water from the pot and keep 1 cup.
3. Grease a heatproof bowl with some olive oil and leave it aside for now.
4. Add cocoa powder, almond extract, honey, salt, eggs and oil to your blender with the beans and puree everything for 1 minute.
5. Transfer mix to greased bowl, spread, place bowl in the steamer basket of your pot, add reserved water from cooking the beans, cover and cook at High for 20 minutes.
6. Release the pressure, take cake out of the pot, leave it aside for 15 minutes, transfer to a plate, sprinkle almonds on top, slice and serve.

Enjoy!
Nutrition:

- Calories 164
- Fat 7.8
- Fiber 4

- Carbs 24
- Protein 4.4

Dulce De Leche

It's a Mexican-style dessert we love!

Preparation time: 10 minutes
Cooking time: 25 minutes
Servings: 6
Ingredients:

- 16 ounces canned sweet condensed milk
- Water to cover

Directions:

1. Put condensed milk can in the steamer basket of your instant pot, add water in the pot to cover and cook at High for 20 minutes.
2. Release the pressure naturally, uncover the pot, take can out of the pot and leave it aside to cool down.
3. Serve your dulce de leche on crackers.

Enjoy!
Nutrition:

- Calories 300
- Fat 10
- Fiber 5
- Carbs 24
- Protein 10

Pears With Wine Sauce

Serve this special dessert with your favorite ice cream.

Preparation time: 10 minutes
Cooking time: 10 minutes
Servings: 6
Ingredients:

- 6 green pears
- 1 vanilla pod
- 1 cloves
- A pinch of cinnamon
- 7 oz sugar
- 1 glass red wine

Directions:

1. In your instant pot, mix wine with sugar, vanilla and cinnamon.
2. Add pears and clove, cover pot and cook at High for 10 minutes.
3. Release pressure, uncover pot and leaves pears to cool down for 10 minutes.
4. Transfer them to serving plates along with the wine sauce and serve.

Enjoy!
Nutrition:

- Calories 151
- Fat 7.7
- Fiber 3
- Carbs 14
- Protein 1.1

Crème Brulee

It's a very popular dessert everyone loves!

Preparation time: 1 hour
Cooking time: 15 minutes
Servings: 6
Ingredients:

- 2 cups fresh cream
- 1 teaspoon cinnamon powder
- 6 egg yolks
- 5 tablespoons white sugar
- Zest from 1 orange
- A pinch of nutmeg for serving
- 4 tablespoons raw sugar
- 2 cups water

Directions:

1. In a pan, mix cream with cinnamon and orange zest, stir and bring to a boil over medium high heat.
2. Take the pan off heat and leave it aside for 30 minutes.
3. In a bowl, mix egg yolks with white sugar and whisk well.
4. Add this to cooled cream and whisk well again.
5. Strain this mix and then divide it into ramekins.
6. Cover with foil, place them in the steamer basket of your instant pot, add 2 cups water to the pot, cover and cook on Low for 10 minutes.
7. Release the pressure naturally, uncover pot, take ramekins out and leave them aside for 30 minutes.
8. Sprinkle nutmeg and raw sugar on top of each and melt this with a culinary torch.
9. Serve right away.

Enjoy!

Nutrition:

- Calories 210
- Fat 10
- Fiber 3
- Carbs 18
- Protein 13

Bread Pudding

This will taste amazing and you will prepare it over and over again for you and your loved ones.

Preparation time: 5 minutes
Cooking time: 25 minutes
Servings: 4
Ingredients:

- 4 egg yolks
- 3 cups brioche, cubed
- 2 cups half and half
- ½ teaspoon vanilla extract
- 1 cup sugar
- 2 tablespoons butter, soft
- 1 cup cranberries
- 2 cups warm water
- ½ cup raisins
- Zest from 1 lime

Directions:

1. Grease a baking dish with some butter and leave aside for now.
2. In a bowl mix, egg yolks with half and half, cubed brioche, vanilla extract, sugar, cranberries, raisins and lime zest and stir well
3. Pour this into greased dish, cover with some tin foil and leave aside for 10 minutes.
4. Put dish in the steamer basket of your instant pot, add warm water to the pot, cover and cook at High for 20 minutes.
5. Release the pressure naturally, uncover pot, take bread out, leave it aside to cool down, slice and serve it.

Enjoy!

Nutrition:

- Calories 300
- Fat 7
- Fiber 2
- Carbs 46
- Protein 11

Rich Ruby Pears

These fruits are extremely versatile, and you can easily prepare an elegant and rich dessert using them! This is one special dessert you should try!

Preparation time: 10 minutes
Cooking time: 10 minutes
Servings: 4
Ingredients:

- 4 pears
- Juice and zest of 1 lemon
- 26 ounces grape juice
- 11 ounces currant jelly
- 4 garlic cloves
- ½ vanilla bean
- 4 peppercorns
- 2 rosemary springs

Directions:

1. Pour the jelly and grape juice in your instant pot and mix with lemon zest and juice.
2. Dip each pear in this mix, wrap them in tin foil and arrange them in the steamer basket of your pot.
3. Add garlic cloves, peppercorns, rosemary and vanilla bean to the juice mixture, cover pot and cook at High for 10 minutes.
4. Release pressure, uncover the pot, take the pears out, unwrap them, arrange them on plates and serve cold with cooking juice on top.

Enjoy!

Nutrition:

- Calories 145
- Fat 5.6
- Fiber 6
- Carbs 12
- Protein 12

Tasty Rice Pudding

This pudding can be served on a hot summer day! You will love the taste and its texture.

Preparation time: 5 minutes
Cooking time: 15 minutes
Servings: 6
Ingredients:

- 1 tablespoon butter
- 7 ounces long grain rice
- 4 ounces water
- 16 ounces milk
- 3 ounces sugar
- A pinch of salt
- 1 egg
- 1 tablespoon cream
- 1 teaspoon vanilla
- Cinnamon to the taste

Directions:

1. Put the butter in your instant pot, set it on Sauté mode, melt it, add rice and stir.
2. Add water and milk and stir again.
3. Add salt and sugar, stir again, cover pot and cook at High for 8 minutes.
4. Meanwhile, in a bowl, mix cream with vanilla and eggs and stir well.
5. Release pressure from the pot, uncover it, and pour some of the liquid from the pot over egg mixture and stir very well.
6. Pour this into the pot and whisk well.
7. Cover pot, cook at High for 10 minutes, release pressure, uncover the pot, pour pudding into bowls, sprinkle cinnamon on top and serve.

Enjoy!

Nutrition:

- Calories 112
- Fat 1.2
- Fiber 0.4
- Carbs 21
- Protein 3.3

Delicious Ricotta Cake

This is a simple and classic dessert but also a very delicious and healthy one! That sounds really good, doesn't it?

Preparation time: 30 minutes
Cooking time: 30 minutes
Servings: 6
Ingredients:

- 1 pound ricotta
- 6 oz dates, soaked for 15 minutes and drained
- 2 ounces honey softened
- 4 eggs
- 2 ounces sugar
- Some vanilla extract
- 17 ounces water
- Orange juice and zest from ½ orange

Directions:

1. In a bowl, whisk ricotta until it softens.
2. In another bowl, whisk eggs well.
3. Combine the 2 mixtures and stir very well.
4. Add honey, vanilla, dates, orange zest and juice to the ricotta mixture and stir again
5. Pour the batter into a heatproof dish and cover with tin foil.
6. Place dish in the steamer basket of your instant pot, add water to the pot, cover and cook at High for 20 minutes.
7. Release pressure, uncover pot, allow cake to cool down, transfer to a platter, slice and serve.

Enjoy!

Nutrition:

- Calories 211
- Fat 8.6
- Fiber 0.5
- Carbs 21
- Protein 12

Pumpkin Rice Pudding

The combination leads to a perfect dessert!

Preparation time: 30 minutes
Cooking time: 35 minutes
Servings: 6
Ingredients:

- 1 cup brown rice
- ½ cup water
- 3 cups cashew milk
- ½ cup dates, chopped
- A pinch of salt
- 1 cinnamon stick
- 1 cup pumpkin puree
- ½ cup maple syrup
- 1 teaspoon pumpkin spice mix
- 1 teaspoon vanilla extract

Directions:

1. Put the rice in your instant pot, add boiling water to cover, leave aside for 10 minutes and drain.
2. Put the water in milk in your instant pot, add rice, cinnamon stick, dates and salt, stir, cover and cook at High for 20 minutes.
3. Release pressure, uncover pot, add maple syrup, pumpkin pie spice and pumpkin puree, stir, set the pot on Simmer mode and cook for 5 minutes.
4. Discard cinnamon stick, add vanilla, stir, transfer pudding to bowls, leave aside for 30 minutes to cool down and serve.

Enjoy!
Nutrition:

- Calories 100
- Fat 1
- Fiber 4
- Carbs 21
- Protein 4.1

Lemon Marmalade

It's a fantastic dessert!

Preparation time: 10 minutes
Cooking time: 15 minutes
Servings: 8
Ingredients:

- 2 pounds lemons, washed, sliced and cut into quarters
- 4 pounds sugar
- 2 cups water

Directions:

1. Put lemon pieces in your instant pot, add 2 cups water, cover and cook at High for 10 minutes.
2. Release the pressure naturally, uncover pot, add sugar, stir, set pot in Simmer mode and cook for 6 minutes, stirring all the time.
3. Divide into jars and serve when needed.

Enjoy!
Nutrition:

- Calories 100
- Fat 2
- Fiber 2
- Carbs 4
- Protein 8

Orange Marmalade

Do you need more great ideas for dessert? Try this one now!

Preparation time: 10 minutes
Cooking time: 25 minutes
Servings: 8
Ingredients:

- Juice from 2 lemons
- 3 pounds sugar
- 1 pound oranges, cut into halves
- 1-pint water

Directions:

1. Squeeze juice from the oranges and cut the peel into pieces.
2. Put peel in a bowl, cover with water and leave aside overnight.
3. In your instant pot, mix lemon juice with orange juice, water and peel.
4. Cover pot, cook at High for 15 minutes, release pressure, uncover, add sugar and set the pot on Simmer mode.
5. Cook until sugar dissolves, divide into jars and serve when needed.

Enjoy!
Nutrition:

- Calories 50
- Fat 0
- Fiber 0.1
- Carbs 12
- Protein 0.1

Berry Jam

Serve this marmalade to your guests, and they will love you!

Preparation time: 60 minutes
Cooking time: 20 minutes
Servings: 12
Ingredients:

- 1 pound cranberries
- 1 pound strawberries
- ½ pound blueberries
- 3.5 ounces black currant
- 2 pounds sugar
- Zest from 1 lemon
- A pinch of salt
- 2 tablespoon water

Directions:

1. In your instant pot, mix strawberries with cranberries, blueberries, currants, lemon zest and sugar.
2. Stir and leave aside for 1 hour.
3. Add salt and water, set the pot on Simmer mode and bring to a boil.
4. Cover pot, cook on Low for 10 minutes and release pressure for 10 minutes.
5. Uncover pot, set it on Simmer mode again, bring to a boil and simmer for 4 minutes.
6. Divide into jars and keep in the fridge until you need it.

Enjoy!
Nutrition:

- Calories 60
- Fat 0
- Fiber 0
- Carbs 12
- Sugar 12
- Protein 0

Tomato Jam

It's something special and very tasty! Try it sometimes!

Preparation time: 10 minutes
Cooking time: 30 minutes
Servings: 12
Ingredients:

- 1 and ½ pounds tomatoes, cored and chopped
- 2 tablespoons lime juice
- 1 cup white sugar
- 1 tablespoon ginger, grated
- 1 teaspoon cinnamon
- 1 teaspoon cumin
- 1/8 teaspoon cloves, ground
- A pinch of salt
- 1 jalapeno pepper, minced

Directions:

1. In your instant pot mix tomatoes with sugar, lime juice, ginger, cumin, cinnamon, cloves, salt and jalapeno pepper, stir, cover and cook at High for 30 minutes.
2. Release the pressure, uncover the pot, divide jam into jars and serve when needed.

Enjoy!

Nutrition:

- Calories 239
- Fat 0
- Fiber 2
- Carbs 59
- Sugar 55
- Protein 0

Pears Jam

You only need a few ingredients and an instant pot to make this special jam!

Preparation time: 10 minutes
Cooking time: 4 minutes
Servings: 12
Ingredients:

- 8 pears, cored and cut into quarters
- 2 apples, peeled, cored and cut into quarters
- ¼ cup apple juice
- 1 teaspoon cinnamon, ground

Directions:

1. In your instant pot, mix pears with apples, cinnamon and apple juice, stir, cover and cook at High for 4 minutes.
2. Release the pressure naturally, uncover the pot, blend using an immersion blender, divide jam into jars and keep in a cold place until you serve it.

Enjoy!

Nutrition:

- Calories 90
- Fat 0
- Fiber 1
- Carbs 20
- Sugar 20
- Protein 0

Tasty Peach Jam

It's one of the best jam recipes ever!

Preparation time: 10 minutes
Cooking time: 5 minutes
Servings: 6
Ingredients:

- 4 and ½ cups peaches, peeled and cubed
- 6 cups sugar
- ¼ cup crystallized ginger, chopped
- 1 box fruit pectin

Directions:

1. Set your instant pot on Simmer mode, add peaches, ginger, and pectin, stir and bring to a boil.
2. Add sugar, stir, cover and cook at High for 5 minutes.
3. Release pressure, uncover pot, divide jam into jars and serve.

Enjoy!

Nutrition:

- Calories 50
- Fat 0
- Fiber 1
- Carbs 3
- Protein 0
- Sugar 12

Raspberry Curd

It's refreshing and delicious!

Preparation time: 10 minutes
Cooking time: 5 minutes
Servings: 4
Ingredients:

- 1 cup sugar
- 12 ounces raspberries
- 2 egg yolks
- 2 tablespoons lemon juice
- 2 tablespoons butter

Directions:

1. Put raspberries in your instant pot.
2. Add sugar and lemon juice, stir, cover and cook at High for 2 minutes.
3. Release pressure for 5 minutes, uncover pot, strain raspberries and discard seeds.
4. In a bowl, mix egg yolks with raspberries and stir well.
5. Return this to your instant pot, set it on Sauté mode, simmer for 2 minutes, add butter, stir and transfer to a container.
6. Serve cold.

Enjoy!

Nutrition:

- Calories 110
- Fat 4
- Fiber 0
- Carbs 16
- Protein 1

Delicious Berry Compote

It's so amazing and tasty!

Preparation time: 10 minutes
Cooking time: 5 minutes
Servings: 8
Ingredients:

- 1 cup blueberries
- 2 cups strawberries, sliced
- 2 tablespoons lemon juice
- ¾ cup sugar
- 1 tablespoon cornstarch
- 1 tablespoon water

Directions:

1. In your instant pot, mix blueberries with lemon juice and sugar, stir, cover and cook at High for 3 minutes.
2. Release pressure naturally for 10 minutes and uncover pot.
3. In a bowl, mix cornstarch with water, stir well and add to the pot.
4. Stir, set the pot on Sauté mode and cook compote for 2 minutes more.
5. Divide into jars and keep in the fridge until you serve it.

Enjoy!

Nutrition:

- Calories 260
- Fat 13
- Fiber 3
- Carbs 23
- Protein 3

Key Lime Pie

It's so creamy and tasty!

Preparation time: 10 minutes
Cooking time: 15 minutes
Servings: 6
Ingredients:
For the crust:
- 1 tablespoon sugar
- 3 tablespoons butter, melted
- 5 graham crackers, crumbled

For the filling:
- 4 egg yolks
- 14 ounces canned condensed milk
- ½ cup key lime juice
- 1/3 cup sour cream
- Cooking spray
- 1 cup water
- 2 tablespoons key lime zest, grated

Directions:
1. In a bowl, whisk egg yolks very well.
2. Add milk gradually and stir again well.
3. Add lime juice, sour cream and lime zest and stir again.
4. In a bowl, whisk butter with crackers and sugar, stir well and spread on the bottom of a spring form greased with some cooking spray.
5. Cover pan with some tin foil and place it in the steamer basket of your instant pot.
6. Add 1 cup water to the pot, cover and cook at High for 15 minutes.
7. Release the pressure for 10 minutes, uncover the pot, take pie out, leave aside to cool down and keep in the fridge for 4 hours before slicing and serving it.

Enjoy!
Nutrition:
- Calories 400
- Fat 21
- Fiber 0.5
- Carbs 34
- Protein 7

Stuffed Peaches

It's such a tasty delight you should try!

Preparation time: 10 minutes
Cooking time: 4 minutes
Servings: 6
Ingredients:

- 6 peaches, insides removed
- A pinch of salt
- ¼ cup coconut flour
- ¼ cup maple syrup
- 2 tablespoons coconut butter
- ½ teaspoon cinnamon powder
- 1 teaspoon almond extract
- 1 cup water

Directions:

1. In a bowl, mix flour with salt, syrup, butter, cinnamon and half of the almond extract and stir well.
2. Fill peaches with this mix, place them in the steamer basket of your instant pot, add the water and the rest of the almond extract to the pot, cover and cook at High for 4 minutes.
3. Release pressure naturally, divide stuffed peaches on servings plates and serve warm.

Enjoy!

Nutrition:

- Calories 160
- Fat 6.7
- Carbs 12
- Fiber 3
- Sugar 11
- Protein 4

Peach Compote

It's much more than a simple compote! Discover why!

Preparation time: 10 minutes
Cooking time: 3 minutes
Servings: 6
Ingredients:

- 8 peaches, chopped
- 6 tablespoons sugar
- 1 teaspoon cinnamon, ground
- 1 teaspoon vanilla extract
- 1 vanilla bean, scraped
- 2 tablespoons grape nuts cereal

Directions:

1. Put peaches in your instant pot and mix with sugar, cinnamon, vanilla bean and vanilla extract.
2. Stir well, cover pot and cook at High for 3 minutes.
3. Release pressure for 10 minutes, add grape nuts, stir well, transfer the compote to bowls and serve.

Enjoy!

Nutrition:

- Calories 100
- Fat 2
- Carbs 11
- Fiber 1
- Sugar 10
- Protein 1

Delicious Cobbler

Pay attention how it's made!

Preparation time: 10 minutes
Cooking time: 12 minutes
Servings: 4
Ingredients:

- 3 apples, cored and cut into chunks
- 2 pears, cored and cut into chunks
- 1 and ½ cup hot water
- ¼ cup date syrup
- 1 cup steel cut oats
- 1 teaspoon cinnamon
- ice cream for serving

Directions:

1. Put apples and pears in your instant pot and mix with hot water, date syrup, oats and cinnamon.
2. Stir, cover and cook at High for 12 minutes.
3. Release pressure naturally, transfer cobbler to bowls and serve it with ice cream on top.

Enjoy!

Nutrition:

- Calories 170
- Fat 4
- Carbs 10
- Fiber 2.4
- Protein 3
- Sugar 7

Simple Carrot Cake

You don't need to be an expert in the kitchen to make this great dessert! We'll show you everything you need to do!

Servings: 6
Preparation time: 10 minutes
Cooking time: 30 minutes
Ingredients:

- 5 ounces flour
- A pinch of salt
- ¾ teaspoon baking powder
- ½ teaspoon baking soda
- ½ teaspoon cinnamon powder
- ¼ teaspoon nutmeg, ground
- ½ teaspoon allspice
- 1 egg
- 3 tablespoons yogurt
- ½ cup sugar
- ¼ cup pineapple juice
- 4 tablespoons coconut oil, melted
- 1/3 cup carrots, grated
- 1/3 cup pecans, toasted and chopped
- 1/3 cup coconut flakes
- Cooking spray
- 2 cups water

Directions:

1. In a bowl, mix flour with baking soda and powder, salt, allspice, cinnamon and nutmeg and stir.
2. In another bowl, mix egg with yogurt, sugar, pineapple juice, oil, carrots, pecans and coconut flakes and stir well.
3. Combine the two mixtures and stir very well everything.
4. Pour this into a spring form greased with some cooking spray, add 2 cups water in your instant pot and place the form into the steamer basket.
5. Cover the instant pot and cook at High for 32 minutes.
6. Release pressure for 10 minutes, remove cake from the pot, leave it to cool down, then cut and serve it.

Enjoy!

Nutrition:

- calories 140
- fat 3.5
- Carbs 23.4
- fiber 4.1
- sugar 5.2
- protein 4.3

Zucchini Nut Bread

Get ready to discover something unique and delicious!

Preparation time: 10 minutes
Cooking time: 25 minutes
Servings: 6
Ingredients:

- 1 cup applesauce
- 3 eggs, whisked
- 1 tablespoon vanilla extract
- 2 cups sugar
- 2 cups zucchini, grated
- 1 teaspoon salt
- 2 and ½ cups white flour
- ½ cup baking cocoa
- 1 teaspoon baking soda
- ¼ teaspoon baking powder
- 1 teaspoon cinnamon
- ½ cup walnuts, chopped
- ½ cup chocolate chips
- 1 and ½ cups water

Directions:

1. In a bowl, mix zucchini with sugar, vanilla, eggs and applesauce and stir well.
2. In another bowl, mix flour with salt, cocoa, baking soda, baking powder, cinnamon, chocolate chips and walnuts and stir.
3. Combine the 2 mixtures, stir, pour into a Bundt pan, place pan in the steamer basket of your instant pot, add the water to the pot, cover and cook at High for 25 minutes.
4. Release the pressure naturally, uncover the pot, transfer bread to a plate, cut and serve it.

Enjoy!

Nutrition:

- Calories 217
- Fat 8
- Fiber 2
- Carbs 35
- Sugar 22
- Protein 3

Samoa Cheesecake

Try a different cheesecake using your instant pot!

Preparation time: 15 minutes
Cooking time: 1 hour
Servings: 6
Ingredients:

For the crust:
- 2 tablespoons butter, melted
- ½ cup chocolate graham crackers, crumbled

For the filling:
- ¼ cup heavy cream
- ½ cup sugar
- 12 ounces cream cheese, soft
- 1 and ½ teaspoon vanilla extract
- ¼ cup sour cream
- 1 tablespoon flour

- 1 egg yolk
- 2 eggs
- Cooking spray
- 1 cup water

For the topping:
- 3 tablespoons heavy cream
- 12 caramels
- 1 and ½ cups coconut, sweet and shredded
- ¼ cup chocolate, chopped

Directions:
1. Grease a spring form pan with some cooking spray and leave it aside.
2. In a bowl, mix crackers with butter, stir, spread in the bottom of the pan and keep in the freezer for 10 minutes.
3. Meanwhile, in another bowl, mix cheese with sugar, heavy cream, vanilla, flour, sour cream and eggs and stir very well using a mixer.
4. Pour this into the pan on top of crust, cover with tin foil and place in the steamer basket of your instant pot.
5. Add 1 cup water to the pot, cover and cook at High for 35 minutes.
6. Release the pressure for 10 minutes, uncover, take the pan, remove tin foil and leave cake to cool down in the fridge for 4 hours.
7. Spread coconut on a lined baking sheet, introduce in the oven at 300 degrees F and bake for 20 minutes, stirring often.
8. Put caramels in a heatproof bowl, introduce in the microwave for 2 minutes, stir every 20 seconds and then mix with toasted coconut.
9. Spread this on your cheesecake and leave aside for now.
10. Put chocolate in another heatproof bowl, introduce in your microwave for a few seconds until it melts and drizzles over your cake.
11. Serve right away.

Enjoy!

Nutrition:
- Calories 310
- Fat 8
- Fiber 2
- Carbs 20
- Protein 10

Pina Colada Pudding

This sounds really interesting, doesn't it?

Preparation time: 10 minutes
Cooking time: 5 minutes
Servings: 8
Ingredients:

- 1 tablespoon coconut oil
- A pinch of salt
- 1 and ½ cups water
- 1 cup Arborio rice
- 14 ounces canned coconut milk
- 2 eggs
- ½ cup milk
- ½ cup sugar
- ½ teaspoon vanilla extract
- 8 ounces canned pineapple tidbits, drained and halved

Directions:

1. In your instant pot, mix oil, water, rice and salt, stir, cover and cook at High for 3 minutes.
2. Release the pressure for 10 minutes, uncover the pot, add sugar and coconut milk and stir well.
3. In a bowl, mix eggs with milk and vanilla, stir and pour over rice.
4. Stir, set the pot on Sauté mode and bring to a boil.
5. Add pineapple tidbits, stir, divide into dessert bowls and serve.

Enjoy!

Nutrition:

- Calories 113
- Fat 3.2
- Fiber 0.2
- Carbs 15
- Protein 4.2

Quick Flan

Try something new and tasty each day! Maybe you'll try this next dessert now!

Preparation time: 10 minutes
Cooking time: 15 minutes
Servings: 6
Ingredients:

For the caramel:
- ¼ cup water
- ¾ cup sugar

For the custard:
- 2 egg yolks
- 3 eggs
- 1 and ½ cups water

- A pinch of salt
- 2 cups milk
- 1/3 cup sugar
- ½ cup whipping cream
- 2 tablespoons hazelnut syrup
- 1 teaspoon vanilla extract

Directions:

1. Heat up a pot over medium heat, add ¼ cup water and ¾ cup sugar, stir, cover, bring to a boil, boil for 2 minutes, uncover and boil for a few more minutes.
2. Pour this into custard cups and coat evenly their bottoms.
3. In a bowl, mix eggs with yolks, a pinch of salt and 1/3 cup sugar and stir using your mixer.
4. Put the milk in a pan and heat up over medium heat.
5. Add this to eggs mix and stir well.
6. Add hazelnut syrup, vanilla and cream, stir and strain this mix.
7. Pour this into custard cups, place them in the steamer basket of your instant pot, add 1 and ½ cups water to the pot, cover and cook at High for 6 minutes.
8. Release pressure, uncover the pot, take custard cups and leave them to cool down.
9. Keep in the fridge for 4 hours before you serve them.

Enjoy!

Nutrition:
- Calories 145
- Fat 4
- Fiber 0

- Carbs 23
- Sugar 20
- Protein 4.5

Delicious Chocolate Pudding

Everyone will love this creamy and textured dessert!

Preparation time: 10 minutes
Cooking time: 20 minutes
Servings: 4
Ingredients:

- 6 ounces bittersweet chocolate, chopped
- ½ cup milk
- 1 and ½ cups heavy cream
- 5 egg yolks
- 1/3 cup brown sugar
- 2 teaspoons vanilla extract
- 1 and ½ cups water
- ¼ teaspoon cardamom, ground
- A pinch of salt
- Crème fraiche for serving
- Chocolate shavings for serving

Directions:

1. Put cream and milk in a pot, bring to a simmer over medium heat, take off heat, add chocolate and whisk well.
2. In a bowl, mix egg yolks with vanilla, sugar, cardamom and a pinch of salt, stir, strain and mix with chocolate mix.
3. Pour this into a soufflé dish, cover with tin foil, place in the steamer basket of your instant pot, add water to the pot, cover, cook on Low for 18 minutes, release pressure naturally.
4. Take pudding out of the instant pot, leave aside to cool down and keep in the fridge for 3 hours before you serve it with crème fraiche and chocolate shavings on top.

Enjoy!

Nutrition:

- Calories 200
- Fat 3
- Fiber 1
- Carbs 20
- Protein 14

Sticky Pudding

It's so amazing and sweet!

Preparation time: 15 minutes
Cooking time: 20 minutes
Servings: 8
Ingredients:

- 2 cups water
- 1 and ¼ cups dates, chopped
- ¼ cup blackstrap molasses
- ¾ cup hot water
- 1 teaspoon baking powder
- 1 and ¼ cups white flour
- A pinch of salt
- ¾ cup brown sugar
- 1/3 cup butter, soft
- 1 teaspoon vanilla extract
- 1 egg

For the caramel sauce:

- 1/3 cup whipping cream
- 2/3 cup brown sugar
- ¼ cup butter
- 1 teaspoon vanilla extract

Directions:

1. In a bowl, mix dates with hot water and molasses, stir and leave aside for now.
2. In another bowl, mix baking powder with flour and salt.
3. In a third bowl, mix sugar with butter, egg and 1 teaspoon vanilla extract and stir using a mixer.
4. Add flour and dates mixtures to this bowl and stir very well.
5. Divide this mix into 8 ramekins which you've greased with some butter, cover with tin foil, place them in the steamer basket of your instant pot, add 2 cups water to the pot, cover and cook on Low for 20 minutes.
6. Meanwhile, heat up a pan with the butter for the caramel sauce over medium high heat.
7. Add cream, vanilla extract and brown sugar, stir and bring to a boil.
8. Reduce temperature to medium-low and simmer for 5 minutes stirring often.
9. Release pressure from the pot, uncover, take ramekins out, remove foil, drizzle sauce over puddings and serve them warm.

Enjoy!
Nutrition:

- Calories 260
- Fat 14
- Fiber 1
- Carbs 33
- Protein 2
- Sugar 21

Rhubarb Compote

This is a light and very delicious compote you should try!

Preparation time: 10 minutes
Cooking time: 30 minutes
Servings: 8
Ingredients:

- 1/3 cup water
- 2 pounds rhubarb, chopped
- 3 tablespoon honey
- Some fresh mint, torn
- 1 pound strawberries, chopped

Directions:

1. Put rhubarb and water in your instant pot, cover, cook at High for 10 minutes, release pressure and uncover pot.
2. Add strawberries and honey, stir, set the pot on Simmer mode and cook compote for 20 minutes.
3. Add mint, stir, divide into jars and serve.

Enjoy!

Nutrition:

- Calories 71
- Fat 0.1
- Fiber 1
- Carbs 18
- Protein 0.5
- Sugar 16

Simple Chocolate Cake

Get ready for a special treat!

Preparation time: 10 minutes
Cooking time: 40 minutes
Servings: 6
Ingredients:

- ¾ cup cocoa powder
- ¾ cup white flour
- ½ cup butter
- 1 cup water
- 1 and ½ cups white sugar
- ½ teaspoon baking powder
- 3 eggs, whites and yolks separated
- 1 teaspoon vanilla extract

Directions:

1. In a bowl, beat egg whites with your mixer.
2. In another bowl, beat egg yolks with your mixer.
3. In a third bowl, mix flour with baking powder, sugar and cocoa powder.
4. Add egg white, egg yolks and vanilla extract and stir very well.
5. Grease a spring form pan with butter, line with parchment paper, pour cake batter, arrange pan in the steamer basket of your pot, add 1 cup water to the pot, cover and cook on Low for 40 minutes.
6. Release the pressure, uncover pot, take the pan out, leave cake to cool down, transfer to a platter, cut and serve it.

Enjoy!

Nutrition:

- Calories 379
- Fat 5
- Fiber 2
- Carbs 53
- Protein 5

Simple Carrot Pudding

It sweet; it's healthy and it's made in an instant pot!

Preparation time: 10 minutes
Cooking time: 1 hours
Servings: 8
Ingredients:

- 1 and ½ cups water
- Cooking spray
- ½ cup brown sugar
- 2 eggs
- ¼ cup molasses
- ½ cup flour
- ½ teaspoon allspice
- ½ teaspoon cinnamon
- A pinch of salt
- A pinch of nutmeg
- ½ teaspoon baking soda
- 2/3 cup shortening, frozen, grated
- ½ cup pecans, chopped
- ½ cup carrots, grated
- ½ cup raisins
- 1 cup bread crumbs

For the sauce:

- 4 tablespoons butter
- ½ cup brown sugar
- ¼ cup heavy cream
- 2 tablespoons rum
- ¼ teaspoon cinnamon

Directions:

1. In a bowl, mix molasses with eggs and ½ cup sugar and stir.
2. Add flour, shortening, carrots, nuts, raisins, bread crumbs, salt, ½ teaspoon cinnamon, allspice, nutmeg and baking soda and stir everything.
3. Pour this into a Bundt pan which you've greased with some cooking spray, cover with foil, place in the steamer basket of your instant pot, add the water to the pot, cover and cook at High for 1 hour.
4. Release the pressure, uncover pot, take pudding out and leave it aside to cool down.
5. Meanwhile, heat up a pan with the butter for the sauce over medium heat.
6. Add ½ cup brown sugar, stir and cook for 2 minutes.
7. Add cream, rum, ½ teaspoon cinnamon, stir and simmer for 2 minutes more.
8. Serve your pudding with this rum sauce.

Enjoy!

Nutrition:

- Calories 316
- Fat 16
- Fiber 5
- Carbs 44
- Protein 7
- Sugar 7

Eggnog Cheesecake

It's such a delicious cheesecake!

Preparation time: 15 minutes
Cooking time: 20 minutes
Servings: 6
Ingredients:

- 2 cups water
- 2 teaspoons butter, melted
- ½ cup ginger cookies, crumbled
- 16 ounces cream cheese, soft
- 2 eggs
- ½ cup sugar
- 1 teaspoon rum
- ½ teaspoon vanilla
- ½ teaspoon nutmeg, ground

Directions:

1. Grease a pan with the butter, add cookie crumbs and spread them evenly.
2. In a bowl, beat cream cheese with a mixer.
3. Add nutmeg, vanilla, rum and eggs and stir very well.
4. Pour this in the steamer basket of your instant pot, add the water to your pot, cover and cook at High for 15 minutes.
5. Release pressure, uncover pot, take cheesecake out, leave aside to cool down and keep in the fridge for 4 hours before slicing and serving it.

Enjoy!

Nutrition:

- Calories 400
- Fat 25
- Fiber 0
- Carbs 30
- Protein 6
- Sugar 19

Poached Figs

You are about to discover a very elegant dessert!

Preparation time: 10 minutes
Cooking time: 7 minutes
Servings: 4
Ingredients:

- 1 cup red wine
- 1 pound figs
- ½ cup pine nuts, toasted
- ½ cup sugar

For the yogurt crème:

- 2 pounds plain yogurt

Directions:

1. Put the yogurt in a strainer, press well, transfer to a container and keep in the fridge overnight.
2. Put the wine in your instant pot, place figs in the steamer basket, cover and cook on Low for 4 minutes.
3. Release the pressure, uncover the pot, take figs out and arrange them on plates.
4. Set the pot on Simmer mode, add sugar and stir.
5. Cook until sugar melts and then drizzle this sauce over figs.
6. Add yogurt crème on top or the side and serve right away.

Enjoy!

Nutrition:

- Calories 100
- Fat 0
- Fiber 1
- Carbs 13
- Sugar 0.6
- Protein 0

Lemon Crème Pots

It's not only delicious! It's also very easy to make in your instant pot!

Preparation time: 30 minutes
Cooking time: 5 minutes
Servings: 4
Ingredients:

- 1 cup whole milk
- Zest from 1 lemon
- 6 egg yolks
- 1 cup fresh cream
- 1 cup water
- 2/3 cup sugar
- Blackberry syrup for serving
- ½ cup fresh blackberries

Directions:

1. Heat up a pan over medium heat, add milk, lemon zest and cream, stir, bring to a boil, take off heat and leave aside for 30 minutes.
2. In a bowl, mix egg yolks with sugar and cold cream mix and stir well.
3. Pour this into ramekins, cover them with tin foil, place them in the steamer basket of your instant pot, add 1 cup water to the pot, cover and cook at High for 5 minutes.
4. Release the pressure for 10 minutes, uncover pot, take ramekins out, leave them to cool down and serve with blackberries and blackberry syrup on top.

Enjoy!

Nutrition:

- Calories 145
- Fat 4
- Fiber 3
- Carbs 10
- Protein 1

Superb Sweet Carrots

Pay attention to this tasty dessert!

Preparation time: 10 minutes
Cooking time: 16 minutes
Servings: 4
Ingredients:

- 1 tablespoon brown sugar
- 2 cups baby carrots
- A pinch of salt
- ½ cup water
- ½ tablespoon butter

Directions:

1. Set your instant pot on Sauté mode, add butter and melt it.
2. Add sugar, water and salt, stir and cook for 1 minute.
3. Add carrots, toss to coat, cover the pot and cook at High for 15 minutes.
4. Release pressure, uncover pot, transfer carrots to plates and serve.

Enjoy!

Nutrition:

- Calories 80
- Fat 1
- Fiber 1
- Carbs 3
- Protein 4

Pineapple And Ginger Risotto Dessert

Can you make such a risotto? Of course you can!

Preparation time: 10 minutes
Cooking time: 12 minutes
Servings: 4
Ingredients:

- ¼ cup candied ginger, chopped
- 20 ounces canned pineapple, chopped
- ½ cup coconut , shredded
- 1 and ¾ cups risotto rice
- 4 cups milk

Directions:

1. In your instant pot, mix milk with rice, coconut, pineapple and ginger, stir, cover and cook at High for 12 minutes.
2. Release the pressure naturally, uncover pot and serve your dessert.

Enjoy!

Nutrition:

- Calories 100
- Fat 2
- Fiber 3
- Carbs 3
- Protein 2

Corn Pudding

It's amazing and very delicious!

Preparation time: 10 minutes
Cooking time: 30 minutes
Servings: 4
Ingredients:

- 11 ounces canned creamed corn
- 2 cups water
- 2 cups milk
- 3 tablespoons sugar
- 2 eggs, whisked
- 2 tablespoons flour
- A pinch of salt
- 1 tablespoon butter
- Cooking spray

Directions:

1. Put the water in your instant pot, set on Simmer mode and bring to a boil.
2. In a bowl, mix corn with eggs, milk, butter, salt, flour and sugar and stir well.
3. Grease a baking dish with some cooking spray, pour corn mix into the pan, cover with foil and arrange in the steamer basket of your instant pot.
4. Cover and cook on High 20 minutes.
5. Release the pressure, uncover pot, take pudding out, leave it aside to cool down and serve.

Enjoy!

Nutrition:

- Calories 200
- Fat 5
- Fiber 2
- Carbs 12
- Protein 9

Conclusion

We know you want to become a master chef in the kitchen! We know you want to impress your guests, your friends and all your loved ones with your cooking skills.

Well, now you can! This magnificent cookbook provides you the tools you were looking for so long! You now know how to make the best dishes in the world in the easiest way possible: using an instant pot.

If you don't have such a wonderful machine yet, it's time to go and purchase one! Then get your hands on this wonderful cooking journal and start making some of the tastiest, unique, rich and flavored dishes ever!

We can assure you that everyone will admire you from now on! Everyone will adore your foods! Your success in the kitchen is guaranteed with just 2 simple tools: this great cookbook and an instant pot!

Have fun!

Made in the USA
Lexington, KY
17 June 2017